Contemporary Issues and the 21st Century Child

edited by

Andre Kurowski
& Sandra Lyndon

Contemporary Issues and the 21st Century Child

New Perspectives on Childhood

1 Oliver's Yard
55 City Road
London EC1Y 1SP

2455 Teller Road
Thousand Oaks
California 91320

Unit No 323-333, Third Floor, F-Block
International Trade Tower, Nehru Place,
New Delhi 110 019

8 Marina View Suite 43-053
Asia Square Tower 1
Singapore 018960

Editor: Delayna Spencer
Editorial assistant: Harry Dixon
Production editor: Victoria Nicholas
Copyeditor: Ritika Sharma
Proofreader: Girish Sharma
Indexer: TNQ Tech Pvt. Ltd.
Marketing manager: Lorna Patkai
Cover design: Wendy Scott
Typesetter: TNQ Tech Pvt. Ltd.
Printed and bound by CPI Group (UK) Ltd
Croydon, CR0 4YY

Library of Congress Control Number: 2024935265

British Library Cataloguing in Publication data

A catalogue record for this book is available from the British Library

ISBN 978-1-5296-1877-8
ISBN 978-1-5296-1876-1 (pbk)

Contents

About the Authors

Linda Cooper is a programme coordinator for the family of Education degree courses at the University of Chichester. Linda has taught and lectured in education for 25 years. She currently teaches across the ITT and education courses. She has published in the fields of early years, technology and humanities education as well as education in crisis contexts. Her PhD thesis focused on opportunities for collaborative and creative talk using play in an immersive learning environment.

Becky Edwards is a Senior Lecturer working in the Institute of Education and Social Sciences. She is also an award-winning children's author and co-founder of the charity PACSO (Parent and Carer's Support Organisation). She is a qualified primary school teacher with a focus on working with children with Special Educational Needs and/or Disability (SEND) and autism and has worked in primary schools and early years settings. Before lecturing, she set up and ran a Childrens Centre based in Chichester Nursery School. Becky has lived and worked all over the world including the United States, France, Germany and Switzerland. She is currently heading up the University of Chichester's from Adversity to University Project. Her first co-authored academic book: *True Partnerships in SEND* was published in 2023.

Heather Green is a Senior Lecturer in Special Education at the University of Chichester, and has 20 years of primary sector experience as a teacher. She established a specialist resourced provision for pupils with difficulties in accessing a mainstream curriculum, served as SENCO and Assistant Head teacher, and held the role of Specialist Leader in Education (SLE) in SEND. Heather's global engagement extends to teaching and research in rural Uganda, fostering an interest in international perspectives on disability and inclusive teaching methods. As a co-author of *True Partnerships in SEND*, she shares insights on collaborative work with children, families and professionals.

Andre Kurowski is a Senior Lecturer and teaches and coordinates on childhood programmes at the University of Chichester. His interests are in social science aspects of childhood including crime and childhood, and the 'digital child', i.e. children in a digital world. His research covers leadership in education and sociocultural issues in language, and he is a regular contributor to European journals.

Debra Laxton is a Senior Lecturer in Education and Early Childhood Lead at the University of Chichester. She has spent her whole career focused on the education of young children. Debra currently teaches across ITT and education provision, focusing on early years education in pre-school settings and primary schools. Debra's research interests explore how translational research can impact on educator practice to improve early childhood education both in global crisis contexts and within the United Kingdom.

Carol Lloyd has over 30 years' experience delivering mental health teaching in Higher Education settings and her private practise as an accredited expressive arts psychotherapist with adults and children. In her early vocational journey, she made the decision to train as an early years teacher, specialising in 3–8 years. However, while undertaking her teacher training, she experienced a life changing event and embarked on the counselling route to help with trauma, leading to the completion of an MA in Transpersonal Arts and Practice (Somatic art psychotherapy) researching cancer and trauma. She completed her PhD on sharing children's sleep dreams within an educational context in 2020. Her research is underpinned by the psychoanalytical work of Carl Jung.

Sandra Lyndon is a reader in Childhood and Social Policy at the University of Chichester. She teaches on a range of Childhood undergraduate programmes as well as taking a lead on supporting research within the department. She is co-chair of the Centre for Childhood in Childhood, Inclusion and Society (CECIS). She is both a qualified teacher and an educational psychologist. She completed her doctoral studies at the University of Sussex and her research interests include poverty, homelessness, mindfulness, child centred approaches, intergenerational practice, and narrative methodologies.

Suzanna McGregor is a Senior Lecturer and Liaison Tutor working across Social Work, Sociology and Early Childhood Studies at the University of Chichester and with partner colleges. Suzanna's background is working in cardiology, and she has been an academic working in Higher Education for over 8 years. Her areas of research interests include: health; education of junior doctors; adult social care; addressing retention and recruitment in key sectors; and food banks.

Sam McNally is a Play Therapist, trauma specialist, and Senior Lecturer at the University of Chichester. She is the programme coordinator for the BA (Hons) Childhood with Therapeutic Play. Sam has previously worked as a primary school teacher and as a mental health practitioner for NHS CAMHS. Her research focuses on the impact of trauma and the importance of professionals accessing supervision.

Eva Mikuska is a Senior Lecturer at the University of Chichester. She has led the Foundation Degree in Early Years programme for the last two decades, hence her interest researching the importance of early years professionalism, learning and teaching in Higher Education, and quality services for children. Eva is an executive member of the Early Childhood Studies Degrees Network (ECSDN) with responsibility for the Research and Knowledge Exchange portfolio where she is sharing the position of the Vice-Chair. Most recently, her research focuses on the digitalisation of the child

Helen Moss has previously worked for a number of local authorities, initially supporting children and families within family centre settings. She is also a former child protection social worker. She leads and teaches on the BA (Hons) Social Work degree, with a particular focus on social work law and child safeguarding. Her research interests include intergenerational practice and the skills used by practitioners in child safeguarding.

Marie Price is a Senior Lecturer in Social Work at the University of Chichester. She lectures at the university part time as well as being involved in end of life and bereavement projects outside of the university. Her research interests include children's responses to grief, spirituality and supervision/support for staff working in these areas. Marie has written about all of these areas in articles and book chapters as well as speaking to, and working with, various groups nationally and locally. She is currently researching the role of Clinical Supervision in Palliative Care for a PhD.

Christopher Smethurst is the Co-Director of the Institute of Education and Social Sciences at the University of Chichester.

Prior to training as a social worker, Chris had been a youth worker, community worker, social care manager, volunteer coordinator, residential care worker and day centre worker (although not necessarily in that order). As a manager and social worker, he developed an interest in topics that he later found were loosely termed under the umbrella of resilience. Working in higher education, Chris has pursued those interests, both in terms of training, but also in direct work with various groups.

Lianna Wilding is a Lecturer within the Institute of Education and Social Sciences at the University of Chichester. She teaches on the BA (Hons) Primary Teaching with Early Years (QTS) and on the PGCE Primary (3–7) degrees, specialising in behaviour, inclusion and working with families. Lianna's professional experience lies within the early years and primary education sectors where she spent time working as a school leader and an Early Years advisor for a local authority as part of a multidisciplinary team. She has research interests in child development and early years policy, particularly the experiences of children aged two. She also has a professional interest in exploring transitions for first-generation students in higher education.

1

Childhood in the 21st Century

Sandra Lyndon

After reading this chapter, readers will be able to:

- Gain a general introduction to the book and be familiar with key terms.
- Begin to explore some of the issues children facing in the 21st century.
- Gain an overview of the book chapters.

Introduction

The aim of this book is to explore a wide range of issues which affect children's lives, both in the United Kingdom and globally. It is written for practitioners and professionals who are working with children, students who are studying childhood or related fields in further or higher education and for academics who are teaching and/or researching in these areas. Each chapter takes a different focus, with the aim of providing both an academic context for issues affecting children as well as how practitioners can support children and families. In this chapter, we introduce some generic terms; provide a general context for some of the issues which are affecting children's lives at the beginning of the 21st century; and an overview of each chapter.

Terminology

Child: For consistency when we use the term 'child' we are referring to UNICEF's (1989) Convention on the Rights of the Child, article 1 which states:

> A child means every human being below the age of eighteen years unless under the law applicable to the child, majority is attained earlier.

While we acknowledge that most countries, including the United Kingdom, consider that adulthood starts at 18, there are some exceptions, with some countries considering adulthood starting as young as 15 or 16. We also recognise that 'age' is not necessarily a good measure of children's development. Each child is unique and will develop at different rates; advances in neuroscience suggest that children's brains do not reach maturity until the mid to late 20s (Blakemore and Choudhury, 2006). Therefore, caution should be applied when making assumptions about age-related child development.

Practitioner: The term 'practitioner' is used throughout this book when referring to those working directly with children; or in a field related to children or childhood. We have chosen to use a generic term, as this book is relevant to those working with children across a broad range of fields (including early years, social work, education and health) where there are many different roles and job titles used.

Issues for Children in the 21st Century

The beginning of the 21st century has brought about change for most children and their families. The onset of the Covid-19 pandemic in March 2020 had a significant detrimental impact on children all over the world, particularly those living in the poorest countries, and for some the impact will be life-long (Save the Children/UNICEF, 2021). In the United Kingdom, children's education and mental health has been especially affected. Enforced lockdowns led to many children experiencing long periods of online learning resulting in significant gaps in learning at all ages. Since a return to face-to-face teaching there has been a noticeable increase in the number of children experiencing anxiety, and increased rates of pupil absence, particularly for those living in low-income families (Holt and Murray, 2021; Taylor, 2021). It is estimated that it will 'take a decade more to return the disadvantage gap to pre-pandemic levels' (HCCPA, 2018: 3). For families on low incomes in the United Kingdom, Covid-19 has exacerbated existing economic issues relating to austerity and Brexit (the United Kingdom's departure from the European Union) (Holt and Murray, 2021), and more recently the war in the Ukraine (Patel, 2022).

However, arguably one of the greatest challenges faced by children and families in the 21st century is climate change. The Intergovernmental panel on Climate Change [IPCC] (2023) states how global warming, caused by humans, has led to worldwide adverse effects including extreme weather, rising sea levels, species loss, wildfires, drought, loss of crop and animal production, poor health and well-being and reduced air quality. In 2022, it was estimated that 31.8 million people were forcibly displaced due to floods, storms, droughts, wildfires, landslides and extreme temperature (Internal Displacement Monitoring Centre [IDMC], 2023). As UNICEF (2021: 7) points out, the 'climate crisis is a child rights crisis', with climate change posing a direct threat to children's lives, affecting their health, nutrition, education and future.

Although all children and families are affected to some extent by climate change, the effects are not distributed equally, often it is the poorest communities who have contributed the least to climate change being affected the most (IPCC, 2023). Although children and families living in the Middle East and North Africa (MENA) region have been severely affected by climate change compared to others (UNICEF, 2021), they have received the smallest amount of funding worldwide (World Bank, 2023). Temperatures are warming faster than in other parts of the world, with some parts expected to research or exceed thresholds of human tolerance by 2071–2100. Key risks to children include an increase in heat waves, water scarcity, decreased food security and physical and environmental threats. The choices that we make now will determine whether these conditions get worse or better, and will have impacts, not just for now, or the next 10 years, but for 'thousands of years' (IPCC, 2023: 24).

For children and young people in the United Kingdom and other parts of the world which have experienced less significant impacts of climate change (so far), anxiety about climate change is becoming an increasingly common phenomenon. Research with young people in the United Kingdom demonstrates how the perceived threat of climate change is linked to poorer mental health and well-being, linked with frustration associated with the perceived lack of action on climate change, concern over the future and a lack of agency (Vercammen et al., 2023).

However, on the positive front increased concerns about climate change is also a motivator for change and taking a proactive approach (Vercammen et al., 2023). One example of this is Greta Thunberg, a Swedish environmental activist, who took a proactive response to her concerns about climate change. At the age of 15, Greta sat outside the Swedish parliament every school day for three weeks to protest against climate change. Greta's postings on social media went viral and started a worldwide youth-led movement, FridaysForFuture (nd). Since then, Greta has addressed the United Nations Climate Change Conference in 2018 and the United Nations Climate Action Summit in 2019 and has twice been nominated the Nobel Peace Prize. However, life for Greta has not been being without its challenges. Greta was diagnosed with Autism, as a teenager, has received criticism for her work and was arrested in London in 2023 at the London oil protest summit. Despite these challenges Greta remains committed to her cause. Not only an advocate for protesting against climate change, she has also become an advocate for those with autism, describing it as her 'superpower'. Speaking to *The Guardian* in 2021 she says:

> Autism can be something that holds you back, but if you get to the right circumstance, if you are around the right people, if you get the adaptations that you need and you feel you have a purpose, then it can be something you can use for good. And I think that I'm doing that now. (Thunberg 2021, cited in Hattenstone, 2021)

Arguably, Greta is a strong advocate for all children and highlights the importance of listening and responding to the voices of children and young people, after all they are the ones who will be inheriting a world which unless action is taken, will be uninhabitable.

Points of Reflection

- Do you think children and young people should be encouraged to be activists?
- What do you think are the potential benefits and challenges?

Listening to Children and Young People

Article 12, 'Respect for the views of the child', in the UN Convention on the Rights of the Child (1989) states that:

> Every child has the right to express their views, feelings and wishes in all matters affecting them, and to have their views considered and taken seriously.

However, opportunities for children and young people, to have their voices heard, listened to and acted on are rare. Even Greta Thunberg who has been described as one of the most influential people in the world and has addressed some of the most influential people in the world, rarely feels listened to or that her words have made a difference. In her speech to Youth4ClimateSummit in Italy in 2021, she describes the words of the world leaders as nothing more than 'blah, blah, blah':

> "Build back better" blah, blah, blah.
>
> "Green economy" blah blah blah.
>
> "Net zero by 2050" blah, blah, blah
>
> "Net zero" blah, blah, blah
>
> This is all we hear from our so-called leaders. Words that sound great but so far have not led to action. Our hopes and ambitions drown in their empty promises. (Thunberg, 2021)

As Bradwell (2019) points out if we are going to be serious about listening to children and young people, we not only need to act on their words, but start with considering what we mean by voice and how we hear voice. Article 13 in the same Convention (UNICEF, 1989) states that:

> The child shall have the right to freedom of expression; this right shall include freedom to seek, receive and impart information and ideas of all kinds, regardless of frontiers, either orally, in writing or in print, in the form of art, or through any other media of the child's choice.

Children and young people communicate in many ways, for some the conventions of written or spoken words are not appropriate for their developmental stage or Special Educational Needs and/or Disability (SEND). Therefore, we need to be open to all forms of communication and start by removing barriers so we can really listen to children and young people (as explored by Edwards and Green in Chapter 8).

Points of Reflection

- To what extent do you think children are 'really' listened to?
- What other approaches could be used to 'hear' children's voices?

Overview of the Book

This book is divided into three sections: Influences on Childhood; Children's Experiences; and Children's Minds. For consistency, each chapter follows a similar format with key objectives stated at the beginning of the chapter, use of case studies and reflective questions and a summary of key points and recommended reading/sources at the end.

In the first section, the influences on children's behaviour are explored, with a particular focus on crime; the influence of digital technology; and the benefits for children in the bringing together of different generations. **Chapter two** by Lianna Wilding and Sandra Lyndon explores children's behaviour in early childhood starting with a consideration of what we mean by 'behaviour', and how constructs of children's behaviour are influenced by both culture and context, as well as the personal experiences and emotions of the person casting judgement. Using their foundation model, they explore how experiences, relationships and biology can influence children's behaviour. They encourage the reader to become an active 'detective' in understanding behaviours as well as discussing practical strategies with a focus on the value of relationships, empathy and safe and stimulating environments. **Chapter three** by Eva Mikuska and Andre Kurowski explores the impact of digital technologies in young children's lives, and how this influences their development and experience. They consider the concept of the 'digital child' and the role of digital technologies within early years settings and schools, as well as from a parent and carers' perspective. **Chapter four** by Andre Kurowski investigates how children are treated within the criminal justice system, and how understandings of children's capacity to commit crimes and criminal responsibility have developed over time. He critically analyses the many factors and theories which are offered as explanations of children's offending. **Chapter five** by Sandra Lyndon explores the construct of family and the role of grandparents and older adults in children's lives. Drawing on her own research about an intergenerational project for young children visiting older adults in a care home for those with dementia, she explores how meaningful connections can be built and the potential benefits for all those involved.

In the second section, a broad range of experiences that affect children's lives are explored including the refugee crisis; special educational needs and disability; health inequalities, loss and bereavement; and safeguarding. **Chapter six** by Helen Moss explores the role of early help in safeguarding children in the early years. She explains the importance of working together to safeguard children, and what can happen to children when this fails to take place. She highlights the barriers to effective safeguarding, and how practitioners can support by recognising the need for and acting quickly so that changes are made early on in the child's life. In **Chapter seven**, Linda Cooper and Debra Laxton explore the global refugee crisis starting with the causes of population movement. They reflect on who should be responsible for children and families who arrive in another country seeking asylum. They consider the impact of being a refugee on children's development, and how a lack of access to education can affect children's life chances. **Chapter eight** by Becky Edwards and Heather Green explores how to break down barriers and provide access to learning for children with SEND. They start by investigating how views of disability have developed historically, and how these have influenced attitudes and legislation. Drawing on the concept of co-production they discuss how a person-centred approach can improve outcomes for children with SEND. Finally assistive technologies are investigated as a way of making education more accessible for children with SEND by taking a strengths-based approach. In **Chapter nine,** Suzanna McGregor explores the inequalities relating to children's health. She starts by taking a global perspective and investigates the social and economic factors that influence children's health. A range of approaches to tackling children's health are considered and how to ensure that all children have equal opportunities and access to health services and support. In **Chapter ten**, Marie Price explores the experiences that children may have when they have or are faced with the death of someone close to them. She investigates how children's reactions and feelings will vary according to their stage of development, as well as how practitioners can support children and their families with their experience of death and experience of bereavement.

In the final section 'Children's Minds', we explore areas relating to children's inner worlds and emotional lives including the importance of dreams, emotional safety, resilience and working therapeutically with children. In **Chapter 11,** 'Dreaming the Child Awake', Carol Lloyd explores the little researched world of children's sleep dreams. Drawing on her research with young children within a school context she explores how the 'dream matrix' can be used to explore the dream worlds of children within an educational context. Her research findings demonstrate that having opportunities to take part in the 'dream matrix' improves children's listening, empathy and prosocial skills. **Chapter 12** by Becky Edwards explores the concept of 'emotional safety' and how having a sense of acceptance and belonging, consistency and predictability, together with an opportunity to build trusting relationships is key to young children's well-being and development. Building on attachment theory Becky explores how secure attachments with trusted people can help to support children when they experience new environments or feel overwhelmed. In the last part of the chapter, she explores how to create a warm and welcoming environment, which supports children's emotional safety. **Chapter 13** by Christopher Smethurst explores children's resilience. He starts by highlighting the complexities of the term 'resilience' and how understandings have been influenced by public discourse and government policy. Drawing on a wide range of research and frameworks, resilience is explored in relation to children's lives, including the importance of taking a wholistic approach and recognising the multiple factors which might affect children's resilience. **Chapter 14** by Sam McNally explores working therapeutically with children. She starts by exploring the increase in children's mental health problems, and the importance of secure relationships for young children. She discusses how working therapeutically with children, drawing on attachment-informed and trauma-informed approaches is a way of providing safety and support for children as well as helping the children to build resilience and emotional well-being. In the last part of the chapter the use of play therapy is explored as an effective medium for young children to make sense of their lives and lived experience. Finally, **Chapter 15,** 'Futures of Childhood', by Andre Kurowski pulls together themes across all three sections, and looks at how childhood is developing both globally and locally and where it is likely to go next.

References

Blakemore, S. and Choudhury, S. (2006) Development of the Adolescent brain: Implications for executive function and social cognition. *Journal of Child Psychology and Psychiatry*, 47(3–4): 296–312.

Bradwell, M. (2019) Voice, views and the UNCRC. *Journal of Early Childhood Research*, 17(4): 423–433.

FridaysForFuture (nd) Fridays for future. Available at: https://fridaysforfuture.org/ (Accessed 18 January 2024).

Hattenstone, S. (2021) The transformation of Greta Thunberg. *The Guardian*. Available at: https://www.theguardian.com/environment/ng-interactive/2021/sep/25/greta-thunberg-i-really-see-the-value-of-friendship-apart-from-the-climate-almost-nothing-else-matters (Accessed 22 January 2024).

Holt, L. and Murray, L. (2021) Children and Covid 19 in the UK. *Children's Geographies*, 20(4): 487–494.

House of Commons Committee of Public Accounts [HCCPA] (2018) *Universal credit: Sixty-fourth report of session 2017–19*. Available at: https://publications.parliament.uk/pa/cm201719/cmselect/cmpubacc/1183/1183.pdf

Intergovernmental Panel on Climate Change [IPCC] (2023) *Climate Change 2023 Synthesis Report: summary for policy makers*. Available at: https://www.ipcc.ch/report/ar6/syr/downloads/report/IPCC_AR6_SYR_SPM.pdf (Accessed 4 January 2024).

Internal Displacement Monitoring Centre [IDMC] (2023) *Internal displacement and food security*. Available at: https://www.internal-displacement.org/sites/default/files/publications/documents/IDMC_GRID_2023_Global_Report_on_Internal_Displacement_LR.pdf#page=9 (Accessed 4 January 2024).

Patel, U. (2022) *The economic consequences of the Ukraine war for UK household incomes*. Available at: https://www.niesr.ac.uk/publications/economic-consequences-ukraine-war-uk-household-incomes?type=uk-economic-outlook-box-analysis (Accessed 14 June 2023).

Save the Children/UNICEF (2021) *Impact of Covid-19 on children living in poverty: A technical note*. Available at: https://data.unicef.org/resources/impact-of-covid-19-on-children-living-in-poverty/ (Accessed 8 January 2024).

Taylor, R. (2021) *Covid-19: Impact on child poverty and on young people's education, health and well being*. Available at: https://lordslibrary.parliament.uk/covid-19-impact-on-child-poverty-and-on-young-peoples-education-health-and-wellbeing/#:~:text=The%20latest%20report%2C%20published%20on,from%2020%25%20to%2023%25

Thunberg, G. (2021) Greta Thunberg mocks world leaders in 'blah, blah, blah' speech. *BBC News*. Available at: https://www.youtube.com/watch?v=ZwD1kG4PI0w (Accessed 22 January 2024).

UNICEF (1989) *United Nations Convention on the Rights of the Child*. Available at: https://www.unicef.org.uk/what-we-do/un-convention-child-rights/ (Accessed 19 January 2024).

UNICEF (2021) *The climate crisis is a child rights crisis*. Available at: https://www.unicef.org.uk/climate-change/ (Accessed 22 January 2024).

Vercammen, A., Oswald, T. and Lawrence, E. (2023) Psycho-social factors associated with climate distress, hope and behavioural intentions in young UK residents. *PLOS Glob Public Health*, 3(8): e0001938.

World Bank (2023) *Climate and development in the Middle East and North Africa, brief*. Available at: https://www.worldbank.org/en/region/mena/brief/climate-and-development-in-the-middle-east-and-north-africa (Accessed 23 January 2024).

Part I
Influences on Childhood

2

Understanding Children's Behaviour in Early Childhood

Lianna Wilding and Sandra Lyndon

After reading this chapter, readers will be able to:

- Critically explore behaviour as a social construct.
- Understand the Foundation Model which examines influences upon children's behaviour.
- Consider how children's experiences, relationships and biology can influence their behaviour.

Introduction

Understanding and supporting children's behaviour is undoubtedly one of the most important roles for early years practitioners. Children's personal, social and emotional development is fundamental to learning and well-being, therefore as early years practitioners we need to make sure that we are listening effectively to children and what their behaviour is telling us. To understand the complexity of children's behaviour, we have developed the Foundation Model which explores how children's behaviour is shaped by their environment, relationships and biology.

What Is Behaviour?

Despite being central to many fields of study, there is a lack of agreement on what does or does not constitute behaviour (Uher, 2016). For example biologists take a broad view defining behaviour as the actions or inactions of animals to internal or external stimuli. In contrast psychologists take a narrower view defining behaviour as verbal utterances or movements that can be seen or heard. To be an effective practitioner it is important to recognise the complexity of children's behaviour, rather than reducing it to an observable action or response to stimuli. Drawing on the work of MacLure et al. (2011), we present children's behaviour as a social construct, shaped by the child's experiences, dominant ideologies, relationships and biology.

Social Constructs of Children's Behaviour

James et al. (1998) suggest there are two western constructs of childhood, the Apollonian child and the Dionysian child. The Apollonian child is pure and naturally good requiring nurturing and protection, almost angelic. In contrast, the Dionysian child is inherently wicked and anarchistic requiring discipline and a 'spare the rod and spoil the child' approach. Both constructs provide a way of understanding children's behaviour as something that needs to be 'controlled' or managed (Smith, 2011). In the case of the Dionysian child control is exercised through discipline or chastisement, whereas in the case of the Apollonian child control is achieved through framing the child as 'vulnerable' and in need of protection (Jenks, 2005).

Within the Early Years Foundation Stage (EYFS) (DfE, 2021; DfE, 2023a; DfE, 2023b) both the Dionysian and Apollonian constructs of the child are apparent. Behaviour is presented as something to be managed by providers and ultimately by children themselves. For example the EYFS framework states that children's behaviour is to be managed 'in an appropriate way' to keep them safe and well (DfE, 2023a: 34). Viewing children as needing protection, reflects an Apollonian construct, where children are innocent and adults are protectors (Aries, 1962; James et al., 1998). Sorin and Galloway (2006: 5) argue that presenting the child as innocent renders them 'incompetent, vulnerable and dependent', ultimately denying children a voice and agency, the opportunity to make their own decisions and learn from their mistakes.

According to the EYFS Early Learning Goals (ELGs) children should know 'right from wrong and try to behave accordingly' by the time they are five years old (DfE, 2021: 12; DfE, 2024: 25). To support children to reach this goal, practitioners are expected to model positive behaviour, highlight 'exemplary behaviour', helping children to recognise when their behaviour does not accord with the rules (DfE, 2021: 56). Arguably by supporting children to develop morality (an understanding of right and wrong) helps to maintain social order within early years settings and in wider society. Applying James et al. (1998) Dionysian discourse of childhood to this context renders adults as moral transmitters of 'good' and child as less than perfect and in need of socialisation. In the same way that the Apollonian discourse has been criticised, the Dionysian discourse can also be criticised for silencing and disempowering the child. Presenting the child as 'evil' or in need of socialisation takes an individualistic view of behaviour, suggesting that the location (or cause) of the child's behaviour is attributable to the child or home rather than considering the negative impact that societal factors, such as structural inequalities, may have on children's behaviour (MacLure et al., 2011).

Social constructs of children's behaviour, shaped by historical discourses of the Apollonian child and Dionysian child, can be unhelpful, viewing children as passive and adults as powerful and responsible for socialising children to be fit for society. They also feed into individualised nature vs nurture debates about whether children are a product of their biology (nature) or shaped by their upbringing and society (nurture), both of which are discussed later in the chapter. In contrast, MacLure et al. (2011) argue that children are not passive subjects but have the potential agency and power through their interactions to determine how their identities are constructed, e.g., whether they are perceived as 'good' or 'bad'. According to the Convention on the Rights of the Child (CRC) (1989) article 12 'Every child has the right to express their views, feelings and wishes in all matters affecting them, and to have their views considered taken seriously'. Understanding the child as having rights to make decisions constructs them as competent and strong (Smith, 2011). One way that we can support a more competent and empowered image of the child is by viewing all behaviour as communication (Grimmer, 2021: 2). Thinking about behaviour as communication respects children's right to be listened to and helps us to explore how children's emotions might affect their behaviour. In summary, we understand children's behaviour as communication (whether or not the child is conscious of what they are trying to communicate) which is shaped and constructed by a complex interaction between their biology (genes) and the environment.

A Model for Behaviour (Understanding Influences)

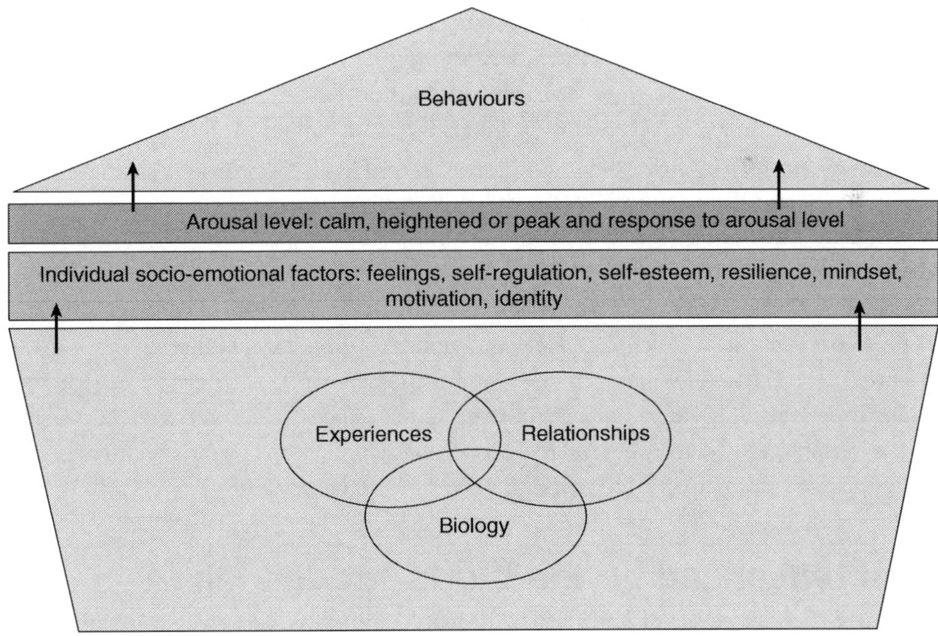

Figure 2.1 Foundation Model for Understanding Children's Behaviour
Source: Created by Wilding and Lyndon, 2023.

The Foundation Model for understanding children's behaviour (Figure 2.1) illustrates the influences on children's behaviour. Often, adults working with young children look to the top of the diagram, the 'roof', at the behaviour itself. Limitations on time, resources and professional knowledge can often explain why this occurs. However, to understand behaviour, a careful examination of the foundations at the bottom of the diagram and the layers that follow is required. The foundations comprise of experiences, relationships and biology. Individual socio-emotional factors comprise the next layer of influence and are informed by the foundations. Finally, it is recognised that the child's stress response, named here the 'arousal level', and the response to this, also inform behaviour. This layer is closer to the tip of the diagram as although it will inform the immediate behaviour that follows, it is the layers beneath that feed this arousal response. This model has clear links to iceberg models of behaviour, such as those by Sackville-Ford (2019) and to psychological theories of child development.

I Am Influenced by Experiences

The first area of the foundation model is experiences. Within the 21st century, environmental influences are multiple and wide-ranging. This section draws upon classic theories of behaviour that are often used to explain children's behaviour within the fields of early childhood, education, psychology and sociology. It is useful to have a contextual understanding of such theories, as they inform many existing systems for children. However, it is acknowledged that commonly cited theories for behaviour are mostly white-centric and based upon western society (see Keller, 2018 for critique of western-centric perspectives on attachment theory).

Although experiences have their own area within the foundation model, they interrelate with the other foundational areas of relationships and biology. For example we now understand the impact of early childhood experiences on the development of the brain. The quality and quantity of relationships in a child's life inform their experiences and vice versa. When using experiences as a lens to inform understanding of a child's behaviour, it is unlikely that a single experience within a child's life alone will provide an explanation. This complexity has the potential to cause discomfort if we are attempting to understand children's behaviour for a 'quick fix'. However, understanding the 'unique child' is good practice (DfE, 2021) and for many children, information gathering as part of transitions and regular reviews is sufficient to understand their unique experiences. Some children benefit from a greater level of 'detective work' and it is for these children that we should invest more time in understanding their experiences.

I Am Influenced by the World Around Me

Exploring the vast array of contextual influences prompts us to avoid a simplistic view of behaviour, where responsibility for a behaviour is placed upon any one system or individual. Families can feel 'othered' by practitioners when it comes to discussing their child's needs (Hughes and MacNaugton, 2000) when in fact both families and education and care are operating within a larger systems and structures around the child. Aynsley-Green (2018) argues that understanding children, means understanding wider society, including political discourses. Often, children are described as making active choices about their behaviour, with adults often using phrases such as 'you chose to do this so now you need to have this consequence'. In reality, young children are rarely making active choices, due to wide-ranging influences.

In the past, when considering environmental influences, media was seen to have an indirect influence upon the child (Bronfenbrenner, 1979). The increase in innovation and access to digital technologies has a direct influence on the young child's experience of the world and their interactions with others (see Figure 2.2). There has been concern about the negative impact of media on children's behaviour, particularly the impact of media portraying violence, on children's levels of aggression (see Bandura, 1977, social learning theory cited in Aubrey and Riley, 2019). However, evidence suggests that media can also have a prosocial effect (Gentile et al., 2009).

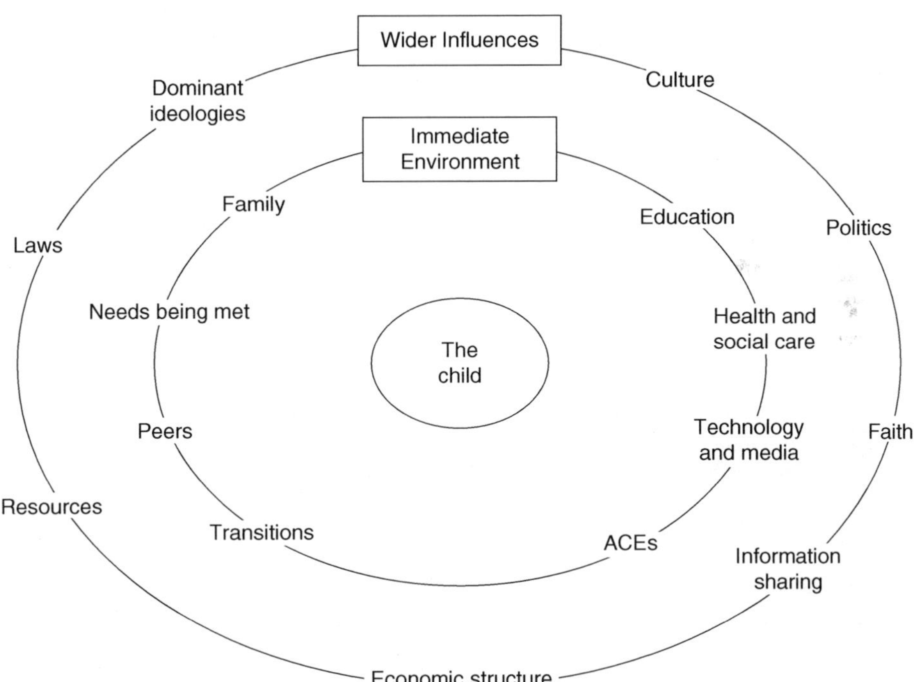

Figure 2.2 Experiences That Shape the 21st Century Child in the United Kingdom
Source: Adapted from Bronfenbrenner's (1979) ecological systems theory.

I Am Influenced by Dominant Ideologies

Within early educational settings, there is a tension between behaviourist systems designed to achieve compliance (Skinner, 1971) and a humanistic needs-based approach. Within behaviourist theories, the educator is viewed as holding the power. Behaviourism centres the needs of the adult and collective, whereas humanism centres the needs of the individual child. As such, behaviourism and humanism are outlined below as lenses through which to understand behaviour.

I Am Conditioned to Behave Like This

Behaviourism describes a range of learning theories that explain behaviour through conditioning. Founded upon animal studies within experimental psychology, such as Skinner's (1971) operant conditioning theory, the behaviourist perspective reflects a mechanistic world view. Through this perspective, children are viewed much like computers, waiting to be programmed. Rather than identifying the underlying factors that contribute to them (Sackville-Ford, 2019), children are presented as passive, with environmental cues and responses conditioning their behaviours. Conditioning relies upon extrinsic motivation, such as rewards and sanctions to shape behaviour and such extrinsic motivation has been long known to be short-lived (Kohn, 1993). Therefore, behaviourism cannot be used alone to understand children's behaviour and as such, is overly simplistic, linking cause to effect, action to consequence and behaviour to response. Despite its limitations, many adults working with children find it beneficial to ask themselves the following behaviourist questions that are most effective when considered over time, rather than relating to a specific snapshot of behaviour.

Points of Reflection

- Are there environmental influences that cause a child to behave in a certain way?
- Are our responses to the child's behaviour, consistent, responsive and proportionate?

Consider, for example the 'STAR' approach (West Sussex County Council, 2021) which is commonly used in the United Kingdom to evaluate environmental conditions and responses to behaviour (Figure 2.3). The reflections upon the observations are then used to amend the environmental cues or the responses to the behaviour. The STAR approach identifies immediate triggers for arousal but does not look at the foundations for behaviour.

Situation	Trigger
What was the environmental context? The children were being dropped off at the setting by their families. Child Y was arriving at the door.	What happened immediately before the behaviour? Y's father said goodbye.
Action What was the behaviour? Y began to run around the room distressed, bumping into furniture and other children.	**Response** What was the response to the behaviour from adults? The adults began to approach/chase Y. Y continued to run and took a long time to calm down. Other adults moved children out of his pathway, with varying levels of success.
Evaluation: Saying goodbye to parents was the trigger. Approaching and chasing Y seemed to prolong the running behaviour as he only ceased this when the adults eventually stopped following him. Adjustments: Key person to consistently meet Y at the door in the morning to support the morning transition. Should Y start to run around the room, adults to not chase him and instead, move the other children into the room next door or the outside area to ensure their safety.	

Figure 2.3 Using 'STAR' to Understand a Child's Behaviour

Because I Need This. . .I Behave Like That

Humanist approaches which link behaviour to a holistic picture of a child's needs are being recognised and adopted in combination with behaviourist approaches in educational settings in the United Kingdom. This school of thought is often attributed to Carl Rogers' (1959) theory of unconditional positive regard and to Maslow's (1970) hierarchy of needs. It can be argued that evaluating whether a child's needs have been met is useful and relevant.

Practitioners often report that the behaviour of two-year olds can be challenging, but when it is considered that only 2.5% of two-year olds cease napping prior to age two (Staton et al., 2020), there is potential for this behaviour to be resolved through establishing an inviting sleeping area. It is useful to ask ourselves, whether our environment meets the child's needs, whether expectations of behaviour are appropriate and if behaviour that feels challenging is due to an un-met need. Consider the parent voice below.

Case Study: My Child Has Autism

'My child has autism' and when he becomes overwhelmed, this is obvious to us at home. We respond by listening to him to determine the reasons. Sometimes we can see he is getting anxious or cross because of an experience he has had, other times because his resilience is low due to ill health. We know which of our responses will help him to calm down and so at home it is very rare that we see aggressive behaviour.

(Continued)

(Continued)

However, he is currently in primary school and has begun to hit other children. His class teacher frequently tells us that 'there were no reasons for this behaviour'. However, each time that it happens, as parents, we can identify a reason. Sometimes this reason is related to the relationships in his life, for example when his supporting adult at school is used to cover other staff.

Other times, it is because he is unwell. But... there is always a reason. Our child has faced public humiliation in assemblies where he has been sanctioned in front of the whole school for his behaviour and has faced exclusions from school. Other parents ask their children to avoid him, so we feel he is now being labelled and targeted. This is frustrating when we feel that if the school tuned into his needs and reviewed their responses, the antisocial behaviour would cease.

- How does the parent view their child's behaviour?
- How does the school view the child's behaviour?
- How could the school behave differently?

Because This Has Happened...I Behave Like That

Colvin and Scott (2015) propose a relationship between prior success or failure and future motivation to learn. In this sense, if a child has not experienced success in their learning, either academically, emotionally or socially, their self-efficacy lowers, and they are less motivated to learn in the future. If a child is repeatedly asked to learn in a way that is not appropriate for their needs, is too challenging or not challenging enough, they will not experience success.

Case Study: Using a Behaviourist Approach

A class of children aged four are expected to sit still and learn poetry and stories by rote for 60 minutes at a time. Their educator reports them to be an 'unruly' class that rarely listens. The manager encourages the educator to adopt a sterner behaviourist approach to control the behaviour.

- Is the learning appropriate for the children?
- What impact does this have on the children's behaviour?

It is known that income poverty, parental mental health and the Covid-19 pandemic are associated with social, behavioural and health outcomes. These specific experiences should be considered when understanding children's behaviour. Brennan (2018, p. 5) explains the importance of considering the effect of adverse childhood experiences (ACEs):

> It is the experiences we find hardest to talk about in our society that have a lasting impact on the mental health and wellbeing of children and young people. Be it bereavement, domestic violence, caring for a parent, or sexual abuse, we must ensure that all services are better able to identify childhood adversity and help to resolve the trauma related to it.

Social, educational and healthcare systems in the United States, Canada and more recently the United Kingdom are adopting 'trauma-informed' approaches to meeting the needs of children with multiple ACEs (Aynsley-Green, 2018). Trauma-informed models of care focus on understanding behaviours and treating children with respect to avoid re-traumatising them (Brennan et al., 2019). However, the impact of these policies is not yet clear due to the recency of these approaches (Berger, 2019). See chapters on Resilience and Therapeutic Approaches.

Responses

The responses that adults give to behaviours have an influence on a child's future behaviour. Not least, because they directly influence the foundations of behaviour by becoming embedded in a child's experiences and relationships. As a result, responses to behaviour also affect the strength of a child's socio-emotional factors such as self-esteem, resilience and growth mindset. The responsibility that comes with being the adult responding to children's behaviour is summarised by Haim Ginott (1993: 1):

> I possess a tremendous power to make a child's life miserable or joyous. I can be a tool of torture or an instrument of inspiration. I can humiliate or heal. In all situations, it is my response that decides whether a crisis will be escalated or de-escalated, and a child humanised or dehumanised.

As part of understanding how the adult's response can affect children's behaviour, it should be considered whether the responses are proportionate, fair and whether they are likely to escalate behaviours, or de-escalate them and what the long-term impact might be (Rogers and McPherson, 2014).

To deliver a response that is proportionate to the behaviour and consider the underlying reasons for behaviour, the adult delivering the response needs to be able to respond as objectively as possible, and be able to self-regulate their emotional responses to the behaviours demonstrated. This is a challenge that should not be underestimated. Each adult that is responding to behaviour will have their own experiences, relationships and maturational influences. As a result, the arousal levels that adults feel in response to behaviours will vary. When in a calm state of arousal, remaining objective, when responding to children's behaviour, is likely to feel manageable. However, when arousal is heightened, perhaps due to not enough sleep, illness or a stressful life event, it becomes more challenging. Practitioners are expected to wear a professional mask at all times, but to ignore the emotional labour that this mask entails would be foolish (Taggart, 2011).

Points of Reflection

Imagine you are on your way to work as a practitioner working with children. Think about the factors that might impact upon your resilience and stress levels before work begins.

- When you arrive at your workplace, which behaviours from young children would you find particularly irritating?
- How would you remain calm and deliver a response that is proportionate and helpful for shaping future behaviour?

Relationships (Making Connections) – Do I Feel Loved and Safe?

The second area in the foundation model of children's behaviour is relationships, drawing on attachment theory we explore how a child's sense of safety and security is shaped by the quality of their bonds and connections with others. Attachment refers to 'emotional ties to the special people who offer us comfort, and in whose company, we feel the happiest' (Doherty and Hughes, 2014: 338). The concept of attachment was developed by John Bowlby in the 1950s, who worked together with Mary Ainsworth, another major contributor to attachment theory. Drawing on psychoanalytic theory, ethology and cognitive and developmental psychology Bowlby and Ainsworth constructed a theory of attachment focusing on how affectional bonds are developed and maintained over time between the caregiver and infant (Ainsworth et al., 1978; Bowlby, 1958, 1960). According to Bowlby (1969), children are born with an innate set of 'proximity' behaviours, which enables them to keep their caregiver close by, for example crying and smiling. Attachment is a two-way process, for bonds to be created the caregiver needs to respond to the infant's behaviours in a sensitive, warm and appropriate way. Trevarthen and Aitken (2001) describe this behaviour as 'intersubjectivity', the ability from birth for newborns and their caregiver(s) to mutually regulate their feelings and interests in harmonious and rhythmic patterns.

Ainsworth (1973) observed how young children use their caregivers as a 'secure base', a safe point from which to explore their environment, and as a 'safe haven', a refuge and comfort when they are distressed. These behaviours are identified in her well known 'strange situation' paradigm test in which a series of brief separations and reunions are observed between the infant (aged between 12 and 18 months) and parent (Ainsworth et al., 1978). The extent to which the infant uses the parent as a 'secure base' and 'safe haven' is used to determine the quality of attachment. Ainsworth et al. (1978) identified three categories of attachment insecure avoidant attachment, secure attachment (the most common type of attachment) and insecure ambivalent or resistant attachment. A fourth category, insecure-disorganised, the most insecure type of attachment, was added later by Main and Solomon (1990).

According to Bowlby (1973), these early experiences of attachment provide 'an internal working model' setting a template for future relationship experiences and whether a child feels 'worthy' of love.

Studies of children's attachment type have found that securely attached children are more likely to have better outcomes than children that are insecurely attached. Stroufe (2005) found in their 30-year longitudinal study with 200 mothers[1] that children who are securely attached tend to be more self-reliant, socially competent, better at problem-solving and have high levels of emotional regulation than children with insecure attachments. These outcomes persist into later childhood, with children with secure attachments being more likely to maintain and have better quality friendships, whereas children with insecure attachments being more likely to have difficulties with peers, experience isolation and more dependent on adults. Despite the outcomes of these studies, caution should be applied and a 'deterministic' approach avoided. Although there is a relationship between early attachment experiences and later attachments, this is not a causal effect. Stroufe (2005) found that, while insecure attachments in early childhood presented risk factors for 'adverse outcomes', this was not the case for all children with insecure attachments. Likewise secure attachments did not necessarily protect children from 'adverse outcomes' and children with secure attachments also presented with behaviour challenges.

As practitioners, it is important that simplistic explanations of children's behaviour are avoided, and to remember that there are a 'myriad of interconnecting factors' which can affect children's development and behaviour (Crowley, 2017). Early attachments alone cannot account for outcomes in later life, other social connections within and outside the home (for example sibling and peer relationships) as well as societal issues such as poverty and family stress can also affect children's outcomes (Crowley, 2017). Therefore, although early attachment is undoubtedly a contributing factor to future outcomes, it is in no way the only factor or deterministic.

The role of the key person in early years setting is fundamental to supporting young children's sense of safety and security through creating close attachments between children and adults (Elfer et al., 2012). The EYFS statutory framework (DfE, 2023a: 28) states that:

> Each child must be assigned a key person. Their role is to help ensure that every that every child's care is tailored to meet their individual needs, to help the child become familiar with the setting, offer a settled relationship for the child, and build a relationship with their parents.

---

[1]The term 'mother' has been used in this context as this is the term which is referenced in this research. However, it is recognised that not all people who carry children may not identify with this term.

While some may disagree with young children being cared for outside of the home, research suggests that attending an early year's setting is not a risk factor for children's future development, as long as the provision is high-quality (Elfer et al., 2012). The Effective Provision of Pre-school Education (EPPE) project (Sylva et al., 2004) and Study of Early Education and Development (SEED) (Melhuish and Gardner, 2021) two longitudinal UK studies of young children's development found that high-quality pre-school provision between the ages of two and four years has a positive effect on young children's cognitive and social/behavioural development, and academic outcomes at Key Stage 1. High quality was associated with how practitioners interacted with children (for example supporting children with conflict resolution and problem-solving), and supporting parents with children's learning at home (Sylva et al., 2004). Goldschmied and Selleck (1996, cited in Elfer et al., 2012) represent the close relationships between the key person, child and parent(s) and/or carer(s) as a triangle of trust and communication. The triangle contains the feelings (both positive and negative) that arise between the key person and the children and families they support. At the heart of this relationship is the key person's 'individuality, personality, warmth and empathy' and professionality (Elfer et al., 2012: 42). Page (2017) conceptualises this as 'professional love', the enacting of professional loving practices used by practitioners to build safety and security with the children in their care. However, enacting professional love is not without its challenges, Page (2017) found that many of her participants experienced tensions within their role of 'loco parentis', particularly with feeling able to express their emotions and affections.

Points of Reflection

- What does professional love mean to you?
- What sort of tensions might arise for practitioners in building close attachments with young children?
- How can practitioners build a triangle of trust and communication with the child and their parent(s) and/or carer(s)?

Biology and Genetics – I Behave the Way I Do Because I'm 'Me'

The third area in the foundation model of children's behaviour is biology and genetics. In this section, we explore the other half of the nature/nurture debate, the extent to which children's behaviour is determined by biology and genes (nature). A nature viewpoint understands children's development as a process of maturation (Crowley, 2017). According to this perspective children's development is pre-determined by genetic factors inherited from their parents. For example, research demonstrates that biology can play an important role in determining children's personality traits (Reuter et al., 2022). Closely related to a 'nature' view of children's behaviour is ethology, the study of animals (including humans) under natural conditions. An underlying premise of ethology is that all animal species are born with biologically programmed behaviours, for example Bowlby (1969) believed that all infants are born with 'proximity' behaviours, which are designed to keep the parent/caregiver close by.

Although the nature vs nurture debate is still referenced in many child development texts, it is generally accepted that it is not one or the other, but the interplay between the two which determines children's development. The link between biology/genes and the environment is complex. Research, including studies with children who are twins, suggests that both genes and environment are important in shaping children's development and behaviour (Doherty and Hughes, 2014). In other words, rather than 'nature vs nurture' it is 'nature via nurture', our 'genes are designed to take their cues from nurture' (Ridley, 2004: 4). From conception, children's brain architecture and gene expression (which genes are switched on or off) are influenced by environmental factors such as stress, physical activity, sleep, diet and where we live (Conkbayir, 2021).

Before the child is born a significant amount of neural development has already taken place. Through a process of 'tuning' and 'pruning' those synapses which are used are strengthened, while those that are not used are discarded. The child's experience and environment help to determine which connections grow stronger and more permanent through repeated use (Brown and Ward, 2013). The policy paper 'The best start for life: a vision for the 1001 critical days' (HM Government, 2021) recognises the importance of the period from 'conception to age two' and how a healthy pregnancy sets up the unborn baby for a healthy life:

> As the baby grows inside the womb, the foetus is susceptible to the environment; it hears what the pregnant person hears, consumes what the pregnant person consumes and may react when the pregnant person is distressed. (HM Government, 2021: 14)

Therefore, the health of the child's brain architecture and gene expression is already shaped before birth by maternal health and their environment.

Points of Reflection

- How would you support parent(s) and carer(s) with building healthy brain architecture for their children?
- How would you support babies in your care to develop healthy brain architecture?

Chapter Summary

Despite being one of the most complex areas of children's development, supporting children's behaviour can be one of the most interesting and rewarding roles for practitioners. Understanding behaviour as communication (rather than trying to manage or control children's behaviour) enables us to really listen to what children are trying to tell us. Although we have not been able to discuss in detail strategies to support children, the Foundation Model provides an effective starting point for exploring the complex interconnectivity between a child's environment, relationships and biology. In the appendix, we provide a template (together with an example) which can be used by practitioners to explore the areas of the Foundation Model. Voices of the child, parents and other professionals should be represented where possible. Although this template focuses on support needs for behaviour perceived to be challenging, it is advised that it should be used within a holistic strength-based approach to evaluating children's progress where children's interests and strengths are celebrated.

Key Points

- Understanding children's behaviour as communication helps to listen to what children are trying to tell us.
- Taking a holistic approach using the Foundation Model enables us to understand the complex interconnection between children's experiences, relationships and biology and how this influences behaviour.
- Using a strength-based approach to reflect on children's behaviour helps to ensure we are child-centred and celebrate children's interests and strengths.

Further Reading

Conkbayir, M. (2021) *Early childhood and neuroscience: Theory, research and implications for practice*, 2nd ed. London: Bloomsbury.

Grimmer, T. (2021) *Supporting emotions and behaviour in the Early Years*. Abingdon: Routledge.

Page, J. (2018) Characterising the principles of professional love in early childhood care and education. *International Journal of Early Years Education*, 26(2): 125–141. DOI: 10.1080/09669760.2018.1459508

References

Ainsworth, M. (1973) The development of infant-mother attachment. In B. Caldwell and H. Ricciuti (eds), *Review of child development research* (Vol. 3). Chicago: University of Chicago Press.

Ainsworth, M., Blehar, M., Waters, E. and Wall, S. (1978) *Patterns of attachment*. Hillsdale: Erlbaum.

Aries, P. (1962) *Centuries of childhood: A social history of family life*. New York: Alfred A. Knopf.

Aubrey, K. and Riley, A. (2019) *Understanding and using educational theories*, 2nd ed. London: SAGE.

Aynsley-Green, A. (2018) *The British betrayal of childhood*. London: Routledge.

Berger, E. (2019) Multi-tiered approaches to trauma-informed care in schools: A systematic review. *School Mental Health*, 11, 650–664.

Bowlby, J. (1958) The nature of the child's tie to his mother. *The International Journal of Psychoanalysis*, 39, 350–373.

Bowlby, J. (1960) Grief and mourning in infancy and early childhood. *The psychoanalytic study of the child*, 15.

Bowlby, J. (1969) *Attachment and loss: Vol 1. Attachment.* New York: Basic.

Bowlby, J. (1973) *Separation and loss.* New York: Basic.

Bronfenbrenner, U. (1979) *The ecology of human development: experiments by nature and design.* Available at: https://ebookcentral.proquest.com/lib/chiuni-ebooks/detail.action?docID=3300702 (Accessed 3 March 2023).

Brown, R. and Ward, H. (2013) Decision making within a child's timeframe. Available at: https://www.gov.uk/government/publications/decision-making-within-a-childs-timeframe-an-overview-of-current-research-evidence-for-family-justice-professionals-concerning-child-development-and (Accessed 20 March 2023).

Brennan, S. (2018) 'Foreword' in Bush, M. (ed.) *Addressing adversity: Prioritising adversity and trauma-informed care for children and young people in England*, pp. 5–6. Available at: https://www.youngminds.org.uk/media/cmtffcce/ym-addressing-adversity-book-web-2.pdf (Accessed 13 April 2023).

Brennan, R., Bush, M., Trickey, D., Levene, C. and Nad Watson, J. (2019) *Adversity and Trauma informed practice: a short guide for professionals working on the frontline.* Available at: https://www.youngminds.org.uk/professional/resources/addressing-trauma-and-adversity/

Colvin, G. and Scott, T. (2015) *Managing the cycle of acting out behaviour*, 2nd ed. London: Corwin.

Conkbayir, M. (2021) *Early childhood and neuroscience: theory, research and implications for practice.* 2nd ed. London: Bloomsbury.

Convention on the Rights of the Child (1989) *Treaty no. 27531.* United Nations Treaty Series, 1577, pp. 3–178. Available at: https://treaties.un.org/doc/Treaties/1990/09/19900902%2003-14%20AM/Ch_IV_11p.pdf (Accessed 20 March 2023).

Crowley, K. (2017) *Child development: a practical introduction.* London: SAGE.

Department for Education (2023a) *Early years foundation stage statutory framework for group and school-based provides. Setting the standards for learning, development and care for children from birth to five.* Available at: https://www.gov.uk/government/publications/early-years-foundation-stage-framework--2 (Accessed 20 May 2024).

Department for Education (2023b) *Early years foundation statutory framework for group and school-based providers.* Available at: https://www.gov.uk/government/publications/early-years-foundation-stage-framework--2 (Accessed 20 May 2024).

Department for Education (2021) *Development matters.* Available at: https://www.gov.uk/government/publications/development-matters--2 (Accessed 1 January 2023).

Department for Education (2024) *Department for Education (2024) Early years foundation stage profile: 2024 handbook.* Available at: https://www.gov.uk/government/publications/early-years-foundation-stage-profile-handbook (Accessed 20 May 2024).

Doherty, J. and Hughes, M. (2014) *Child development: Theory and practice 0–11*, 2nd ed. Harlow: Pearson Education Ltd.

Elfer, P., Goldschmied, E. and Selleck, D. (2012) *Key persons in the early years*, 2nd ed. Abingdon: Routledge.

Gentile, D., Anderson, C.A., Yukawa, S., Ihori, N., Saleem, M., Ming, L. K., Shibuya, A., Liau, A. K., Khoo, A., Bushman, B. J., Rowell Huesmann, L., and Sakamoto, A. (2009) The effects of prosocial video games on prosocial behaviors; international evidence from correlational, longitudinal and experimental studies. *Personality and Social Psychology Bulletin*, 35(6), 752–763.

Ginnot, H. (1993) *Teacher and child: A book for parents and teachers*. New York: Collier.

Grimmer, T. (2021) *Supporting emotions and behaviour in the Early Years*. Abingdon: Routledge.

HM Government (2021) *The best start for life: a vision for the 1, 001 critical days*. Available at: https://www.gov.uk/government/publications/the-best-start-for-life-a-vision-for-the-1001-critical-days (Accessed 20 March 2023).

Hughes, P. and MacNaughton, G. (2000) Consensus, dissensus or community: The politics of parent involvement in early childhood communication. *Contemporary Issues in Early Childhood*, 1(3), 241–258.

James, A., Jenks, C., and Prout, A. (1998) *Theorizing childhood*. Cambridge: Polity Press.

Jenks, C. (2005) *Childhood*, 2nd ed. London: Routledge.

Keller, H. (2018) Universality claim of attachment theory: Children's socio-emotional development across cultures. *Anthropology*, 115(45), 11414–11419.

Kohn, A. (1993) *Punished by rewards: The trouble with gold stars, incentive plans, A's, praise and other bribes*. New York: Hughton Mifflin.

Maclure, M., Jones, L., Holmes, R., and MacRae, C. (2011) Becoming a problem: Behaviour and reputation in the early years classroom. *British Educational Research Journal*, 38(2), 447–471.

Main, M. and Solomon, J. (1990) Procedures for identifying infants as disorganized/disorientated during the Ainsworth Strange situation. In M. Greenberg, D. Cicchetti and E. Cummings (eds), *Attachment in the pre-school years: Theory, research and intervention* (pp. 121–160). Chicago: University of Chicago Press.

Maslow, A. (1970) *Motivation and Personality*. New York: Harper and Row.

Melhuish, E. and Gardner, J. (2021) Study of early education and development (SEED): impact case study on early education use and child outcomes up to age seven years. Available at: https://www.gov.uk/government/publications/early-education-use-and-child-outcomes-up-to-age-7 (Accessed 7 February 2023).

Page, J. (2017) Re-framing infant toddler pedagogy through a lens of professional love: exploring narratives of professional love: exploring narratives of professional practice in early childhood settings in England. *Contemporary Issues in Early Childhood*, 18(4), 387–399.

Reuter, M., Plieger, T. and Netter, P. (2022) The question why and how people differ in personality cannot be answered satisfactorily while neglecting biological approaches. *Current opinion in behavioral sciences*, 43, 181–186.

Ridley, M. (2004) *Nature via nurture: Genes, experience and what makes us human*. London: Fourth Estate.

Rogers, B. and Mcpherson, E. (2014). *Behaviour management with young children: Crucial first steps with children 3–7 years*, 2nd ed. London: SAGE.

Rogers, C. (1959) Significant learning: In therapy and in education. *Educational Leadership*, 16, 232–242.

Sackville-Ford, M. (2019). How might we frame behaviour in primary schools. In C. Carden (ed.), *Primary teaching*. London: SAGE, pp. 244–260.

Skinner, J. (1971) *Beyond freedom and dignity*. Indianapolis: Hackett Publishing.

Smith, K. (2011) Producing governable subjects: images of childhood old and new. *Childhood*, 19(1), 24–37.

Sorin, R. and Galloway, G. (2006) Constructs of childhood: Constructs of self. *Children Australia*, 31(2), 12–21.

Staton, S., Rankin, S. R., Harding, M., Smith, S., Westwood, E., LeBourgeois, M. and Thorpe, K. (2020) Many naps, one nap, none: A systematic review and meta-analysis of napping patterns in children 0–12 years. *Sleep Medicine Reviews*, 50.

Stroufe, L. (2005) Attachment and development: A prospective, longitudinal study from birth to adulthood. *Attachment & Human Development*, 7(4), 349–367.

Sylva, K., Melhuish, E., Sammons, P., Siraj-Blatchford, I. and Taggart, B. (2004) The effective provision of pre-school education (EPPE) project: Findings from preschool to end of key stage 1. Available at: https://dera.ioe.ac.uk/8543/7/SSU-SF-2004-01.pdf (Accessed 20 March 2023).

Taggart, G. (2011). Don't we care? The ethics and emotional labour of early years professionalism. *Early Years*, 31(1), 85–95.

Trevarthen, C. and Aitken, K. (2001) Infant intersubjectivity: Research, theory and clinical applications. *Journal of Child Psychology and Psychiatry*, 42(1), 3–48.

Uher, J. (2016) What is behaviour? And (when) is language behaviour? A metatheoretical definition. *Journal for the Theory of Social Behaviour*, 46(4), 475–501.

West Sussex County Council (2021) West Sussex ordinarily available inclusive practice: A co-produced guide for all mainstream staff working in education settings. Available at: https://schools.local-offer.org/inclusion/ordinarily-available-inclusive-practice/ (Accessed 19 July 2023).

Appendix

Detecting Influences on Behaviour Using the Foundation Model (Example)

Behaviour: Hitting others

Arousal level: Heightened. X does not hit children when calm. X moves from calm to heightened arousal very rapidly. X describes this as feeling 'wobbly'.

Socio-emotional factors: X is four-years old and has been diagnosed with autism so they are developing their regulation of behaviour and emotions. X has not experienced much prior success in relation to his behaviour fitting the expectations of the setting and we are starting to see this impact upon his self-esteem. He has begun to shout 'I can't do it' when we discuss rules. We need to review the support we are putting in place to help him achieve success with his behaviour.

Experiences

After some detective work, we have realised that X regularly hits others when he is ill or tired. X has disturbed sleep and colds regularly which impact behaviours. X has an Education Health and Care Plan (EHCP) in place which has resulted in him receiving 1:1 support when communicating.

Relationships

Relationships contribute to X's feeling of safety and security. X's parents report that X hits children when stressed because his key person is working with other children, rather than staying close to him.

Biology

X has autism so his developmental pathway is atypical and we need to recognise that his development of behavioural regulation is unlikely to follow a typical trajectory. X needs support to communicate with others and frustration with communication could impact upon their self-regulation.

Review and Next Steps

We now have a better understanding of why X hits other children. Moving forward, we will use a home-parent log book to enhance communication about when illness or tiredness could influence behaviours. An additional secure relationship with an adult is required to minimise distress for X when his key person is unavailable.

3

The Digital Child

Eva Mikuska and Andre Kurowski

After reading this chapter, readers will be able to:

- Outline the benefits and drawbacks for children in a digital age.
- Comment on issues facing parents in a digital age.
- Evaluate attempts to protect children from online harms.

Introduction

The role of digital technology (DT) is complex and dynamic, and it has become a significant element of early childhood education and care professional practices and philosophy. Children are early adopters and frequent users of the internet for play, communication and access for information (UNICEF, 2017). DT supports children learning and literacy skills (Flewitt et al., 2015; Kucirkova et al., 2019), digital creativity and digital play (Sakr, 2019), but it has been associated with social problems such as addiction (Ding and Li, 2023; Hermawati et al., 2018). Undheim's (2022) definition of DT refers to electronic tools, various digital devices, including digital resources and digital content. The term 'digital child' refers to those children who have grown up with DTs including digital environment and digital space and little experience without DT. Digital literacy refers to the knowledge, skills and attitudes that allow children to be both safe and empowered in an increasingly digital world. This encompasses their play, participation, socialising, searching and learning through DTs. This chapter will examine children in a world changing faster than ever, and the development of the 'digital child'.

The Way Childhood Is Changing: The Concept of the Digital Child

The use of DT can have unintended positive and negative consequences that are rarely evenly distributed throughout the society. For example, ECEs often struggle to think about digital play as 'real play'. Edwards (2016) explains how to tackle this issue by developing a 'web-mapping' tool that enables ECE to recognise how children develop interests through play in various contexts using various resources including DT. Children can also use DT in distributed ways across the various activities and rooms in the ECEC settings and include DT in their play (Fleer, 2020). It can be argued that when DT became part of the social practices in the ECEC setting, play has become more complex, for example when the children record each other's play. Afterwards, when watching their recorded play, the children experienced a form of 're-play'. This process contributes to the development of the 'digital child'.

For children DT has several advantages. In an era of increased supervision and restrictions on young people's access to actual public spaces, digital media provides alternatives for self-expression, friendship-building, learning and knowledge acquisition, creativity and digital play (Sakr, 2019; Wilson, 2016). However, children's ability to understand the complicated workings and ramifications of using DT, according to Stoilova et al. (2020) and Orben et al. (2022), is constrained by their cognitive aptitude. Children are unable to comprehend what they see and do online until they are between the ages of 10 and 11 years (Abrams, 2022) despite, in some cases, the potential consequences on their lives (Orben et al., 2022). Therefore, participation in internet activities by children less than 11 years is cognitively juvenile, consistent with Piaget's (1929) formal operational stage. Children from the age 11 can think abstractly and methodically, utilising moral reasoning to create a plausible explanation for their online behaviours. Therefore, only children who are at least 11 years old can fully comprehend online activities and engage effectively and safely (Orben et al., 2022). As a result, children under 11 years are more vulnerable to danger and harm from the online environment (Kidron and Rudkin, 2017). Craft (2012) argues, as technology evolves, childhood and adolescence also change. Children are constantly connected and have a parallel existence in a virtual space, interacting on social networks, playing online games and creating and modifying content (Craft, 2012). The constant exposure to digital communications has resulted in children being instantly connected to the digital world from birth (King, 2022; UNICEF, 2017) which has contributed to the digitalisation of childhood (Craft, 2012).

Yet, the benefits or dangers of this phenomenon are yet to be established. The effect of DT on childhood experiences has never been more pronounced than it is right now (UNICEF, 2017). Online technologies are frequently referred to as digital media (Guinibert, 2021) and in modern civilisation's current digitalisation phase, digital media is extremely important (Musuik and Bognor, 2019). While some argue the development of digital technology has opened limitless opportunities for communication, education and self-expression, others argue it endangers children's well-being (UNICEF, 2017). Digital technology is transforming childhood (Coleman, 2022), influencing how children engage with people, participate in the discussion and express themselves online (Norman et al., 2015).

Points of Reflection

Children can view content not intended for them online. Neil Postman (1994) wrote about children's access to the wider adult world through technology, and the effect on what we have come to regard as 'childhood'.

- What online content should be regarded as inappropriate for children?
- What online content should children be protected from?
- To what extent can online activities threaten our ideas of childhood?

The Role and Impact of Digital Technologies in Early Childhood and Education

According to Childwise (2022), 94% of children have a computer at home, 73% have a touchscreen tablet, 69% have a laptop or netbook and most children sleep with their mobile phone beside their bed. Children aged 5–15 spend around 15 hours each week online (Ofcom, 2020), and are what Weiler (2005) calls 'e-ready'. However, not all young people have equal access to technology; in the United Kingdom, if you are living in poverty, there is less chance of being online. The chances of having access to the internet from home increase with income; only 51% of households with earnings between £6000 and 10,000 have home internet access, whereas 99% of households with an income of over £40,001 (University of Cambridge, 2023).

There is limited research with a critical focus as to how the digital influx is shaping children's development and experience (Hatzigianni et al., 2023), and whether some children are excluded if their homes lack smartphones or access to the internet (Baltaki and Ersoz, 2022; D'Lima and Higgins, 2021). Research suggests that the potential of new technologies for young children's literacy development remains largely untapped in educational settings with a 'digital divide' where children have different experiences at the setting and at home (Wolfe and Flewitt, 2010).

Early childhood education and care (ECEC) primarily uses DT for pedagogical purposes, as a tool to support and advance the quality of teaching and learning in areas, such as early literacy (Kucirkova et al., 2019; Neumann et al., 2022) and early mathematics (Sinclair, 2018). There has also been an increasing focus to integrate DT to encourage problem-solving thinking in young children (Murcia et al., 2020).

Children's immersion in digital communication and the use of DT occurs at a critical period in their lives when their emerging literacy skills and identities as effective and competent learners are being moulded by the conventions of the social and cultural worlds in which they live (Flewitt et al., 2015). Generation Z, or 'zoomers', born between 1996 and 2010, have been shaped by the digital age (Merriam-Webster Dictionary,

2023). The European Commission et al. (2018) acknowledged that babies and young children observe and mirror the behaviour of adults and older children close to them, and a four-year old is perfectly capable of mimicking the taking digital photos and to use smartphone, digital camera or a digital video recorder. Neumann et al. (2022) argue that young children diversify their digital skills, and those children who attend educational environments that integrate DT meaningfully and develop digital literacy are more aware of risks.

Primary school children are using social media apps more now than ever, affecting how they interact and communicate with others (Neumann et al., 2022). Social media in today's digital age includes several online social media sites each with a different way to connect, communicate and share material (Boyd and Ellison, 2007). This provides several advantages; children can use social media to learn virtually and connect with others locally and globally which was beneficial during the Covid-19 pandemic (Mikuska et al., 2021), although differences in access to DT were highlighted during the Covid-19 lockdowns in 2020–2021 (Kurowski, 2022).

DT can also play a major role in supporting early childhood educators (ECE) with planning, documentation and observations of children's learning and development (Lyons and Tredwell, 2015). Beaumont-Bates (2017) suggests that educators are increasingly adopting digital resources to allow ECEC settings to streamline processes and communicate more effectively with parents and carers. DT also provides opportunities to connect to the world (Hoehe and Thibaut, 2020), and Greater Manchester Combined Authority (2022) use an 'Early Years App' to connect health professionals with parents and carers; the aim is to make services more efficient, reduce costs, identify support needs and to empower people.

Case Study: Online Learning During Lockdown

- During the Covid-19 lockdown, some children were excluded from education through lack of online access and/or lack of effective support from home (Kurowski, 2022) resulting in differential outcomes for children from different socio-economic backgrounds.
- What are the implications for children from different socio-economic backgrounds?
- What expectations can schools realistically place on parents to support their children with online learning?
- What could the consequences be for the widespread use of technology in children's learning?

The Child and Digital Dependency

According to Levine and Munsch (2018), children are active explorers who continually do investigations on the world around them to better understand it and use their findings to develop conceptual frameworks. Hence, it could be claimed that children are using DT to learn about the world in a novel way. With constant exposure to DT, children are increasingly curious about the function of technology; however, in many countries, internet addiction has become a serious problem for mental health. Ding and Li (2023) found addiction is mainly among adolescents aged between 9 and 19 years. However, Hermawati et al. (2018) found that children under two-years old who used more than 3 hours of screen time every day, had symptoms such as attention problems and hyperactivity, but most frequent symptom of addiction across all age groups is depression. Also, Beyens and Nathanson (2019) argue that overuse of DT affects children's sleeping and eating patterns, causing substantial damage to their health and brain function.

Lockdowns during the Covid-19 pandemic led to a sharp increase in digital addiction, especially in children and young adolescents. Addiction is often associated with substance misuse but can also be extended to other compulsive behaviours including sex, internet use, television, gambling, food and shopping. Within these categories of addiction, a common diagnostic scale involves tolerance, withdraw and cravings (Muller et al., 2013). With widespread use of home-based online teaching and learning, hundreds of millions of children worldwide have also been transformed into 'online learners'. Children and their teachers were not ready for such a sudden paradigm shift (Mikuska et al., 2021), theoretically and practically resulting safeguarding issues (Khan and Mikuska, 2021) nor were parents prepared for digital learning at home. Ding and Li (2023) argue that home-schooled children were particularly vulnerable due to excessive or unrestricted use of digital devices and contributed to digital addiction. Even so, digital addictions are very rare, especially in children and adolescents (Ding and Li, 2023).

In recent years writers have been referring to the phenomenon of Problematic Internet Use (PIU) (Anderson et al., 2017). There are certain predictors for PIU and these include psychiatric disorders, affective disorders (including depression), anxiety disorders, attention deficit hyperactivity disorder (ADHD), personality traits, parenting and familial factors, alcohol use and social anxiety (Weinstein and Lejoyeux, 2010). Males are at higher risk, and some personality traits have been identified (Anderson et al., 2017). These include extroversion and neuroticism, impulsive behaviour, expression of hostility and aggression and preferences for visual stimuli.

Cyberbullying

The arrival of new DT has resulted in a new type of bullying, cyberbullying (CB) in various forms including spreading malicious rumours to intimidation and blackmail, from posting embarrassing or humiliating images or videos without consent to repeated harassment (National Bullying Helpline, 2023). New terms have emerged from cyberbullying, including 'trolling', menacing messages on social media (Ineqe, 2021) and 'doxing', the posting of private information about someone else online, which could include the victim's real name, home address, phone number, email address, photos or other personal information (Bernard, 2022).

The effects of CB on health and well-being are unclear. Li et al. (2022) claim that children affected by bullying in cyberspace may experience emotional and behavioural issues. However, it is evident that the volume of CB has increased in parallel with the increased use of DT, which is considered a serious public health concern (Ferrara et al., 2018). CB poses new challenges for ECEC regarding how to effectively provide young children with appropriate cyber safety education (Edwards et al., 2016) with bullying causing self-harm and, at worst, suicide (NSPCC, 2020). Children's capacity to utilise technologies, particularly social media, efficiently and safely, is reduced due to unfavourable consequences and negative outcomes. Abrams (2022) and Orben et al. (2022) claim that children should not be allowed the freedom to use digital media until they are of a responsible age since they do not understand the significant harm it can cause. As incidents of cyberbullying are anticipated to increase with the growing importance of the internet (Mahanta and Khatoniyar, 2019), putting measures in place to protect children is urgent. Li et al. (2022) established that CB victimization among youths is a public health concern. They argue that rapid change and increased use of DT could be a marker of greater 'psychopathological severity, particularly suicide-related issues'.

Developing teachers and parents' digital competency skills is particularly controversial in school and early years settings (Merchant, 2012); access to DTs in early years settings and schools potentially gives marginalised and disadvantaged children opportunities to learn vital skills and bridge socio-economic status and educational attainment gaps. However, several issues arise as digital media continues to innovate, and CB is one of these. It is evident that in the digital era we all live, more studies that explore the impact of CB are necessary to inform the development of educational and public policies devoted to mitigating the impact of CB.

Points of Reflection

'Some people just use like Facebook and Instagram and things like that just to promote how good their life is and make it seem much better than it actually is and make other people ... feel really bad' (Kidron and Rudkin, 2017).

- How far does cyberspace provide more convenient opportunities for children to engage in bullying?
- How can online bullying be compared with other, offline, forms of bullying?
- To what extent has cyberspace replaced other, offline, forms of bullying?

Parenting in a Digital Age

From the early days of DT to today's social networks, tablets and multiplayer online games, DT has always entered discourses of parenting and raised new hopes and fears affecting parenting. Ofcom (2022) found that of 3–4-year olds, 17% have their own mobile phones, although the main devices used are tablets. Eighty nine percent of this group use video-sharing platforms, and 24% have their own social media profile. In the 5–7 age range, 93% use video-sharing platforms and 33% have their own social media profile. Where such young children are using DT to this extent, it might be asked what role the parents have in this.

Many parents and carers are increasingly anxious about what these changes will mean for their children now, and in the future. Livingstone and Blum-Ross (2020) argue, parents are clear that the future will be digital. With informal education starting in the home for children, parents have more power to influence their children's beliefs, attitudes and behaviours than teachers in the school environment. However, 'turning it off' is no longer feasible, especially in a post-pandemic world where childhood has become digital by default. Parent's main concerns are that their children are using social media sites too young, concerns about cyberbullying, the content of video-sharing sites and online purchasing (Agechecked.com, 2016).

In addition, a new contradiction is raising concern; the more society relies on parents to find ways and means to bring up their children for a digital future, the greater the digital inequalities will be, due to family's diverse circumstances and incomes. More than a third of parents (36%) said their primary school-age children did not always have access, and 11% rarely had access to an 'appropriate device' in the home. Of secondary school children, just 17% did not always have access and 3% rarely had access to an appropriate device (Ofcom, 2022). Providing homes with adequate DT, even if achievable, is far from realised. Therefore, it is vital that the key government, education and welfare institutions that rely on parents to provide a digital home, 'should build a supportive infrastructure, tailored to diverse circumstances and responsive to parents' concerns' (Livingstone and Blum-Ross, 2020: 33). Parental responsibilities are changing in line with the needs of the digital age. In the digital age, parents try to resist or to balance change while at the same time trying to embrace the development of DT in ways that meet the needs of their family.

While parents encourage their children to use digital media for educational and social purposes, they also attempt to minimise risks and control the potential negative consequences developing digital literacy. Nine out of ten children have been told about online safety, usually by a parent or teacher (Ofcom, 2022). Parental control is vital in preventing and reducing the risks and threats children may encounter in their online activities (Nouwen and Zaman, 2018). This implies that parents need to perceive and use technology in an effective way, prepare their children for the requirements of the information age, and encourage them to acquire and properly use information. Parents (75%) tend to feel they know enough to keep their children safe online, and half of the parents speak to their children about online safety regularly (every few weeks) (Ofcom, 2022). Therefore, parents should have sufficient knowledge about their children's internet use, the online risks and threats and the safe use of the internet.

However, the advice parents receive is fundamentally contradictory according to Livingstone and Blum-Ross (2020). For example the use of internet for 'screen time' including schoolwork, but also sustaining friendships and family. Parents see benefits from being online in that it helps their child with their schoolwork or homework, and the older the child the more perceived benefit. Also, more than half of the parents feel that their child benefits from learning new skills or developing their creative skills, across all age groups for children (Ofcom, 2019). However, Livingstone and Blum-Ross (2020) found that parents report significantly more conflict about screen time than about how children use the technologies. They found that parents tend to support more of their children's digital learning opportunities if schools integrate DT in their homework and tend to have more positive views upon technologies.

A child's interaction with digital media can be influenced by reinforcement from family members. McPake et al. (2013) advise that this is due to young children learning about social media by observing their family and friends. Children who grow up in a culture where a variety of technology is used and where social media usage is common will normalise these traits and will want to emulate them, resulting in many children using social media before they are old enough to have an account. Navarro and Tudge (2022) argue that interactions with families, communities and cultures affect children's experiences, attitudes and behaviours on social media. Taani et al. (2017) argues that it is common knowledge that social media sites are used by parents to communicate with their children. As a result, children start their own social media and gain more understanding about the various types of applications, online games and social interactions available to them. A rising number of young people worldwide are equipped with mobile devices like smartphones and tablets, keeping them connected to their parents, social peer groups and accessibility to photo and video capabilities (Bork- Hüffer et al., 2020). For them, the internet is thoroughly ingrained into their daily spaces rather than existing as a distinct 'cyberspace' (Vanden Abeele, 2016). Simultaneously, because digital devices and media may present new threats (George and Odgers, 2015), young people should have media competency skills. Strandell (2014) argues that the lack of media competency skills results in parents and teachers frequently questioning the use of mobile devices and their related activities. Adigwe and van der Walt (2020) argue that parents should support their children to develop digital literacy skills that mitigate possible digital risks and facilitate online safety. Young children can develop the technical abilities necessary to send text messages and emails, and transmit and receive digital information. Hence, parents and teachers can play a significant role in the development of children's social media abilities in terms of personal safety, information sharing and privacy settings by providing the appropriate guidance and direction (Donelle et al., 2021).

Points of Reflection

Parents' main concerns about their children's online activities include pornography, cyber-bullying and video-sharing sites that contain violent or inappropriate content (Agechecked, 2016).

- How can parents control the online activities of children?
- What other online content should parents be concerned about?
- To what extent are parents able to supervise or control the online content their children access?

The Law, Policy and Technological Development

The ease with which children use DT raises questions about whether they completely comprehend the need for online safety. Being online offers a wealth of new opportunities for realising children's rights, but also poses new risks for their violation and abuse. Legislation already exists but is continually trying to keep up with changing technology. The Communications Act 2003 (Crown Prosecution Service, 2022) provides for dishonestly obtaining access to the internet, sending malicious communications, causing 'annoyance' or 'needless anxiety' and sending grossly offensive or obscene messages. However, with what we know about DT and children, more relevant legislation is necessary.

To be safe online, children need to develop digital literacy, to differentiate online opportunities and risks, and how to manage harms and threats online. In England and Wales, the Online Safety Act 2023 (UK Parliament, 2023) was first published as a draft in 2021, and has recently passed as legislation. One of the main barriers to it becoming law is the balance between protection for children and free speech (Chartered Institute for IT, 2023). A distinction has been developed between 'illegal' and 'harmful' content (UK Parliament, 2022); however, some content may not break any laws, but it may still be harmful. Duties placed on large technology platforms to tackle 'legal but harmful' content have been removed from the Bill after challenges about adults 'free speech' (Chartered Institute for IT, 2023), and young children may continue to be exposed to harmful images or online bullying because legal but harmful content is not prohibited (NSPCC, 2023); children may continue to see inappropriate or explicit content due to algorithms, the technical method of sorting content based on the likelihood of engagement (Golino, 2021). Children's safety is put in jeopardy by this kind of content because there is no guarantee that their online activities are safe.

Case Study: Molly Russell

Fourteen-year-old Molly Russell took her own life after viewing disturbing material about depression, suicide and self-harm. It has been suggested that, even though the content she accessed was legal, Molly's death was caused by social media firm's use of algorithms to supply more similar, harmful, material (NSPCC, 2022a).

- Can young people have a full understanding of the implications of their online consumption?
- To what extent can social media platforms be responsible for the content that children access online?
- To what extent can legislation be used to promote the safety of children?

Chapter Summary

This chapter has examined how the rapid influx of DT has influenced the digitalisation of childhood and placed childhood within the distinctive context of the digital age. It is difficult to determine the effect of DT on children; instead, the focus should be on the balanced relationship between DT and children environment/society as one aspect of the society that is in constant change. Children's aptitude has been raised as a crucial consideration in assessing the extent of children's capacity to engage in digital activities safely and productively in the online environment. It has been suggested that while the digital world presents children and young people with a variety of new opportunities, it also exposes them to a variety of new harms and dangers (NSPCC, 2022b). This chapter has emphasised the need for wider DT use as well as upskilling for early childhood educators and parents, but also how to use DT more safely and this involves teaching children about digital literacy. Additionally, training parents/carers on the value of talking and spending time with their children and enabling parental controls on devices is important. In addition, it is key to limit children's access to adult content and educate them on the potential dangers and harms of the digital world.

Key Points

- The technological age has brought with it benefits and drawbacks for children.
- Legislation needs to keep up with developments in technology to protect children.
- Parents and educators need to play a role in educating children about safe and effective online activities.

Further Reading

Luttrell, R. (2021) Social media: How to engage, share, and connect. Maryland: Rowman and Littlefield Publishers.

Online Safety Act (2023) Legislation. Gov. UK. https://www.legislation.gov.uk/ukpga/2023/50/enacted

Ofcom (2020) Online Nation. https://www.ofcom.org.uk/__data/assets/pdf_file/0027/196407/online-nation-2020-report.pdf

References

Abrams, Z. (2022) Why young brains are especially vulnerable to social media: The science behind why apps like TikTok, Instagram, and Snapchat impact your child's brain in a different way than your adult brain. Available at: https://www.apa.org/news/apa/2022/social-media-children-teens (Accessed on 01.04.2023).

Adigwe, I. and Van der Walt, T. (2020) Parental mediation of online media activities of children in Nigeria: A parent-child approach. *Computers in Human Behavior Reports*, 2(3)

Agechecked.com (2016) Parents' Concerns for 'Generation Internet, A research study by Agechecked.com 2016. Available at: https://images.agechecked.com/agechecked_report_print.pdf (Accessed on 04.07.2023).

Anderson, E. L., Steen, E. and Stavropoulos, V. (2017). Internet use and problematic internet use: A systematic review of longitudinal research trends in adolescence and emergent adulthood. *International Journal of Adolescence and Youth*, 22(4), 430–454.

Baltaki, S. and Ersoz, A. R. (2022) Social media engagement, fear of missing out and problematic internet use in secondary school children. *International Online Journal of Educational Sciences*, 14(1), 197–210.

Beaumont-Bates, J. R. (2017) E-portfolios: Supporting collaborative partnerships in an early childhood centre in Aotearoa/New Zealand. *Educational Studies*, 52, 347–362. https://doi.org/10.1007/s40841-017-0092-1 (Accessed on 04.07.2023).

Bernard, C. (2022) *What is doxxing? How to keep children safe*. Internet Matters. Available at: https://www.internetmatters.org/hub/news-blogs/what-is-doxxing-and-how-can-you-keep-your-child-safe/?gclid=CjwKCAiAyfybBhBKEiwAgtB7fqZr4WoyB_pRaqChOFQ1aFzfqKYh7kH8xRSKzZNRSMnxjt-XRpSAvhoCj_oQAvD_BwE (Accessed on 04.07.2023).

Beyens, I. and Nathanson, A. I. (2019) Electronic Media Use and Sleep Among Preschoolers: Evidence for Time-Shifted and Less Consolidated Sleep, *Health Communication*, 34(5), 537–544.

Bork-Hüffer, T., Mahlknecht, B. and Kaufmann, K. (2020). (Cyber)Bullying in schools – When bullying stretches across cON/FFlating spaces. *Children's Geographies*, 19(2), 1–13. https://doi.org/10.1080/14733285.2020.1784850 (Accessed on 04.07.2023).

Boyd, D. M. and Ellison, N. B. (2007) Social network sites: Definition, history, and scholarship. *Journal of Computer-Mediated Communication*. 13(1), 210–230. https://doi.org/10.1111/j.1083-6101.2007.00393.x (Accessed on 04.07.2023).

Chartered Institute for IT (2023) *The online safety bill – Where are we as the Bill reaches the Lords?* Available at: https://www.bcs.org/articles-opinion-and-research/the-online-safety-bill-where-are-we-as-the-bill-reaches-the-lords/ (Accessed on 04.07.2023).

Childwise (2022) *Childwise Monitor Report*. Available at: https://www.childwise.co.uk/monitor.html (Accessed on 04.07.2023).

Coleman, C. (2022). *Social media: potential harm to children.* Available at: https://lordslibrary.parliament.uk/social-media-potential-harm-to-children/ (Accessed on 01.03.2023).

Craft, A. (2012). Childhood in a Digital Age: creative challenges for educational futures. *London Review of Education*, 10(2), 173–190.

Crown Prosecution Service (2022) *Social media and other electronic communications.* Available at: https://www.cps.gov.uk/legal-guidance/social-media-and-other-electronic-communications (Accessed on 04.07.2023).

Ding, K. and Li, H. (2023) Digital addiction intervention for children and adolescents: A scoping review. *International Journal of Environmental Research and Public Health*, 20(6), 4777. https://doi.org/10.3390/ijerph20064777 (Accessed on 04.07.2023).

D'Lima, P. and Higgins, A. (2021) Social media engagement and fear of missing out (FOMO) in primary school children. *Educational Psychology in Practice*, 37(3), 320–338.

Donelle, L., Facca, D., Burke, S., Hiebert, B., Bender, E. and Ling, S. (2021) Exploring Canadian children's social media use, digital literacy, and quality of life: Pilot cross-sectional survey study. *JMIR Formative Research*, 5(5), 18771.

Edwards, S., Nolan, A., Henderson, M., Skouteris, H., Mantilla, A., Lambert, P. and Bird, J. (2016) Developing a measure to understand young children's Internet cognition and cyber-safety awareness: A pilot test. *Early Years*, 36(3), 322–335. https://doi.org/10.1080/09575146.2016.1193723 (Accessed on 04.07.2023).

Edwards, S. (2016) New concepts of play and the problem of technology, digital media and popular-culture integration with play-based learning in early childhood education. *Technology, Pedagogy and Education*, 25 (4), 513–532.

Edwards, S., Mantilla, A., Grieshaber, S., Wood, E. (2020) Converged play characteristics for early childhood education: Multi-modal, global-local, and traditional-digital. *Oxford Review of Education*, 46(12), 1–24.

European Commission, Joint Research Centre, Chaudron, S., Di Gioia, R., Gemo, M. (2018) *Young children (0-8) and digital technology: a qualitative study across Europe*, Publications Office. Available at: https://data.europa.eu/doi/10.2760/294383 (Accessed on 04.07.2023).

Ferrara, P., Lanniello, F., Villani, A. and Corsello, G. (2018) Cyberbullying a modern form of bullying: Let's talk about this health and social problem. *Journal of Paediatrics*. 44(14). Available at: https://ijponline.biomedcentral.com/articles/10.1186/s13052-018-0446-4 (Accessed on 28.02.2023).

Fleer, M. (2020) Studying the relations between motives and motivation – How young children develop a motive orientation for collective engineering play. *Learning, Culture and Social Interaction*, 24. https://doi.org/10.1016/j.lcsi.2019.100355

Flewitt, R., Messer, D. and Kucirkowa, N. (2015) New directions for early literacy in a digital age: The iPad. *Journal of Early Childhood Literacy*. 15(3), 289-310.

George, M.J. and Odgers, C.L. (2015) Seven fears and the science of how mobile technologies may be influencing adolescents in the digital age. *Perspectives on Psychological Science*, 10(6), 832–851. https://doi.org/10.1177/1745691615596788 (Accessed on 04.07.2023).

Golino, M. (2021) *Algorithms in social media platforms.* Available at: https://www.internetjustsociety.org/algorithms-in-social-media-platforms (Accessed on 01.03.2023).

Greater Manchester Combined Authority (2022) *Giving children the best start in life through digital*. Available at: https://www.greatermanchester-ca.gov.uk/what-we-do/digital/empowering-people/early-years-digitisation/ (Accessed on 04.07.2023).

Guinibert, M. (2021) Defining digital media as a professional practice in New Zealand. *Kōtuiui: New Zealand Journal of Social Sciences*, 17(2), 185–205.

Hatzigianni, M., Stephenson, T., Harrison, L.J., Wanigayage, M, Li, P., Barblett, L., Hadley, F., Andrews, R., Davis, B. and Irvine, S. (2023) The role of digital technologies in supporting quality improvement in Australian early childhood education and care settings. *ICEP*, 17(5), 2–23. https://doi.org/10.1186/s40723-023-00107-6 (Accessed on 04.07.2023).

Hermawati, D., Rahmadi, F.A., Sumekar, T.A. and Winarni, T.I. (2018) Early electronic screen exposure and autistic-like symptoms. *Intractable and Rare Diseases Research*. 7 (1), 69–71.

Hoehe, M.R. and Thibaut, F. (2020) Going digital: how technology use may influence human brains and behavior, *Dialogues in Clinical Neuroscience*, 22:2, 93-97, https://doi.org/10.31887/DCNS.2020.22.2/mhoehe (Accessed on 04.07.2023).

Ineqe (2021) *What is trolling? What is trolling? - Ineqe safeguarding group*. Available at: https://ineqe.com/2021/11/12/trolling/ (Accessed on 04.07.2023).

Khan, T. and Mikuska, E. (2021) The first three weeks of lockdown in England: The challenges of detecting safeguarding issues amid school closures. *Social Science and Humanities Open*. 3(1). https://doi.org/10.1016/j.ssaho.2020.100099 (Accessed on 04.07.2023).

Kidron, D. and Rudkin, A. (2017) *Digital childhood: Addressing childhood development milestones in the digital environment*. Available at: https://www.ormiston.org/the-link/wp-content/uploads/2019/03/Digital-Childhood-2017.pdf (Accessed on 20.02.2023).

King, L. (2022) *Raising children in a digital age*. Available at: https://www.life.ca/lifelearning/1506/raising-children-in-digital-age.htm (Accessed on 02.03.2023).

Kucirkova, N., Wells Rowe, D., Oliver, L. and Piestrzynski, L. E. (2019) Systematic review of young children's writing on screen: What do we know and what do we need to know. *Literacy*, 53(4), 216–225. https://doi.org/10.1111/lit.12173 (Accessed on 04.07.2023).

Kurowski, A. (2022) *Covid, home schooling, and inequalities*. Lubelski Rocznik Pedagogicny T. XLI, z. 2 – 2022. Available at: https://www.researchgate.net/publication/363650186_Covid_Home_Schooling_and_Inequalities#fullTextFileContent

Levine, L.E. and Munsch, J. (2018) *Child development from infancy to adolescence: an active learning approach*. London: SAGE.

Li, C., Wang, P., Martin-Moratinos, M., Bella-Fernandez, M and Blasco-Fontecilla (2022) Traditional bullying and cyberbullying in the digital age and its associated mental health problems in children and adolescents: A meta-analysis. *European Child Adolescent Psychiatry*. https://doi.org/10.1007/s00787-022-02128-x (Accessed on 04.07.2023).

Livingstone, S. and Blum-Ross, A. (2020) *Parenting for a digital future. How hopes and fears about technology shape children's lives*. Oxford: Oxford University Press.

Lyons, C.D. and Tredwell, C.T. (2015) Steps to implementing technology in inclusive early childhood programs. *Computers in the Schools*, 32(2), 152–166. https://www.learntech lib.org/p/157636/ (Accessed on 04.07.2023).

Mahanta, D. and Khatoniyar, S. (2019) Cyberbullying and its impacts on mental health of adolescents. *International Journal in Management and Social Science*. 14(2), 1–10.

McPake, J., Plowman, L. and Stephen, C. (2013) Pre-school children creating and communicating with digital technologies in the home. *British Journal of Educational Technology*, 44(3), 421–431.

Merchant, G. (2012) Mobile practices in everyday life: Popular digital technologies and schooling revisited. *British Journal of Educational Technology*, 43(5), 770–782. https://doi.org/10.1111/j.1467-8535.2012.01352.x (Accessed on 04.07.2023).

Mikuska, E., Khan, T. and Kurowski, A. (2021) Home-schooling during the lockdown in England. *Journal of Applied Technical and Educational Sciences,* 11 (3), 1–18. Available at: https://doi.org/10.24368/jates.v11i3.280 (Accessed on 04.07.2023).

Miriam Webster Dictionary (2023) *Words We're Watching: 'Zoomer'*. Available at: https://www.merriam-webster.com/words-at-play/words-were-watching-zoomer-gen-z (Accessed on 04.07.2023).

Murcia, K., Pepper, C., Joubert, M., Cross, E., & Wilson, S. (2020) A framework for identifying and developing children's creative thinking while coding with digital technologies. *Issues in Educational Research*, 30(4), 1395.

Musuik, C. and Bognor, A. (2019) Digitalization & society. *Austrian Journal of Sociology*, 44, 1–14. Available at: https://link.springer.com/article/10.1007/s11614-019-00344-5 (Accessed on 02.04.2023).

National Bullying Helpline (2023) *Cyberbullying and online harassment advice.* Available at: https://www.nationalbullyinghelpline.co.uk/cyberbullying.html (Accessed on 04.07.2023).

Navarro, J.L. and Tudge, J.R. (2022) Technologizing Bronfenbrenner: neo-ecological theory. *Current Psychology*, 1–17, https://doi.org/10.1007/s12144-022-02738-3 (Accessed 20.05.2023).

Neumann, M.M., Park, E., Soong, H., Nichols, S. and Selim, N. (2022) Exploring the social media networks of primary school children. *Education*, 13(3), 1–15. https://doi.org/10.1080/03004279.2022.2144404 (Accessed on 04.07.2023).

Norman, H., Nordin, N., Din, R., Ally, M. and Dogan, H. (2015) Exploring the roles of social participation in mobile social media learning: A social network analysis. *International Review of Research in Open and Distance Learning*, 16(4), 205–224.

Nouwen, M and Zaman, B. (2018) Redefining the role of parents in young children's online interactions. A value-sensitive design case study. *International Journal of Child-Computer Interaction*, 18, 22–26.

NSPCC (2020) *Bullying and cyberbullying*. NSPCC. Available at: https://www.nspcc.org.uk/what-is-child-abuse/types-of-abuse/bullying-and-cyberbullying/#effects (Accessed on 28.04.2023).

NSPCC (2022a) *Molly Russell Inquest findings*. Available at: https://www.nspcc.org.uk/about-us/news-opinion/2022/response-molly-russell/ (Accessed on 04.04.2023).

NSPCC (2022b) *Parliament briefing: The importance of the online safety Bill.* Available at: https://www.nspcc.org.uk/globalassets/documents/policy/online-safety-bill-briefing-nspcc-oct-2022.pdf (Accessed on 04.05.2023).

NSPCC (2023) *Inappropriate or explicit content.* Available at: https://www.nspcc.org.uk/keeping-children-safe/online-safety/inappropriate-explicit-content/ (Accessed on 02.04.2023).

Ofcom (2019) *Children and parents: Media use and attitudes report 2019.* Available at: https://www.ofcom.org.uk/__data/assets/pdf_file/0023/190616/children-media-use-attitudes-2019-report.pdf (Accessed on 03.07.23).

Ofcom (2020) *One Nation 2020 Report-Raising awareness of online harms.* Available at: https://www.ofcom.org.uk/__data/assets/pdf_file/0027/196407/online-nation-2020-report.pdf (Accessed on 04.07.2023).

Ofcom (2022) *Children and parents: media use and attitudes report 2022.* Available at: https://www.ofcom.org.uk/__data/assets/pdf_file/0024/234609/childrens-media-use-and-attitudes-report-2022.pdf (Accessed on 04.07.2023).

Orben, A., Przybylski, A., Blakemore, S. and Kievit, R. (2022). Windows developmental sensitivity to social media. *Nature Communications*, 13, 1–10. Available at: https://www.nature.com/articles/s41467-022-29296-3 (Accessed on 03.05.2023).

Piaget, J. (1929) *The child's conception of the world.* London: Routledge.

Postman, N. (1994) *The disappearance of childhood.* London: Vintage.

Sakr, M. (2019) *Digital play in early childhood: What's the problem?* London: SAGE.

Sinclair, N. (2018) Time, immersion and articulation: Digital technology for early childhood Mathematics. In Elia, I., Mulligan, J., Anderson, A., Baccaglini-Frank, A., Benz, C. (eds), *Contemporary Research and Perspectives on Early Childhood Mathematics Education.* ICME-13 Monographs. Springer. https://doi.org/10.1007/978-3-319-73432-3_11 (Accessed on 04.07.2023).

Stoilova, M., Livingstone, S. and Nandagiri, R. (2020) Digital by default: Children's capacity to understand and manage online data and privacy. *Media and Communication*, 8(4), 197–207.

Strandell, H. (2014) Mobile phones in children's after-school centres: Stretching of place and control. *Mobilities*, 9(2), 256–274. https://doi.org/10.1080/17450101.2013.802488 (Accessed on 04.07.2023).

Taani, I., Ong, Z.Q., Pahuja, A. and Heng, C.S. (2017) Social media in families: A qualitative inquiry from the perspectives of parents and children. In *2017 Pacific Asia Conference on Information Systems: PACIS 2017.* Available at: http://eprints.lse.ac.uk/108643/ (Accessed on 20.05.2023).

Undheim, M. (2022) Children and teachers engaging together with digital technology in early childhood education and care institutions: a literature review, *European Early Childhood Education Research Journal*, 30(3), 472–489. https://doi.org/10.1080/1350293X.2021.1971730 (Accessed on 04.07.2023).

UK Parliament (2022) *World-first online safety laws introduced in Parliament.* https://www.gov.uk/government/news/world-first-online-safety-laws-introduced-in-parliament#:~:text=Changes%20to%20requirements%20on%20'legal%20but%20harmful'%20content&text=If%20companies%20intend%20to%20remove,by%20both%20Houses%20of%20Parliament

UK Parliament (2023) *Safety Act 2023.* https://www.legislation.gov.uk/ukpga/2023/50/enacted#:~:text=(1)This%20Act%20provides%20for,individuals%20in%20the%20United%20Kingdom.&text=(b)confers%20new%20functions%20and,powers%20on%20the%20regulator%2C%20OFCOM

University of Cambridge (2023) *"Pay the wi-fi or feed the children": Coronavirus has intensified the UK's digital divide.* Available at: https://www.cam.ac.uk/stories/digitaldivide#:~:text=As%20an%20aspect%20of%20deprivation,income%20of%20over%20%C2%A340%2C001. (Accessed on 04.07.2023).

UNICEF (2017) *Children in a Digital World.* Available at: https://www.unicef.org/media/48601/file (Accessed on 20.05.2023).

Vanden Abeele, M.M., (2016) Mobile youth culture: A conceptual development. *Mobile Media and Communication*, 4(1), 85–101. https://doi.org/10.1177/2050157915601455 (Accessed on 04.07.2023).

Weiler, A. (2005) Information seeking behaviours in Generation Y students: motivation, critical thinking, and learning theory. *The Journal of Academic Librarianship*, 31, 46–53.

Weinstein, A. and Lejoyeux, M. (2010, September) Internet addiction or excessive internet use. *The American Journal of Drug and Alcohol Abuse*, 36(5), 277–83.

Wilson, S., (2016) Digital technologies, children and young people's relationships and self-care. *Children's Geographies*, 14(3), 282–294. https://doi.org/10.1080/14733285.2015.1040726 (Accessed on 04.07.2023).

Wolfe, S. and Flewitt, R. S. (2010) New technologies, new multimodal literacy practices and young children's metacognitive development. *Cambridge Journal of Education*, 40(4), 387–399.

4

Childhood and Crime

Andre Kurowski

After reading this chapter, readers will be able to:

- Outline the legal status of the child in the criminal justice system.
- Analyse explanations for children committing crimes.
- Evaluate the treatment of children in the criminal justice system.

Introduction

This chapter will focus on how the treatment of children in the criminal justice system has developed, and explanations for this. It will examine elements of criminal law, child development and scrutinise children's capacity to commit crimes. It will consider how children are treated in courts and sanctions available, and responses by the public and the media to child offending. Ideas of the social construction of childhood will be used and historic and contemporary attitudes towards child offending will be explored. Theories on criminal behaviour will be outlined and discussed to determine their application to children and criminal behaviour.

Case Study: County Lines

County lines drug dealing describes organised crime groups who supply drugs to suburban areas including market and coastal towns. This type of drug dealing is strongly associated with the coercion of children and vulnerable people. The dealers use children and vulnerable people to move drugs, money and sometimes weapons between their hometown and the costal and market towns they are dealing in.

- *Why do you think children are used for these purposes?*
- *Drug dealing can result in ruining people's lives, but should the children be treated as criminals, or as victims themselves?*
- *What should be done about County Lines crime?*

The Law and the Child

Criminology is the study of crime, those who commit crime and the criminal justice system (Scottish Centre for Crime and Justice Research, 2023), and criminal law is a distinct part of legal system separate from, for example civil law (UK Government, 2023a). Criminal law goes beyond the personal and into the public sphere where the intervention of the police, courts and prison service is needed (Scott and Marshall, 2009). Crime can be differentiated form the social concept of 'deviance' which is rule breaking behaviour (Muncie, 2015). Deviance can attract social disapproval but is not necessarily illegal, and some illegal acts can break laws but are not necessarily considered deviant. For example some minor driving offences may be technically illegal but not seen as deviant behaviour; some tax evasion may not break tax laws, but some will consider it morally wrong to pay tax that is due.

A child is defined by English law as anyone who has not yet reached their 18th birthday (NSPCC, 2022). Most countries reserve special legal measures for children who commit criminal acts or are involved in the criminal justice system in some way. Although this varies across countries and cultures, the United Nations claim that children should have inalienable rights and 'the child, by reason of his physical and mental immaturity, needs special safeguards and care, including appropriate legal protection, before as well as after birth' (United Nations, 1989).

Childhood may be a biological fact but can be 'understood and made meaningful' differently (Prout and James, 1997: 7). Likewise, the definition of a crime reflects and reinforces political and social forces (Garside, 2011). These distinctions are significant when deciding on accountability for children in criminal cases.

Children and Criminal Responsibility

The minimum age of criminal responsibility (MACR) is the age at which people can face the full weight of criminal law (Muncie, 2015) and it varies across time and cultures. In England and Wales, the MACR is 10 years old, in Northern Ireland it is also 10 years old (Department for Justice NI, 2023); however, in Scotland the MACR is 12 years old (UK Government, 2023a). Attempts to raise the MACR in England and Wales have not been successful. These include the Children and Young Persons Act 1969 (Fitz-Gibbon, 2016), the Royal Society (2011) and the Centre for Social Justice (2012). Reasons given are that flexibility is needed and that children should understand that criminal actions are serious matters (McGuinness, 2016). The MACR in England and Wales remains at 10 since the Children and Young Persons Act 1963 (UK Government, 2023b) and, despite various efforts to raise it, Northern Ireland also remains at 10 (Department of Justice NI, 2022). The UN Committee on the Rights of the Child (2007) has repeatedly called for the MACR to be raised to a minimum of 12 on the grounds of intellectual and emotional development, and that drawing children at 10 years into the justice system can have negative long-term impact on their lives.

In addition to the MACR, there was an added protection for children in England and Wales known as 'doli incapax'. This is the presumption that a child between the age of 10 and 14 years is 'incapable of committing an evil act' (Arthur, 2010: 43) unless it can be demonstrated that they are able. Doli incapax required the prosecution to demonstrate that a child understood what they were doing was seriously wrong and aimed to protect the child from 'the criminal justice system' (Bandalli, 1998).

In criminal law, to qualify as a crime, the prosecution needs to exhibit two elements; it needs to establish that an act has taken place, e.g., stealing, assault etc. It also needs to demonstrate 'intent', in other words that the defendant meant to carry out the act. In law these principles are known as 'actus reus' and 'mens rea' (Incorporated Council of Law Reporting, 2023). There is much debate about the capacity of children to commit crimes, not least neurological research on the adolescent brain (Arain et al., 2013), but courts need to show that children have a 'mental element' in a crime or 'malice aforethought' as well as demonstrating they carried out the act. The burden of proof, or onus, in criminal cases, is on the prosecution, who need to prove the case against the defendant 'beyond reasonable doubt' and is a higher standard from other types of law (Incorporated Council of Law Reporting, 2023).

This raises the question of whether children should be held accountable, due to their emotional and mental maturity, and whether courts can demonstrate beyond reasonable doubt that the child not only performed the act, but whether they had intent. The current reasoning in England and Wales conflicts with most European countries who have a MACR well above 10 (Child Rights International Network, 2023).

Children, Crime and History

In the Tudor period, children were subjected to the same punishments as adults for similar crimes, including the death penalty. Records exist that show John Dean, who was between eight and nine years old, was hanged for arson (Captialpunishment, 2023) in 1629. The judge found evidence of malice, revenge and cunning and this was reason not to recommend a reprieve. Alice Glaston was hanged at the age of 11 in 1546 and is believed to be the youngest girl to be executed. Michael and Ann Hamond, ages 7 and 11, respectively, are recorded in the History of Lynn (Richards, 1812), as being hanged together in 1709 for an undisclosed crime. At the time, the MACR was seven, and children were still being executed in the 18th century, although records are scarce, and registrations of births were not required before 1837.

Executions of teenagers were continued into the 19th century, but the Children's Act 1908 raised the minimum age for execution to 16 (Intriguing History, 2023) and introduced separate courts for juveniles for the first time. The last youth to receive a death sentence was 16-year-old Harold Wilkins in 1932, but the sentence was reprieved because of his age. Shortly after this, the Children and Young Person's Act, 1933 raised the MACR to eight and the minimum age for execution to 18.

The MACR was raised to 10 by the Children's and Young Persons Act 1963 (English Legal History, 2013), leaving only children over 10 accountable in criminal law (Goldson, 2013). However, the presumption of doli incapax was abolished in England and Wales by section 34 of the Crime and Disorder Act 1998 (Fitz-Gibbon, 2016). Since then, all children over the age of 10 who commit a criminal offence are left 'open to the full rigours of the criminal law' (Ashworth, 2003: 178) to make children realise the consequences of their actions. This was a result of the killing of James Bulger by two ten-year-old boys. This case was a watershed and seen as a catalyst for a rhetoric of toughness as proposed by successive governments in the 1990s (Goldson, 2013), as well as debates about children as demons rather than innocents (Haydon and Scraton, 2000).

Timeline of Childhood and Crime

- 1485–1603 – children were punished in the same way as adults.
- 1889 – last known execution of a person under 18, Charles Dobell 17, hanged at Maidstone.
- Pre-20th century – children under 7 were deemed incapable of crime, children aged 7–14 years were presumed to be doli incapax.
- 1908 – the Children Act 1908 banned the execution of juveniles under the age of 16.
- 1932 – last juvenile, aged 16, sentenced to death for a sexually related murder, but reprieved due to his age.
- 1933 – the Children and Young Person's Act, 1933 raised the minimum age of criminal responsibility to 8, and the minimum age for capital punishment to 18.
- 1963 – Child and Young Persons Act 1963 raised the minimum the age of criminal responsibility from eight years to ten years.
- 1992 – the United Nations Convention on the Rights of the Child came into force in the United Kingdom, and states that the minimum age of criminal responsibility should be at least 12.
- 1998 – doli incapax abolished in England and Wales under the Crime and Disorder Act 1998.
- 1998 – The Crime and Disorder Act 1998 lays out statutory requirements for youth offending teams.
- 2019 – Age of Criminal Responsibility (Scotland) Act 2019 raised the age to 12.

Inventing Innocence

Ariès (1962) views childhood as dating back only to the Middle Ages. Before this, children were treated the same as adults, were employed and shared responsibilities with adults, and therefore the age of criminal responsibility was low (LawTeacher, 2023). Prout and James (1997) also challenge the Piagetian biological view (Goswani, 2008) of childhood as universal and natural. In the 16th Century puritanical doctrine placed children as being born evil and stubborn and in need of civilisation (Shahar, 1990).

However, Locke (1996) took the empiricist view that children start life with a 'blank slate' and that knowledge comes from experience or perception (Locke, 1996). Ideas from the enlightenment are different; Rousseau in the 18th century viewed children as 'noble savages' who were naturally endowed with a sense of right and wrong (Redford, 1991) and children's behaviour as the corruption by society of an innocent.

In the 20th century, Shorter (1976) argued that modern ideas about childhood started with industrialisation, and the rise of the nuclear family. Where families moved to cities in small units, one member (usually the male) would secure employment and leave child rearing responsibilities to (usually) the female. This, Shorter argues, is how ideologies of maternal love and domesticity developed in the way we understand them today, although DeMause (1976) and Pollock (1983) claim that attachments between parents and children have always existed and that children. Postman (1994) claims that a so-called golden age of childhood is disappearing. With the introduction of the printing press, boundaries between childhood and adulthood were emphasised by those who could and those who could not read, leading to splits between childhood and adult experiences. With the advent of television and technology, Postman argues that children have regained access to the cultural world of adults and are becoming more like adults again. As a result, western concepts of childhood developed over hundreds of years are disappearing.

Case Study: James Bulger

The killing of three-year-old James Bulger by two ten-year-old boys highlights fault line between our understanding of childhood. On one hand children are seen as innocent, as in the victim, but on the other, the killers were vilified as evil.

- How does this affect our views of what childhood should be?
- What effect should this have on how we deal with children in criminal cases?
- To what extent are children in the modern world 'innocent'?

Childrens' Criminal Capacity

If the puritanical view is taken about restrictive and harsh childcare practices to tame the depraved child, and children have their own (Piagetian) view of the world, then perhaps children can be held accountable. On the other hand, if children are blank slates who are corrupted by social experience, then perhaps children cannot be held solely accountable for their actions. If a golden age of childhood is in decline, then perhaps ideas to protect them as innocents should be discarded, and they should be treated the same as adults.

Whatever way we look at the concept of childhood, western societies are child centred; children are protected by domestic and international legislation, children are no longer treated as adults and have fewer responsibilities. However, Fionda (2005) argues that the setting of a MACR must reflect a consensus on the social construction of childhood, with children maturing differently than in previous times.

One question for deciding if children can be held responsible for a crime is whether they know their behaviour is disapproved of by others. Piaget (1932) was interested in how children think about morality and placed moral reasoning into different ages and stages. Before the age of five, children have little understanding of rules, in other words they are in a pre-moral stage. Between the ages of five and ten years, children are in the heteronomous stage – otherwise known as moral realism. At this stage, children regard morality as conforming to the rules of others, and that breaking permanent and unchangeable rules will inevitably lead to punishment. Behaviour is judged by the severity of the consequences, rather than the motive for doing it in the first place.

When children reach nine or ten, and the stage of autonomous morality or moral relativism, they recognise that there is no absolute right or wrong, and morality depends on the intentions one has rather than the consequences. At this post-egocentric stage, children can appreciate internal responsibility, and can take intention and circumstances of the act into account. An act that was malicious in intention but did little damage was more serious than a well-intentioned act that did more damage. Kohlberg's (1984) concept of moral reasoning is also significant; at above nine years old, children recognise different viewpoints and behave in a way as to gain the approval of others and to uphold the wider rules of society and the law. These two theories fit well with the MACR at ten years, as well as the legal requirement of intent or mens rea.

Bandura's (1973) classic research with the bobo doll illustrates that children can learn to be aggressive from observing others, the noble savage (Redford, 1991) can be influenced or corrupted by society. If this is the case, then perhaps society should take some responsibility for actions that it has influenced. However, Bandura (2001) also wrote about human agency, the power to originate action, or subjective awareness of one's actions (Hilppö et al., 2016). Bandura identifies four aspects to agency: intention, forethought, self-regulation and self-reflectiveness (Bandura, 2006), and research has demonstrated 9–10-year-old children have a sense of self-agency (Hilppö et al., 2016). Other arguments about children's capacity are provided by neurological research. Griffin (2017) found that brain development in adolescents can lead to urges to experiment and explore boundaries, heightened sensitivity to reward, risk-taking or impulsive behaviour, creativity and openness to novel solutions and learn about their limits.

These ideas are contradictory and leave some room for doubt over children's capacity in criminal cases and whether intent can be demonstrated. So, developmental explanations are inconclusive.

Case Study: Mary Bell

In 1968, between the ages of 11 and 12, Mary Bell strangled and mutilated the bodies of two young boys. Mary was known to be a dangerous bully in the schoolyard. At the trial she showed no emotion and bantered with prosecution; she took great pleasure in tormenting the victim's families. Mary was sentenced to life in prison.

- To what extent did Mary really know what she was doing in these cases?
- How can a life sentence be justified for a child of Mary's age?
- How can we know if a child has been successfully rehabilitated and fit for release?

Factors in Offending

Age and Crime

Farrington (1986) found that the percentage of offenders in a population tends to increase sharply from late childhood, peaks at around 15–19 year olds and declines gradually from the early 20s. However, it is uncertain whether more young people are committing crimes overall, or a proportionately larger number of younger people are committing crimes when compared to the overall population (Tremblay and Nagin, 2005), but the overall trend is unambiguous. Some writers claim that this is due to economic reasons, that young people are poorer than adults (Shulman et al., 2013), but this depends on the nature of the crime, socio-economic status and gender. According to Fagan and Western (2005), for offences such as vandalism, the incidence is higher in adolescence than adulthood, whereas vehicle crime and drug use is higher in adulthood than adolescence. There are also variations within the childhood/adolescent phase; from around 6–10 year olds physical aggression tends to increase, and this tends to decrease from 10–13 years as young people mature. The peak of offending is higher at an earlier age for those from lower socio-economic status (Fagan and Western, 2005), and female offending rates are far lower than those for males (Bottoms, 2016).

Moffitt (1993) also sees age as a factor in offending and distinguishes between adolescent limited offenders and life-course persistent offenders. Antisocial behaviour is only committed in adolescence, whereas life-course persistent offenders begin to offend early in childhood and persist into early adulthood (Martens, 2000). According to Moffitt (Chamberlain, 2015), adolescents experience tension over attractive behaviours around sex, alcohol and drugs, and are influenced by peers to act. One of the reasons children are treated differently is because the authorities take the view that the young person should be diverted out of the criminal justice system if possible and that they can be rehabilitated. As Moffitt states:

> An adult criminal career, by and large, requires childhood anti-social behaviour, yet not all antisocial children become antisocial adults or offenders. (Moffitt in Chamberlain, 2015: 156)

Neutralisation Theory

Matza and Sykes (1961) developed the concept of subterranean values where deviant behaviour, such as excitement and thrill seeking, are latent values of mainstream society. These values are suppressed except in certain appropriate, legal settings. Delinquent behaviour is viewed as an expression of these latent values at inappropriate times. According to Matza and Sykes, most people are able suppress these 'delinquent' values, but this is a learnt skill, so people are more likely to engage in deviant behaviour when they are young and less so when they age.

Adverse Childhood Experiences

Other social factors that can contribute to young people's offending are adverse childhood experiences (ACEs) (Ellis and Dietz, 2017). These include direct ACEs, such as abuse and neglect by parent/caregiver, parental divorce or separation, a caregiver in prison, food, clothing and housing insecurities and drug/alcohol problems of caregiver. ACEs are linked to a wide range of harmful behaviours including smoking, harmful alcohol use, drug use, risky sexual behaviour, violence and crime (Local Government Association, 2018). A young person with four or more adverse childhood experiences is eight times more likely to have committed a violent act than those with none (The Centre for Youth and Criminal Justice, 2018).

Inclusion and Offending

Ethnicity can be a factor in offending although the evidence is not clear and not conclusive. Bowling and Phillips (2002) offer explanations why black people are over-represented in robberies, and these centre around black culture. However, Sharp and Budd (2005) conducted a survey of self-reported antisocial behaviour by 10–25-year olds and found that levels of engagement by white and mixed race were higher than young black people.

Mental Health

Young people with Attention Deficit and Hyperactivity Disorder (ADHD) become involved with the criminal justice system at an earlier age than others and have higher rates of recidivism (Young and Cocallis, 2021). Also, Lennox and Khan (2021) found that over one quarter of young people in the youth justice system have a learning disability, and for those in custody, depression, anxiety and psychotic symptoms are not rare.

Labelling Theory

Young people are not usually publicly named and there are limits to who can attend youth trial. One explanation is labelling theory (Becker, 1963). According to Becker:

> Deviance is not a quality of the act the person commits, but rather a consequence of the application by others of rules and sometimes to an 'offender'. The deviant is one to whom that label has successfully been applied; deviant behaviour is people so label. (Winfree and Abadinsky, 2010: 227)

Labelling theory concentrates on the reputation or the social standing of the person who has been through the criminal justice system. Becker refers to the 'master status' that people acquire upon conviction; this overrules all other positions in society that the person has and becomes a form of stigma. In a process of self-fulfilling prophecy, the individual may see their options as limited, their personal self-concept as a 'deviant' and go on to commit more offences. With anonymity and with a focus on rehabilitation, the authorities try to steer the young person away from crime at a young age to prevent them from adopting a criminal identity leading to further offending. In terms of custody, young people will not share prisons with older or adult offenders until the age of 21 to try to avoid influence by adult offenders.

Points of Reflection

The judge who presided over the trial of teenage murderer Aaron Campbell lifted a ban on naming the offender because of the revulsion of the case.

- What circumstances are appropriate for judges to name young offenders?
- How could being named as an offender affect a young person?
- To what extent does the severity of the crime affect how young people should be sentenced?

Treatment in the Criminal Justice System

Children between 10 and 17 can be arrested and taken to court if they commit a crime (Youth Justice Legal Centre, 2023a). They are dealt with by youth courts, given different sentences and sent to special secure centres for young people, not adult prisons. Children in police stations must have an appropriate adult present and a parent or guardian contacted on arrest. They should be transferred to local authority accommodation overnight and isolated from adults in cells. Children who admit less serious offences can be offered out of court disposals, such as triage. Triage means that the child will not be prosecuted but be dealt with by way of a community resolution or a youth caution. The police should always consider an out of court resolution, especially for first-time child offenders. No further action will be taken, and this is to try to keep the children out of the criminal justice system (Youth Justice Legal Centre, 2023b).

Children between 10 and 17 appear in special magistrates' courts called youth courts (UK Government, 2023c). These courts are informal and confidential; children are addressed by their first names and the public is not permitted to the courtroom. The press can report on the case, but the young person should not be named, unless in exceptional cases. For serious crimes, such as murder or rape, the case will be started in the magistrates' court but referred to a Crown Court. If found guilty, the court will take a range of factors into account; these include age, criminal record and the plea. In court, a young person can receive one of several non-custodial sentences (Sentencing Council, 2023).

Table 4.1 Sentencing Young People

	Types of Discharges
Absolute discharge	Decision not to impose a punishment.
Conditional discharge	Given a second chance, but conditional on any further offending.
	Non-custodial Sentences
Fines	Reflecting ability to pay, the parent/guardian pays the fine for those under 16.
Referral orders	Requirement to attend a youth offender panel and agree a contract lasting between three months and one year.Could include reparation or restitution to the victim, as well as interventions and activities to address their offending (UK Government, 2023e).
	Community Sentencing
Youth rehabilitation order	Order to comply with e.g., curfew, supervision, unpaid work, electronic monitoring, drug treatment, mental health treatment and education (Sentencing Council, 2023).

There is a range of custodial sentencing powers for children aged between 10 and 18 years (Youth Justice Legal Centre, 2023b). If refused bail, a child may be sent to Youth Detention Accommodation (YDA) as decided by the Youth Custody Service.

Incarceration can have a negative effect on young people. Apart from the loss of liberty, goods and services, these can be 'profound threats to the inmate's personality or sense of worth' (Sykes, 1958: 64), and this is just as painful as any physical condition inmates may suffer. In the year 2020–2021, there was an average of 560 children in custody at any one time in England and Wales (UK Government, 2022), and young people are at a disadvantage in custody compared to adults. They are more likely to miss family members (Skinns and Wooff, 2020), and suffer boredom because of near-total lack of stimulation or prisoner underload (Toch, 1982). Children can be totally dependent on staff for basic items, such as toilet paper, and loss of autonomy and sense of helplessness can lead to resentment and anger (Bevan, 2022).

The Nuffield Family Justice Observatory (Roe et al., 2022) questions the purpose of depriving children of their liberty apart from punishment and expresses doubts over rehabilitation. This falls far short of the requirements of the United Nations Convention on the Rights of a Child (United Nations, 1989), which states that the best interests of the child should be a priority, laws should promote children's rights and justice systems should enable children to reintegrate into society. However, in Scotland a commitment has been made to end the placement of 16- and 17-year olds in Young Offenders' Institutions (YOI) (Scottish Government, 2022), in favour of a care-based system that puts 'love and relationships' at the centre of the experiences and outcomes for every child.

Case Study: Child Q

In 2020, Child Q, a black female teenager, was strip searched by female police officers from the Metropolitan Police Service. It took place on school premises without an appropriate adult present (CHSCP, 2022), and involved the exposure of Child Q's intimate body parts. Between 2018 and 2020, 650 children, some as young as 10, were strip searched – at a rate of nearly one a day in 2020. A quarter were aged 15 or under (Children's Commissioner, 2022).

- How can the police be justified in the way the search of Child Q was conducted?
- How else might the situation have been dealt with?
- What issues arise when police treat young black people as they did Child Q?

Chapter Summary

This chapter has introduced various issues concerning legal issues and child offending. It has shown the rationale for youth justice and linked this to developmental issues. It has prompted the reader to think critically about concepts of childhood and children's accountability as well as the treatment of children by the police, the courts and the sanctions available. The reader should be able to take a critical view of childhood and crime, and make judgements about how children are viewed and treated in criminal cases.

Key Points

- Western societies have developed legal processes to treat children differently from adults.
- There are ongoing debates around children's capacity to commit crimes.
- Factors in children's offending are wide-ranging and diverse.

Further Reading

Crown Prosecution Service: *Youth crime.* https://www.cps.gov.uk/crime-info/youth-crime

Green, D. (2012) *When Children Kill Children: Penal Populism and Political Culture.* Oxford: Oxford University Press.

Youth Justice. https://justice.org.uk/youth-justice/

Youth Justice Board. https://www.gov.uk/government/organisations/youth-justice-board-for-england-and-wales

References

Arain, M., Hague, M., Johal, L., Mathur, P., Nel, W., Rais, A., Sandhu, R. and Sharma, S. (2013) Maturation of the adolescent brain. *Neuropsychiatric Disease and Treatment*, 9: 449–461. https://www.ncbi.nlm.nih.gov/pmc/articles/PMC3621648/ (Accessed on 04.07.2023).

Ariès, P. (1962). *Centuries of Childhood.* London: Cape.

Arthur, R. (2010) The age of criminal responsibility and the defence of doli incapax. In Arthur, R. (ed.) *Young Offenders and the Law: How the Law Responds to Youth Offending.* Hoboken. NJ: Taylor and Francis.

Ashworth, A. (2003) *Principles of Criminal Law.* Oxford: Oxford University Press.

Bandalli, S. (1998). Abolition of the presumption of Doli Incapax and the Criminalisation of Children. *The Howard Journal of Criminal Justice*, 37(2): 114–123.

Bandura, A. (1973). *Aggression: A social learning analysis.* Englewood Cliffs, NJ: Prentice-Hall.

Bandura, A. (2001). Social cognitive theory: An agentic perspective. *Annual Review of Psychology*, 52:1–26. doi: 10.1146/annurev.psych.52.1.1

Bandura, A. (2006). Toward a psychology of human agency. *Perspectives on Psychological Science*, 1:164–180.

Becker, H. (1963) *Outsiders: Studies in the Sociology of Deviance.* Free Press, New York.

Bevan, M. (2022) The pains of police custody for children: A recipe for injustice and exclusion? *British Journal of Criminology*, 2022(62):805–82.

Bottoms, A. (2016) Crime prevention for youth at risk: Some theoretical considerations. https://www.researchgate.net/publication/265530215_CRIME_PREVENTION_FOR_YOUTH_AT_RISK_SOME_THEORETICAL_CONSIDERATIONS (Accessed on 04.07.2023).

Bowling, B. and Phillips, C. (2002) *Racism, Crime and Justice.* London: Longman.

Captialpunishment (2023) http://www.capitalpunishmentuk.org/child.html (Accessed on 04.07.2023).

Centre for Youth Criminal Justice (2018) *National Youth Justice Conference 2018.* https://www.cycj.org.uk/resource/youth-offending-perceptions-of-the-problem-137/

Centre for Social Justice (2012, January) *Rules of Engagement: Changing the Heart of Youth Justice*, p. 201. https://www.centreforsocialjustice.org.uk/wp-content/uploads/2012/01/CSJ_Youth_Justice_Full_Report.pdf (Accessed on 14.08.2023).

Child Rights International Network (2023) *Minimum Ages of Criminal Responsibility in Europe.* https://archive.crin.org/en/home/ages/europe.html (Accessed on 27.01.2023).

Children's Commissioner (2022) *Strip Search of Children by the Metropolitan Police Service – New Analysis by the Children's Commissioner for England.* https://www.childrenscommissioner.gov.uk/blog/strip-search-of-children-by-the-metropolitan-police-service-new-analysis-by-the-childrens-commissioner-for-england/ (Accessed 14.08.2023).

Chamberlain (2015) *Criminological Theory in Context.* London: SAGE.

Children and Young Person's Act (1933) https://www.legislation.gov.uk/ukpga/Geo5/23-24/12 (Accessed on 03.02. 2023).

City of London and Hackney Safeguarding Children Partnership (2022) *Child Q.* https://chscp.org.uk/wp-content/uploads/2022/03/Child-Q-PUBLISHED-14-March-22.pdf (Accessed on 14.08.2023).

Department of Justice NI, (2022) https://www.justice-ni.gov.uk/ (Accessed 1st July 2024).

Department for Justice NI (2023) https://www.justice-ni.gov.uk/news/long-launches-public-consultation-minimum-age-criminal responsibility#:~:text=The%20consultation%20will%20ask%20the,to%20meet%20international%20children's%20standards. (Accessed on 26.01.2023).

De Mause, L. (1976) *The History of Childhood. The Evolution of Parent-Child Relationships as a Factor in History.* London: Souvenir Press.

Ellis, W. and Dietz, W. (2017, September-October) A new framework for addressing adverse childhood and community experiences: The building community resilience model. *Academic Paediatrics*, 17(7S): S86–S93.

English Legal History. (2013). *Age of Criminal Responsibility.* Available at: https://englishlegalhistory.wordpress.com/2013/05/25/age-of-criminal-responsibility (Accessed on 03.02. 2023).

Fagan, A. A., and Western, J. (2005). Escalation and deceleration of early offending behaviours from adolescence to early adulthood. *Australian and New Zealand Journal of Criminology*, 38, 59–76.

Farrington, D. (1986) Age and crime. In Tonry M. and Morris N. (eds) *Crime and Justice: An Annual Review of Research, Vol 7.* Chicago University Press, Chicago, pp 189–250.

Fionda, J. (2005). *Devils and Angels: Youth Policy and Crime.* Oxford: Hart.

Fitz-Gibbon, K. (2016) Protections for children before the law: An empirical analysis of the age of criminal responsibility, the abolition of doli incapax and the merits of a developmental immaturity defence in England and Wales. *Criminology and Criminal Justice*, 16(4):391–409.

Garside, R. (2011) Crime: Myth or reality? *Criminal Justice Matters*, 83(1):18.

Goldson, B. (2013) 'Unsafe, unjust and harmful to wider society': Grounds for raising the minimum age of criminal responsibility in England and Wales. *Youth Justice*, 13(2): 111–130.

Goswani, U. (2008) *Cognitive Development.* Hove: Psychology Press.

Griffin, A. (2017) Adolescent neurological development and implications for health and well-being. *Healthcare*, 5(4):62.

Haydon, D. and Scraton, P. (2000). 'Condemn a little more, understand a little less': The political context and rights' implications of the domestic and European rulings in the Venables-Thompson case. *Journal of Law and Society*, 27(3):416–448.

Hilppö, J., Lipponen, L., Kumpulainen, K. and Virlander, M. (2016) Sense of agency and everyday life: Children's perspective. *Learning, Culture and Social Interaction*, 10:50–59.

Incorporated Council of Law Reporting (2023) Burden and standard of proof. https://www.iclr.co.uk/knowledge/glossary/standard-and-burden-of-proof/#:~:text=In%20criminal%20cases%2C%20the%20burden,defendant%20%E2%80%9Cbeyond%20reasonable%20doubt%E2%80%9D (Accessed on 03.02.2023).

Intriguing History (2023) https://intriguing-history.com/childrens-act/ (Accessed on 03.02. 2023).

Kohlberg, L. (1984) *The Psychology of Moral Development: The Nature and Validity of Moral Stages* (Essays on Moral Development, Volume 2). Harper and Row.

LawTeacher (2023) https://www.lawteacher.net/free-law-essays/criminal-law/evaluation-of-the-age-of-criminal-responsibility-in-england-and-wales-4006.php (Accessed on 03.02.2023).

Lennox, C. and Khan, L. (2021) *Youth Justice. Annual Report of the Chief Medical Officer 2012, Our Children Deserve Better: Prevention Pays.* https://assets.publishing.service.gov.uk/government/uploads/system/uploads/attachment_data/file/252662/33571_2901304_CMO_Chapter_12.pdf (Accessed on 14.08.2023).

Local Government Association (2018) *Adverse Experiences in Childhood.* https://www.local.gov.uk/case-studies/adverse-experiences-childhood#:~:text=A%20growing%20body%20of%20research%20is%20revealing%20the,drug%20use%2C%20risky%20sexual%20behaviour%2C%20violence%20and%20crime (Accessed on 03.02.2023).

Locke, J. [1689] (1996) *An Essay Concerning Human Understanding* (edited by K. P. Winkler). Indianapolis: Hackett Publishing Company.

Martens, W. (2000). Antisocial and psychopathic personality disorders: Causes, course, and remission-a review article. *International Journal of Offender Therapy and Comparative Criminology*, 44(4):406–430.

Matza, D. and Sykes, G. (1961, October) Juvenile Delinquency and Subterranean Values. *American Sociological Review*, 26(5).

McGuinness, T. (2016, August 15) *The Age of Criminal Responsibility.* Briefing Paper Number 7687. House of Commons Library.

Moffitt, T. (1993) Adolescence-limited and life-course persistent antisocial behavior: A developmental taxonomy. *Psychological Review*, 100:674–701.

Muncie, J. (2015) *Youth Crime* (3rd ed.). London: SAGE.

NSPCC (2022) *Children and the Law.* https://learning.nspcc.org.uk/child-protection-system/children-the-law (Accessed on 09.02.2023).

Piaget, J. (1932). *The Moral Judgment of the Child.* London: Kegan, Paul, Trench, Trubner and Co.

Pollock, L. (1983) *Forgotten Children: Parent-Child Relations from 1500 to 1900.* Cambridge: Cambridge University Press.

Postman, N. (1994) *The Disappearance of Childhood.* London: Vintage.

Prout, A. and James, A. (1997) A new paradigm for the sociology of childhood? Provenance, promise and problems. In Prout, A. and James, A. (eds) *Constructing and Reconstructing Childhood.* London: Routledge Falmer.

Redford, K.H. (1991) The Ecologically Noble Savage. *Cultural Survival Quarterly*, 15(1):46.

Richards, W. (1812) *History of Lynn.* https://archive.org/stream/historylynntowh00richgoog/historylynntowh00richgoog_djvu.txt (Accessed on 04.07.2023).

Roe, A., Ryan, M. and Powell, A. (2022). *Deprivation of Liberty: A Review of Published Judgments*. Report summary. Nuffield Family Justice Observatory. https://www.nuffieldfjo.org.uk/resource/deprivation-of-liberty-a-review-ofpublishedjudgments (Accessed on 09.02.2023).

Scott, J. and Marshall, G. (2009) *A Dictionary of Sociology* (3rd ed.). Oxford: Oxford University Press.

Scottish Centre for Crime and Justice Research (2023) *What Is Crime?* http://www.sccjr.ac.uk/wp-content/uploads/2015/10/SCCJR-What-is-crime.pdf (Accessed on 04.07.2023).

Sentencing Council (2023) *Types of Sentences for Children and Young People*. https://www.sentencingcouncil.org.uk/sentencing-and-the-council/types-of-sentence/types-of-sentences-for-young-people/ (Accessed on 09.02.2023).

Scottish Government (2022) *Keeping the Promise Implementation Plan*. https://www.gov.scot/publications/keeping-promise-implementation-plan/pages/2/ (Accessed on 09.02.023).

Shahar, S. (1990) *Childhood in the Middle Ages*. London: Routledge.

Sharp, C. and Budd, T. (2005) *Minority Ethnic Groups and Crime: Findings from the Offending, Crime and Justice Survey 2003*. Home Office. https://www.researchgate.net/publication/242489635_Minority_ethnic_groups_and_crime_Findings_from_the_Offending_Crime_and_Justice_Survey_2003 (Accessed on 14.08.2023).

Shorter, E. (1976) *The Making of the Modern Family*. London: Basic Books.

Shulman, E, Steinberg, L, Piquero, A. (2013 June) The age-crime curve in adolescence and early adulthood is not due to age differences in economic status. *Journal of Youth and Adolescence*, 42(6):848-60. doi: 10.1007/s10964-013-9950-4. Epub 2013 Apr 18. PMID: 23595417.

Skinns, L. and Wooff, A. (2020) Pain in police detention: A critical point in the penal painscape? *Policing and Society*, 31:245–62.

Sykes, G. (1958) *The Society of Captives: A Study of a Maximum-Security Prison*. Princeton: Princeton University Press.

Toch (1982) *The Pains if imprisonment*. London: Sage.

Tremblay, R.E. and Nagin, D.S. (2005) The developmental origins of physical aggression in humans. In Tremblay R.E., Hartup W.H. and Archer J. (eds) *Developmental Origins of Aggression*. New York: Guilford Press.

UK Government (2022) *Youth Justice Statistics: 2020 to 2021*. https://www.gov.uk/government/statistics/youth-justice-statistics-2020-to-2021/youth-justice-statistics-2020-to-2021-accessible-version (Accessed on 09.02.2023).

UK Government (2023a) *Civil Legal Advice*. https://www.gov.uk/civil-legal-advice (Accessed on 25.01.2023).

UK Government (2023b) *Children and Young Persons Act 1963*. https://www.legislation.gov.uk/ukpga/1963/37 (Accessed on 26.01.2023).

UK Government (2023c) *Criminal Courts*. https://www.gov.uk/courts/youth-courts (Accessed on 09.02.2023).

United Nations (1989) *Convention on the Rights of the Child*. https://www.ohchr.org/sites/default/files/crc.pdf (Accessed on 25.01.2023).

United Nations Committee on the Rights of the Child, General Comment No. 10 (2007) – Children's Rights in Juvenile Justice, CRC/C/GC/10. https://www.refworld.org/legal/general/crc/2007/en/43085 (Accessed on 25.04.2007).

Winfree, L. and Abadinsky, H. (2010) *Understanding Crime: Essentials of Criminological Theory*. Boston: Cengage.

Young, S, Cocallis, K. (2021, July) ADHD and offending. *Journal of Neural Transmission*. 128(7):1009–1019.

Youth and Criminal Justice, (2018) https://www.gov.uk/government/statistics/youth-justice-statistics-2018-to-2019 (Accessed 1st July 2024).

Youth Justice Legal Centre (2023a) *Age*. https://yjlc.uk/resources/legal-terms-z/age (Accessed on 09.02.2023).

Youth Justice Legal Centre (2023b) *Triage*. https://yjlc.uk/resources/legal-terms-z/triage (Accessed on 09.02.2023).

5

Family, Grandparents and Intergenerational Practice

Sandra Lyndon

After reading this chapter, readers will be able to:

- Explore the social construct of 'family' and the role of grandparents and older adults in children's lives.
- Discuss the benefits and challenges of intergenerational (IG) practice (the bringing together of children and older adults).
- Consider how IG practice can support meaningful connections between children and older adults.

Introduction

Working effectively with families is fundamental to any practitioner within the childhood sector. This chapter analyses the social construct of 'family' and the role of grandparents and older adults in children's lives. It explores how an increase in segregation between the generations has contributed to IG misunderstanding, loneliness and a lack of trust for both young and old. The benefits and challenges of bringing together different generations are considered, with reference to recent and emerging research in the area. Drawing on the author's own research, a case study of an IG project between a nursery school and residential care home is explored, including how meaningful encounters are created for both children and their 'older friends'. Finally, the challenges for IG practice are considered and how barriers can be overcome.

What Is Family?

Defining 'family' is challenging as understandings of family are constructed in different ways. For some, 'family' has a broad meaning, for example family might include close friends, whereas for others the adage 'It takes a village to raise a child' suggests that family includes those that live and work in the community (Wilson, 2016). Families are diverse and range from the nuclear family of parents and children to extended families of three or more generations living together; as well as same-sex parents; families with one child or families with multiple children; blended families (where different families come together); and children who are protected (for example living with foster carers) (Mason and Tipper, 2008).

Points of Reflection

- How do you define family?
- How can you adapt your definition to reflect the diversity of families in the United Kingdom?

Bronfenbrenner's Bio-ecological Systems Theory

All members have an influence on the family, including the children within the family. Bronfenbrenner and Morris' (2006) bio-ecological systems theory provides a useful framework for understanding how these interactions influence children's development. The theory builds on Bronfenbrenner's early models (1979; 1989) and recognises the interaction between biology ('bio'), what the child brings to the process from their biological make up, and the 'ecological', the interactions with and influence from others (Doherty and Hughes, 2014). Positive reciprocal interactions with significant others help to support the child's development, fostering curiosity, responsiveness and engagement, by the same token, negative interactions are likely to have the opposite effect. Bronfenbrenner and Morris' (2006) bio-ecologial systems theory is presented as a model of concentric circles, with those closest to the child having the most direct influence (see Figure 5.1). The arrows denote the bidirectional of the relationships and interactions within and across the systems.

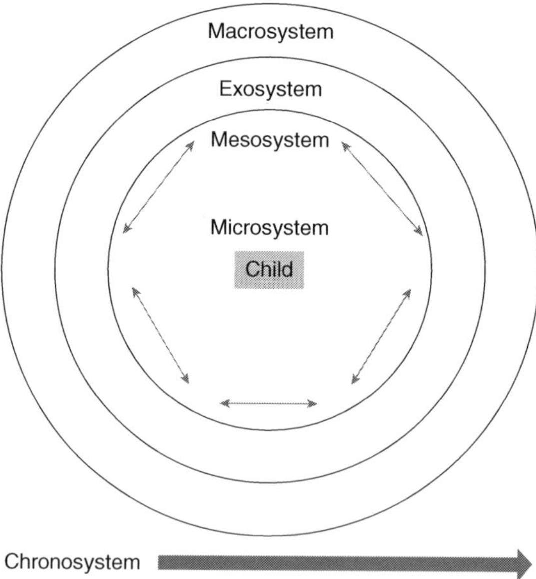

Figure 5.1 Model of Bronfenbrenner's Ecological Systems Theory

The system which has the most direct influence on the child is the **microsystem**; this consists of the child's immediate relationships and social activities. Research from the Effective Provision of Pre-school Education (EPPE) (Sylva et al., 2012: 1) demonstrates that what 'parent(s) do (at home with their babies and young children) is more important than who parents are' and has the greatest impact on the child's social, emotional and cognitive outcomes throughout childhood. The nature of the microsystem will vary, for example for some children this may consist of many people (for example several siblings, grandparents, children and adults at a pre-school setting, other pre-school activities). For others the microsystem may be small, for example parents of children with Special Educational Needs and/or Disability (SEND) often report experiencing isolation and separation from other parents and families who do not have a child with SEND (Green and Edwards, 2023). For all children the relationships within the microsystem are reciprocal, with the child's behaviour influencing the family and the family influencing the behaviour of the child. The microsystem sits within the **mesosystem**, which has a less direct influence on the child. The mesosystem is formed of the interactions and connections between the elements of the microsystem. For a young child, this may be the interactions between the family members and the pre-school setting and the interactions between the family members. The nature and strength of these relationships will have an influence on the child; for example research demonstrates that a trusting and open relationship between the parent(s) and the child's key person at the setting is likely to have positive outcomes for the child (Elfer et al., 2012; Sylva et al., 2012). The microsystem and the mesosystem sit within the **exosystem**, although not a direct member of this system the interactions within this system will still have an impact on the child. This system may include the parent(s) relationships with others in the workplace; the relationships with local health services (for example the relationship with the General Practitioner, health visitor and local hospital). The outer layer is the **macrosystem**; this consists of the child's broader society such as the laws, values, government policies and economic systems. Although the child is not directly part of the macrosystem, this will still have an influence. For example years of under investment in education and cuts to children's services has had a significant impact on the children's educational outcomes, particularly for children living in low-income families with the educational outcomes between poorer children and their more affluent peers increasing more than ever (Pro Bono Economics, 2022). The final system is the **chronosystem**, recognising how the four systems are dynamic and change over time, for example the child's microsystem changes as key milestones are met (e.g., learning to walk and talk) and transitions occur (e.g., starting school, moving house, birth of a sibling and experience of bereavement or loss).

The Role of Grandparents and Older Adults in Children's Lives

As discussed, the quality and nature of interactions in the microsystem play a central role in creating a solid foundation for a child's well-being, development and long-term outcomes. Research about families has typically concentrated on the role that parent(s) play in children's development; however there is increasing recognition of the importance grandparents have in raising the next generation. Overall, people in the United Kingdom are living longer and more healthier lives, and therefore for many families Grandparents are more available than in previous generations (Buchanan and Rotkirch, 2018). With the increased cost and lack of Early Childhood Education and Care (ECEC) provision, the role of grandparents has become more important in providing informal care for grandchildren. Drawing on both international and UK research, the next section explores how social and cultural change has shaped the role of grandparents.

How Social and Cultural Change has Shaped the Role of Grandparents

Although life expectancy varies globally, on average people are living longer and more healthy lives, and it is expected that this trend is likely to continue (World Health Organisation [WHO], 2019). In the United Kingdom children born in 2018 are expected to live into their late 80s or early 90s (Office for National Statistics [ONS], 2019). The 'Grey Dawn' (a healthier and longer living population) means there is more support available for bringing up the next generation (Buchanan and Rotkirch, 2018). Globally more women than ever before are participating in the labour force, and therefore affordable childcare is an essential requirement for many families. Research published in the United Kingdom by the International Longevity Centre (2017) found that a significant number of grandparents (65%), who took part in the survey provide childcare for their grandchildren. On average grandparents (many of whom who were also working) provided 11.3 hours of childcare per week. Nearly all Grandparents (96%) received no payment from their children to cover the cost of looking after the grandchildren, and in addition many contributed financially towards the cost of toys, activities, holidays and pocket money. Affordable childcare is a particular challenge for lone parents (most of whom are women), who are particularly vulnerable to poverty as many are in low paid jobs and work part time hours (Millar and Ridge, 2013). Increase in the numbers of lone parents has placed further demands on Grandparents who support with childcare, homework and meetings at school (Buchanan, 2017).

Despite the important contribution that grandparents make to bringing up the next generation, attitudes towards ageing are not always positive (Buchanan and Rotkirch, 2018). In Western cultures attitudes towards ageing tend to be negative, reinforced by stigmatising stereotypes of fragility, senility and vulnerability. While in non-western cultures such as Asian, African and Latin American societies tend to adopt a more positive attitude, with older adults and grandparents holding a high status within families and communities. Research suggests that people who have positive attitudes towards ageing are more likely to live longer and more healthier lives than those who hold negative beliefs (McGuire, 2017). In addition, grandparental involvement has many positive impacts for both the well-being of grandparents and the grandchildren (Rotkirch, 2018). For children in particular, research suggests that grandparental involvement contributes to improved mental health, increased resilience and positive behaviour (Attar-Schwartz and Buchanan, 2018; Tan, 2018; Wild, 2018). Therefore, good relationships between grandchildren and grandparents are both beneficial for a child's microsystem, and likely to contribute to positive outcomes in later life.

Case Study: A Grandfather and Granddaughter (Created by Molly's Grandmother)

Vik was in his early 70s when his Granddaughter Molly was born. It was soon apparent that there was a delay in her in terms of her speech and physical development. When Molly was 7, she went to a school that specialised in language development, where she was very happy. Vik lived in London with Lisa (Molly's Grandmother) and Molly lived on the South coast with her parents and her brother and sister. Molly saw her Grandparents about once a month. Molly had a special relationship with both her Grandparents, but particularly with her Grandfather. Vik was very patient with Molly and he enjoyed being with her. Equally Molly enjoyed Vik's company and liked to help him. More than anything they were friends. Reflecting on their relationship, Molly's Grandmother recounts how this was one of equals. When Vik retired, he and Lisa moved to the South coast. Molly often came over to visit her Grandparents. One of Vik and Molly's favourite things was making up stories together. Molly would ride round and round the close where Vik and Lisa lived on Vik's mobility scooter; together Vik and Molly would make up stories and adventures about where Molly might be travelling. When Vik died in his early 90s the family held a celebration in memory of his life. Molly was the first person to ask if she could make a speech at the celebration. On the day of the celebration, Molly had so much to say about her Grandfather she didn't want to stop.

Points of Reflection

- What were the benefits for Vik and Molly in terms of their special relationship?
- What might have been the challenges?

Kinship Care

Kinship care is when a child who is not able to live with their parents is brought up by a family member or close family friend. In the United Kingdom, kinship care is often provided by grandparents and (McGrath and Ashley, 2021). Most of these carers are older adults (aged 55–85), often with support needs of their own. Kinship care can be challenging, many of the children have experienced abuse or neglect before coming to live with their grandparents, and many have long-term additional mental and physical needs (Buchanan and Rotkirch, 2018; Turner, 2022). Grandparents who provide kinship care are often on low incomes, and receive little financial, practical or emotional support

(Turner, 2022). Unfortunately, kinship carers have few rights and are not entitled to flexible working arrangements or parental leave in the same way as adoptive parents; this can result in being forced to leave work permanently or reduce working hours (Turner, 2023). Despite the challenges, outcomes for children are often better when being raised by their grandparents, than those who are given care by strangers, for example foster care placements (Buchanan and Rotkirch, 2018).

Point of Reflection

- How could grandparents who provide kinship care be better supported?

Contact With Grandparents

Another challenge for grandparents is when parents decide they no longer want grandparents to be involved in their children's lives, this can sometimes be the case when parents' divorce or separate. In England and Wales grandparents do not have an automatic legal right to see their grandchildren (Gov.UK, nd). When informal arrangements and mediation fail, grandparents' only recourse is to apply for a court order which can be costly and time consuming. It is estimated that there are at least one million grandparents who do not have access to their grandchildren (Buchanan and Rotkirch, 2018). Despite pressure in 2018 for the Minister of Justice to make changes to the Children Act 1989, which would include a child's right to have a close relationship with members of their extended family, there are no current plans to change the law. As Buchanan and Rotkirch (2018) argue by denying children the right to contact their grandparents is denying them the valuable support and resources a relationship with their grandparents could provide.

Points of Reflection

- Do you think that grandchildren should have a legal right to see their grandparents? Why?
- Do you think that grandparents should have a legal right to see their grandchildren? Why?

Intergenerational (IG) Practice

Despite the many children who have positive and regular contact with their grandparents and other older adults in their extended family, there are many who have little contact or no contact at all. For young children who might spend long hours in ECEC provision, or extended hours after school there is a reduced amount of time to build relationships with older family members (Holmes, 2009). For others who have moved away from families, close contact with grandparents is more difficult due to geographical distance (Crawford, 2018). During the Covid-19 pandemic these circumstances were exacerbated due to social distancing and increased health risks for those in higher age categories (Gov.UK, 2021). For older adults, particularly those living on their own or in care homes loneliness and social isolation is a significant issue (Alzheimer's Society, 2020; Sutin et al., 2018).

One way of addressing loneliness for older generations and a lack of contact with older adults for children is IG practice. IG practice aims to create positive relationships between different generations by bringing together children and older adults to participate in shared experiences (Drury et al., 2017). In recent years, one way this has been addressed for children and older adults is through establishing contact between educational settings (such as, nursery schools and schools) and residential care homes. The Channel 4 (2017) mini-series 'Old People's Home for 4-year olds', where 10 elderly care home residents were brought into a classroom for 10 pre-schoolers was instrumental in creating popular media coverage of the potential benefits that friendships across the generations affords for both children and older adults. This type of IG practice is often referred to as 'co-located', where the interactions between the children and older adults take place in the same location. It is this type of IG practice we will be focusing on in the rest of the chapter.

Benefits, Challenges and Supporting Successful IG Practice

Emerging research suggests that there are positive benefits for both children and older adults who engage in IG practice (Lyndon and Moss, 2022). For older adults, benefits include enhanced well-being, increased social interaction and engagement, a sense of purpose, confidence, self-worth and improvements in memory. For children, research has tended to focus on how contact with older adults has improved negative attitudes towards ageing and age-related conditions (such as dementia) (Di Bona et al., 2017). However, broader outcomes also include friendship, enjoyment, empathy, communication skills and self-esteem.

Despite evidence which indicates clear benefits for both children and older adults who take part in IG practice, there are also challenges. For young children in particular, interactions with older adults who are very frail or have significant dementia may have a negative impact on children's attitudes towards ageing unless they are well-prepared and supported by practitioners (Crawford, 2018). Therefore, to be successful IG practice needs to be well-planned and careful consideration given to the needs of the children and older adults. In their review of IG projects, Drury et al. (2017) found several key factors for determining positive outcomes, these include:

- Joint activities which are appropriate for both age groups.
- Frequent and regular contact so that meaningful relationships can be built.
- Skilled facilitator(s) who can support interactions between the children and older adults

The most significant of these is the role of the facilitator, in the case of IG practice where children meet with older adults in a care home they are likely to be supported by pre-school practitioners and the activity providers working in the care home. Drury et al. (2017) found that paying careful attention to both age groups, modelling positive interactions and treating everyone as equal were essential skills for the role of the facilitator.

An evaluation of an IG Project between a Nursery School and Residential Care Home for Older Adults With Dementia

In 2019, I was fortunate to be part of a small research study evaluating how meaningful interactions are created between pre-school children, older adults and nursery school practitioners who engage in IG practice (Lyndon and Moss, 2022; Lyndon and Moss, 2021). At the time of the research, the project between the nursery school and residential care home had been running for two years. The nursery school and care home were very enthusiastic about the project and were interested in exploring the benefits of IG practice for children and older adults. A group of six children took part in the study; all were 3 years old and were spending 30 hours or more at the nursery school. They visited a group of older adults in the care home once a week over the course of one academic year (September to July). They were supported by three practitioners from the nursery school and two activity leaders from the care home. None of the staff who were involved in the project had received any training about IG practice, but all were experienced and skilled practitioners. A variety of rooms were used for the sessions, depending on which space was available. The sessions were 30 minutes long and adult-led, a typical session included the following:

- Hello song to introduce the children, older adults and practitioners;
- Singing activities;
- Drink and biscuit for the children;
- Goodbye song.

The number of older adults who took part in the group varied from week to week, although there were some residents who were regular attenders.

Data Collection and Analysis

We visited the care home once a month between November 2019 and February 2020 to observe the children and older adults. We planned to continue our monthly observations during the summer but due to the first Covid-19 lock down in March 2020 and the closure of the care home to outside visitors, we were no longer able to visit. During April and May 2020, we interviewed each of the nursery school practitioners about their experiences of the project. Before we started the research, we gained ethical approval from our university and consent from everyone who participated in the study. Riessman's (2008) narrative dialogic approach was used to analyse the observations and interviews. This approach focused on how interactions between our participants (the children, older adults and staff) were co-produced. In line with this approach, we considered how the physical environment (e.g. the room); the structure of the sessions, activities and use of objects informed the interactions during the observations. For the interviews we focused on how meanings were created between our participants (the staff) and ourselves. For further information about the data analysis, please see Lyndon and Moss (2021) and Lyndon and Moss (2022).

Although this was a small case study, the findings were wide ranging and highlighted how the IG sessions supported meaningful connections for everyone involved in the project. From our analysis we identified several key factors which helped to facilitate meaningful connections between the children, older adults and staff. These included the type of activity; the space (where the IG sessions took place); use of objects; and structure of the session.

Singing was the main focus of nearly all the IG sessions we observed. A picture board with picture cards of well-known nursery rhymes and songs was used to support the children and older adults' choice of songs. The singing activity was a time when everyone was involved, and provided opportunities for the children to demonstrate their capabilities and support the adults. In this observation Simon and Alfie (both aged three) support Judy (nursery school practitioner) and Charlie (older adult) with an unfamiliar song:

> When Judy (nursery school practitioner) forgets the words, Simon (child) helps her.
>
> Judy helps Peter (older adult) by supporting him hand over hand with the chopping action
>
> Alfie (child) supports Charlie (older adult) in the same way (Observation 1)

However, it was in the unstructured moments, outside of adult-led activities where meaningful interactions and building friendships between the young children and older adults were more likely to occur. Over the course of our visits, we observed a strong friendship developing between Alfie (child) and Charlie (older adult). Alfie would regularly seek out Charlie to be his partner in the singing activities. As time progressed Alfie and Charlie supplemented the structured activities with their own unscripted activities, which typically occurred at the beginning or end of the session. This often took the form of a 'high-5' game, where Charlie held up this hand for Alfie to slap and then Charlie taking his hand away at the last second so that Alfie misses his hand. Both Charlie and Alfie clearly enjoyed this activity.

The space where the session occurred had a strong influence on the interactions between the children, older adults and staff. A variety of rooms were used for the sessions, the size and accessibility contributed to the level of enjoyment, physical movement and opportunities for interaction. The first session we observed took place in a room which was 'small, hot and enclosed' (observation 1) where adults were sat in a circle and children were sitting on adults' laps (as there were not enough chairs for everyone). There was little opportunity for spontaneous interaction between the children and older adults. In our later visits the sessions took place in larger and more accessible spaces which supported greater interaction and more spontaneous activity. We noted in our observations how:

> The new room again alters the interactions and dynamics of the session – this time allowing more movement and more joining in for the older adults.
> (Observation 3)

In addition to the singing board, there were several occasions where we observed how objects provided a focus for engagement and interaction and helped the children engage with the past lives of the older adults. During our first visit to the care home, the older adults were wearing name badges with a picture which symbolised their past life, for example Diana had a picture of a tractor because she used to work on a farm as a 'land girl' during World War II. Natalie (nursery school practitioner) recounts in her interview how the children's interest was sparked by Peter's badge which had an image of a ship, representing the time he had spent in the Royal Navy:

> One of the children said, 'On your boat did you see sharks?' Because obviously they were really interested in sharks and he said, 'Yes, we saw lots' and then we said, 'Oh we could all sing baby shark' [. . .]
>
> We are started singing baby shark and they all got up and joined in . . . it was amazing.

At the time 'Baby Shark' was the most played song on YouTube and known to both the children, older adults and staff, enabling the generations to connect and share one of the most popular songs at that moment in time.

The most meaningful connections between the children and older adults took place when key factors occurred at the same time, for example where the room was large enough to afford movement and spontaneity; where objects afforded personal connections to be made; and where staff stepped back to enable spontaneous activity between the children and older adults. Our last visit took place in an open space on the first floor, which was set out as an informal lounge, easily accessible to older adults, staff and the children. As we were sat waiting for the session to start, Rose, one of the older adults unexpectedly takes the lead and starts talking to the children about her large colourful knitting bag. Natalie (who normally led the session) watches and gently supports Rose with her interactions with the children. The children watch avidly as Rosie reveals and talks about the objects in her bag. As the session progresses Natalie (nursery school practitioner) notices a small, knitted bag around Rose's neck:

Natalie: Rose has something round her neck.
Rose: I knitted it – it has my mobile phone. Sometimes I forget where I put things [...] my daughter is called the same as our Queen.
Child 1: Are you the Mum?
Rose: Who is the Queen? Is she called Queen Mary? Is she called Queen Elizabeth? Yes... my daughter is the same as the Queen . I can ring her on my phone [...]
[Rose mimes talking on the phone to her daughter]
Rose: I say 'Hello, Liza how are you?' and she says, 'It's snowing' and I say, 'It's sunny here' and that's just the way God made the big world.
[Rose makes a circular movement with her hands to represent the world]
Rose: Now you don't get much snow...
Child 1: I get lots of them
Child 2: From the sky...
Child 3: Father Christmas
Child 2: I do [raising her hand] ... I do at my house outside.

Natalie chooses to abandon the usual structure of the session, to give Rose space to talk about her knitting bag. The mystery of what might be inside Rose's bag sparks the children's interest, providing an opportunity for Rose to engage in dramatic story telling and for the children to learn about her daughter's life on the other side of the world. As the session becomes less structured and more informal, there is opportunity for the children and Rose to construct new understandings across the different generations of their past and present lives.

Spontaneous activity was often referred by the nursery school practitioners as 'going with the moment', the ability to be flexible and adapt quickly to the behaviour and activity of the children and older adults. As well as supporting positive interactions (as in the example with Rose's knitting bag), this was also important when interactions were more challenging. Despite the good connection between Alfie (child) and Charlie (older adult), as evidenced in the earlier example of their High-5 game, there were also times when there was frustration and disconnection. This was particularly evident when the effects of Charlie's dementia and memory loss were more noticeable:

Charlie: 'What's your name?' [to Alfie]
Alfie: 'You know my name!' [in a weary voice]
Charlie: 'Come on, what's your name?'
Alfie: 'Alfie' [elongating the 'Al']
(They high-5 again and this time Alfie slaps Charlie's hand quite hard.)
Natalie: 'Do it nice and gently'
Alfie 'high-5s' again but this time more gently.

(Observation 3)

On this occasion Alfie becomes frustrated when Charlie fails to remember his name, expressed by hitting his hand too hard. Natalie supports the interaction by reminding Alfie to be more gentle.

In summary the key factors we found that supported meaningful connections between the young children and older adults were as follows:

- Activities which can be enjoyed and are appropriate for young children and older adults are particularly important for building connections. We found that singing supported with visual prompts (such as picture cards) and signing (for example use of Makaton) was an activity which engaged everyone during the IG sessions. There was also opportunity to extend activities through use of props (for example using a big piece of blue material for everyone to hold and wave for songs such as 'Over the deep blue sea').
- The space where the IG session takes place needs to big enough to allow easy access and space for both children and adults to move around. This is particularly important for older adults who may want to join or leave the session before it is finished and to provide space for spontaneous activity, for example dancing or moving to music.
- Objects provide a way for older adults to share their former lives and identities with children, tell stories and extend children's knowledge of other places. We found that objects which were the most meaningful were often the ones that the older adults and children chose themselves (such as Rose's knitting bag).
- 'Going in the moment' and allowing space for child-led and older adult-led activities provide opportunities for children and older adults to connect in meaningful ways (as in the case of Alfie and Charlie's High-5 game).

Points of Reflection

- How would you set up an IG project between a nursery school and a care home?
- What would you need to consider?
- Who would you involve in the planning?

Challenges of IG Practice

One of the greatest challenges for IG practice has been the Covid-19 pandemic. During the pandemic all care homes were closed to visitors, and any IG face-to-face activities were stopped because of the risk of infection and particular vulnerability of older people. During this time the lack of social contact caused deterioration in the health and well-being particularly for older adults with dementia (Alzheimer's Society, 2020). The highest incident of deaths occurred in people aged 75 years or older, potentially leaving many children without grandparents of great grandparents (ONS, 2021). Therefore, re-establishing connections and building new connections between children and older adults within the community is of benefit to both older adults and young children's health and development. There are many ways that this could be addressed; below I give a couple of examples, one from the case study of the nursery school and care home and the other from an established innovative project in Chester.

When we asked the nursery school practitioners about how the IG project could develop, a common theme across the interviews was about the use of outdoor spaces. The nursery school and care home were neighbours which allowed easy access between the two locations. Although the IG sessions took place in the care home, there had been occasions when residents from the care home had visited the children at the nursery school and taken part in reading activities with the children. The practitioners talked about creating an 'intergenerational gate' between the two premises, as a way of removing the physical barriers between the two settings and allowing more spontaneous interactions between the children and older adults. Although for many education and care settings and care homes an 'intergenerational gate' is not a possibility (unless they happen to be neighbours), arguably outdoor and public spaces could provide opportunities for children and older adults to meet together. Public and outdoor spaces are typically age segregated, for example playgrounds designed for children; housing designed for older adults. IG approaches to planning and designing public and outdoor spaces which are 'age-friendly' and suitable for both young and old would help to support meaningful connections across the generations (Nelischer and Loukaitou-Sideris, 2023). The 'Nursery in Belong' in Chester, run by the charity Ready Generations is one example of how the generations can be brought together in a meaningful way through careful planning and design. The 25 space Nursery School opened in 2022 and is based in the Belong Chester care village. The care village is in the centre of Chester and provides dementia and nursing care, support available across extended family sized households and independent living apartments (Belong Chester, nd). The nursery is designed to support connections across the generations through both planned and informal encounters. Examples of IG activities on their website include a choir, storytelling, art and dance and stay and play sessions.

Chapter Summary

The definition of family adopted in this chapter is broad and dynamic and one which has changed significantly over time and continues to evolve. Globally and in the United Kingdom, family takes many different forms, all of which should be respected and acknowledged. Bronfenbrenner and Morris's (2006) bio-ecological systems theory is a useful framework for understanding how the family (and broader influences) shapes children's development. As healthy ageing increases, the role of grandparents have become increasingly important in children's lives and central to raising the 'next generation'. However, for some grandparents and grandchildren there are significant challenges, including the lack of funding and support for those who provide kinship care, and for those grandchildren who have been denied access to their grandparents. IG practice has the potential to provide significant benefits for both children and older adults, provided this is carefully planned and appropriate activities are provided for those involved. One way to help build meaningful connections across the generations is through the planning and design of 'age-friendly' outdoor and public spaces, suitable for those of all ages.

Key Points

- Globally and in the United Kingdom, family takes many different forms, all of which should be respected and acknowledged.
- The role of grandparents should be acknowledged as an important and essential resource in terms of bringing up the next generation.
- IG practice and 'age-friendly' spaces are a way of building connections across the generations with positive benefits for all those involved.

Further Reading

Belong Chester (nd) *Belong*. Available at: https://www.belong.org.uk/ (accessed 31.8.23).

Buchanan, A. and Rotkirch, A. (2018) Twenty-first century grandparents: Global perspectives on changing roles and consequences. *Contemporary Social Science*, 13(2): 131–144.

Lyndon, S. and Moss, H. (2022) Creating meaningful interactions for young children, older friends, and nursery school practitioners within an intergenerational project. *Early Childhood Education Journal*, 51(4): 755–764.

References

Alzheimer's Society (2020) *The impact of Covid-19 on people affected by dementia*. Available at: https://www.alzheimers.org.uk/sites/default/files/2020-08/The_Impact_of_COVID-19_on_People_Affected_By_Dementia.pdf (accessed 25.8.23).

Attar-Schwartz, S. and Buchanan, A. (2018) Grandparenting and adolescent well-being: Evidence from the UK and Israel. *Contemporary Social Science*, 13(2): 219–231. https://doi.org/10.1080/21582041.2018.1465200

Belong Chester (nd) *Belong*. Available at: https://www.belong.org.uk/ (accessed 31.8.23).

Bronfenbrenner, U. (1979) *The ecology of human development: Experiments by nature and design*. Cambridge: Harvard University Press.

Bronfenbrenner, U. (1989) Ecological systems theory. In R. Vasta (Ed.) *Annals of child development*, Vol. 6, pp. 187–249.

Bronfenbrenner, U. and Morris, P. (2006) 'The bioecological model of human development'. In W. Damon and R. Lerner (Eds.), *Handbook of child psychology, Vol. 1: Theoretical models of human development*, 6th ed., pp. 793–828. New York: John Wiley.

Buchanan, A. (2017) Changing roles of grandparents in the United Kingdom; the emergence of the 'new Grandfather. In D. Shwalb and Z. Hossain (Eds.), *Grandparents in cultural context* (Chapter 6). New York: Routledge.

Buchanan, A. and Rotkirch, A. (2018) Twenty-first century grandparents: Global perspectives on changing roles and consequences. *Contemporary Social Science*, 13(2): 131–144.

Channel 4 (2017) *Old people's home for 4 year olds*. Available at: https://www.channel4.com/press/news/channel-4-returns-old-peoples-home-4-year-olds (accessed 25.8.23).

Crawford, P. (2018) Focus on elementary rock of ages: Developing health perspectives of aging in the elementary grades. *Childhood Education*, 91(5): 395-401.

Di Bona, L., Kennedy, S. and Mountain, G. (2017) Adopt a care home: An intergenerational imitative bringing children into care homes. *Dementia*, 1–16.

Doherty, J. and Hughes, M. (2014) *Child Development: Theory and practice 0-11*, 2nd ed. Harlow: Pearson Education Limited.

Drury, L., Adams, D. and Swift, H. (2017) *Making intergenerational connections: What are they, why do they matter and how to make more of them*. London: Age UK. Available at: https://www.researchgate.net/publication/318223654_Making_intergenerational_connections_What_are_they_why_do_they_matter_and_how_to_make_more_of_them (accessed 25.8.23).

Elfer, P., Goldschmied, E. and Selleck, D. (2012) *Key persons in the early years*, 2nd ed. Abingdon: Routledge.

Gov.UK (nd) *Contact with your grandchild if their parents' divorce or separate*. Available at: https://www.gov.uk/contact-grandchild-parents-divorce-separate (accessed 24.8.23).

Gov.UK (2021) *Guidance on protecting people who are clinically extremely vulnerable from COVID-19*. Available at: https://www.gov.uk/government/publications/covid-19-guidance-for-people-whose-immune-system-means-they-are-at-higher-risk (accessed 24.8.23).

Greeen, H. and Edwards, B. (2023) *True Partnerships in SEND: Working Together to Give Children, Families and Professionals a Voice*. London: Routledge.

Holmes, C. (2009) An intergenerational program with benefits. *Early Childhood Education Journal*, 37(2): 113–119.

International Longevity Centre (2017) *The Grandparent Army*. Available at: https://ilcuk.org.uk/the-grandparent-army/ (accessed 25.8.23).

Lyndon, S. and Moss, H. (2021) Meaning-making in an intergenerational project: A dialogic narrative analysis of young children's interactions with older adults. *International Journal of Early Years Education*. https://doi.org/10.1080/09669760.2021.2010519

Lyndon, S. and Moss, H. (2022) Creating meaningful interactions for young children, older friends, and nursery school practitioners within an intergenerational project. *Early Childhood Education Journal*, 51(4): 755–764.

Mason, J. and Tipper, B. (2008) Being related: How children define and create kinship. *Childhood*, 15: 441–460.

McGrath, P. and Ashley, L. (2021) *Kinship care: State of the nation survey 2021*. Available at: https://kinship.org.uk/wp-content/uploads/Kinship-State-of-the-Nation-2021-FINAL.pdf (accessed 24.8.23).

McGuire, S. (2017). Aging Education: A worldwide imperative. *Creative Education*, 8(12): 1878–1891. https://doi.org/10.4236/ce.2017.812128

Millar, J. and Ridge, T. (2013) Lone mothers and paid work: The family-work project, *International Review of Sociology*, 23(3): 564–577.

Nelischer, C. and Loukaitou-Sideris, A. (2023) Intergenerational public space design and policy: A review of the literature. *Journal of Planning Literature*, 38(1): 19–32. https://doi.org/10.1177/08854122221092175

Office for National Statistics [ONS] (2019) *Past and projected period and cohort life tables, 2018-based, UK: 1981 to 2068*. Available at: https://www.ons.gov.uk/peoplepopulationandcommunity/birthsdeathsandmarriages/lifeexpectancies/bulletins/pastandprojecteddatafromtheperiodandcohortlifetables/1981to2068 (accessed 25.8.23).

Office for National Statistics [ONS] (2021). *Coronavirus (COVID-19) latest insights: Deaths: July 2021*. https://www.ons.gov.uk/peoplepopulationandcommunity/healthandsocialcare/conditionsanddiseases/articles/coronaviruscovid19latestinsights/deaths#deaths-by-age

Pro Bono Economics (2022) *Stopping the spiral: Children and Young People's services spending 2010-11 to 2020–21*. Available at: https://media.actionforchildren.org.uk/documents/CSOC03_-_Childrens_Services_Funding_Alliance_Final_1.pdf (accessed 23.6.23).

Reissman, C. (2008) *Narrative methods for the human sciences*. London: SAGE.

Rotkirch, A. (2018) Evolutionary family sociology. In R. Hopcroft (Ed.), *Oxford handbook of evolution, biology, and society* (Chapter 21). New York: Oxford University Press.

Sutin, A., Stephan, Y., Luchetti, M. and Terracciano, A. (2018) Loneliness and risk of dementia. *Innovation in aging*, 2(1): 966–967.

Sylva, K., Melhuish, E., Sammons, P., Siraj-Blatchford, I. and Taggart, B. (2012) *Effective pre-school provision of pre-school education (EPPE) project: Technical paper 12 – the final report: Effective pre-school education*. London: Department for Education and Skills/Institute of Education, University of London.

Tan, J. (2018) Do grandparents matter? Intergenerational relationships between grandparents and Malaysia adolescents. *Contemporary Social Science*, 13(1): 1–15.

Turner, S. (2022) *The cost of loving: Annual survey of kinship carers 2022*. Available at: https://kinship.org.uk/cost-of-loving/ (accessed 24.8.23).

Turner, S. (2023) *Forced out: Delivering equality for kinship carers in the workplace*. Available at: https://kinship.org.uk/forced-out/ (accessed 24.8.23).

Wild, L. (2018) Grandparental involvement and South African adolescents' emotional and behavioural health. *Contemporary Social Science*, 13(2): 1–14.

Wilson, T. (2016) *Working with parents, carers and families in the early years: The essential guide*. Abingdon: Routledge.

World Health Organisation [WHO] (2019) *GHE life expectancy and health life expectancy*. Available at: https://www.who.int/data/gho/data/themes/mortality-and-global-health-estimates/ghe-life-expectancy-and-healthy-life-expectancy (accessed 25.8.23).

Part II
Children's Experiences

6

Safeguarding Children – The Case for Early Help in the Early Years

Helen Moss

After reading this chapter, readers will be able to:

- Discuss the role of early help in safeguarding children in the early years.
- Have an understanding of different levels of safeguarding intervention, from early help to child protection.
- Assess the changing policy context for early help/family support services for children and families in relation to safeguarding.

Introduction

It should be the right of every child to grow up in an environment where they are safe and receive appropriate care to meet their needs, and where they can form positive relationships with parents/carers who will support their journey through childhood. Children's experiences and care in their early years are associated with health, educational and well-being outcomes in later childhood and throughout life; early childhood can therefore be seen as the time when the foundations on which child's future life are built. This chapter will focus on the safeguarding of younger children and the additional support and intervention that some families may need to keep children safe and promote their welfare. The increased vulnerability and risk that can be experienced in the early years will be explored, including the role and safeguarding duties of all professionals who work with children. The function and effectiveness of early help in the early years will be discussed in terms of current safeguarding policy and practice.

Context

Most children grow up in families where they do not experience harm and/or abuse, enabling them to have opportunities to grow, develop and reach their potential. Some children will require extra support, including effective safeguarding intervention, due to concerns, or specific risks, within their home or wider environment. Young children can be particularly vulnerable, or at risk of abuse, and can experience lifelong consequences if their day-to-day needs are not met, or they experience harm. They are highly dependent on the safe and effective care provided in the first instance by their primary carers, but this can also be day-to-day care provided by wider family members or substitute carers (for example foster carers). Young children's development is also enhanced and supported by contact with external services and professionals beyond their family, such as universal health services, early years settings and schools. Bronfenbrenner's (1979) Ecological Systems Model can be helpful in thinking about children growing up within the context of their immediate family but also wider contexts, all of which can impact their development and experience throughout childhood.

Currently in the United Kingdom there are a high number of children who are vulnerable and require additional support beyond their family. This may be due to living in households where they are exposed to issues such as domestic abuse, parental substance misuse, have a parent with a mental health need or living in families under extreme stress due to issues such as poverty or discrimination. A report from the Children's Commissioner (2019) on childhood vulnerability in England estimates that 723,000 children are known to services that work with children and are receiving support or intervention. The Report highlights that 2.3 million children are living with risk because of a vulnerable family background. Hence, the report claims there are significant numbers of children who are vulnerable but who are not receiving help and support, and would benefit from services.

Children Have the Right to Grow up Safely and Be Protected From Harm

The United Kingdom is a signatory to the United Nations Convention on the Rights of the Child. The United Kingdom signed this convention in 1990, ratified it in 1991 and it came into force in 1992 (UNCRC, 1989). Our commitment as a society, and the role of government specifically, is to ensure that children are protected from violence, abuse and neglect by their parents, or anyone else who looks after them as specified under Article 19 of the Convention:

> States Parties shall take all appropriate legislative, administrative, social and educational measures to protect the child from all forms of physical or mental violence, injury or abuse, neglect or negligent treatment, maltreatment or exploitation, including sexual abuse, while in the care of parent(s), legal guardian(s) or any other person who has the care of the child (UNCRC, 1989: Article 19).

In addition, the state should provide 'help and support to meet the needs of children as soon as problems emerge '(Department for Education, 2023b: 7). Subsequently, the

Committee on the Rights of the Child (2011) has stressed that this support should encompass a proactive approach.

In the United Kingdom, the government fulfils these commitments to children's protection, safety and well-being by enacting legislation and policy to safeguard all children and young people. Under such legislation (supported by statutory guidance/frameworks, local policy and procedures) everybody involved the care of children has a responsibility to safeguard them and protect them from harm. Therefore, a fundamental right of all children is the right to safety and protection.

Safeguarding Is Everyone's Responsibility

All practitioners who work with children have safeguarding responsibilities. Current statutory guidance (DfE, 2023b: 7) states that 'Nothing is more important than children's welfare. Every child deserves to grow up in a safe, stable and loving home. Children who need help and protection deserve high quality and effective support'. Safeguarding and promoting the welfare of children is defined within this guidance as:

- providing help and support to meet the needs of children as soon as problems emerge;
- preventing impairment of children's mental and physical health or development;
- ensuring that children grow up in circumstances consistent with the provision of safe and effective care;
- promoting the upbringing of children with their birth parents, or otherwise their family network through a kinship care arrangement, whenever possible and where this is in the best interests of the children;
- taking action to enable all children to have the best outcomes in line with the outcomes set out in the Children's Social Care National Framework. (DfE, 2023b: 8)

This can be viewed as a holistic safeguarding approach which goes beyond just protecting children from maltreatment or harm but also providing early help to children and their families/carers when safeguarding concerns begin to emerge. We will revisit this point when we explore how professionals work together at different levels to safeguard children.

This statutory guidance also reinforces the need for all agencies that work with children and families to work together:

> Safeguarding partners are under a duty to work together, and with other partners locally including education providers and childcare settings, to safeguard and promote the welfare of children in their area (DfE, 2023b: 7).

Within safeguarding is child protection. This refers to activity undertaken to protect specific children who are suffering, or who are likely to suffer, significant harm because of abuse and/or neglect. When a child suffers, or is at risk of, significant harm the law places specific duties on the Local Authority to make enquiries and take such action as required to protect the child. These duties can be found in section 47 of the Children Act 1989. On a continuum of safeguarding interventions, early help seeks to offer targeted interventions to children and families, to avoid or minimise harm and/or mitigate family crisis. Early help seeks to prevent children living with adversity over longer periods of time and should be provided prior to the point of statutory intervention, for example child protection inquiries. Intervention prior to child protection is carried out to prevent impairment of a child's health or development and promote circumstances for children to grow up with the provision of safe and effective care, wherever possible within their families.

Point of Reflection

- Why is it important that all professionals and agencies that work with children, work together to safeguard children?

Risk and Younger Children – With Reference to Child Safeguarding Practice Reviews

Children and young people of all ages can experience abuse and neglect, but risks and impact can vary depending on the age and environment of the child. Too frequently media headlines make us aware of tragic outcomes for children who have been harmed or killed in the care of their families. Often, these children have been known to a range of professionals, but timely intervention to protect them from harm has either been inadequate or lacking sufficient urgency, resulting in these children experiencing harm or even being killed by those who should offer them care and safety. When considering significant risks to young children, a summary of key findings of case reviews into the deaths of children under 2 between 2018 and 2022, the NSPCC (2023) stated that children under the age of 2 years are particularly vulnerable in respect of non-accidental injuries, neglect and the dangers associated with unsafe sleeping.

At the beginning of the 2020s, the tragic deaths of two young children in the care of family members, Arthur Labinjo-Hughes and Star Hobson, prompted widespread public and professional concern about the effectiveness of the safeguarding and child protection systems that could have intervened to protect them. In the year 2020 the United Kingdom experienced Covid-19 lockdowns; Arthur was 6-years old and Star was 16-months old. They both died as a result of harm inflicted by an adult within their household. A key theme of the safeguarding practice reviews, following their deaths, highlights that practitioners must always see the child first and maintain a child-centred approach. The Review into the deaths of Arthur and Star opens with the following statements:

> Arthur Labinjo-Hughes was a little boy who loved playing cricket and football. He enjoyed school, had lots of friends, and was always laughing. Arthur died in Solihull aged six on 17 June 2020.
>
> Star Hobson was an inquisitive toddler who loved to listen to music and would dance in her baby walker, laughing and giggling. Star died in Bradford aged 16 months on 22 September 2020. (The Child Safeguarding Practice Review Panel[1], 2022: 8)

The deaths of the two children led the government to commission a detailed investigation into the circumstances surrounding their deaths. This formed part of a wider national review of Child Protection (Child Protection in England, The Child Safeguarding Practice Review Panel, 2022). The Child Safeguarding Practice Review (2022) examined the circumstances surrounding the death or injury of babies under one year by their fathers or males in a caring role. It identified that 37% of referrals relating to all serious incident notifications in 2020 involved babies under one and were in relation to physical injury or death. Babies under one year were the largest age category of all notifications that the panel received. Therefore, those working within in the early years sector need to be particularly aware of factors that can make babies and young children particularly vulnerable and at risk of harm. These factors also include their high level of dependency on their primary carer/s to meet all basic daily needs. Before children become verbal, they are unable to verbally tell anyone what is happening to them or even have awareness that what they are experiencing is abuse or neglect. Younger children may not be seen by services on a regular basis, hence making them relatively invisible to people outside of the family home, who can pick up on safeguarding concerns. This was a heightened safeguarding concern during Covid-19 lockdown restrictions, when children where not seen regularly by professionals, as was the case for Arthur Labinjo-Huges. The report by the Children's Commissioner (2020: 10) noted that when schools closed, this did not only impact children's education but 'left children more vulnerable and at risk of harm'.

Point of Reflection

- What factors may lead to babies and young children being vulnerable to harm and abuse?

[1]The Child Safeguarding Practice Review Panel is an independent body that reviews cases where children have been seriously harmed, and abuse or neglect is known or suspected.

Overview of the Legal Framework to Safeguard Children

The Children Act 1989 provides the main legal framework for the safeguarding and protection of children and contains key legal powers and duties to do this. It introduced the threshold for when a local authority must make enquiries about, and decide what action is required, to safeguard and protect a child's welfare. It places a duty on all local authorities to provide services to support children and families. A fundamental principle of the Children Act 1989 is that the welfare of the child is paramount (Part 1, s1). The Children Act 1989 introduced important legal concepts that have shaped professional roles and responsibilities for the safeguarding and protection of children. These include the concepts of 'child in need' and 'significant harm' which are key in determining the involvement of Children's Social Care to conduct an assessment to determine either family support and/or plans to protect children from harm.

The Children Act 1989 places 'a duty on local authorities to safeguard and promote the welfare of children in their area who are in need and, so far as is consistent with that duty, to promote the upbringing of such children by their families'. The term 'child in need' has a statutory definition and is the point at which a child is entitled to family support from the Local Authority, under s17, Children Act 1989. This section of the Act defines a 'child in need' as a child who is:

> Unlikely to achieve or maintain, or have the opportunity of achieving or maintaining, a reasonable standard of health or development without the provision for him of services by the local authority; the child's health or development is likely to be significantly impaired, or further impaired, without the provision of such services; or the child is disabled S17 (10) Children Act 1989

The threshold of 'significant harm' triggers compulsory intervention by the local authority to make enquiries and determine if action is required to protect the child. These enquiries would be conducted under s47, Children Act 1989. In s31 Children Act 1989, as amended by the Adoption and Children Act 2002:

> Harm means ill-treatment, or the impairment of health or development, including, for example, impairment suffered from seeing or hearing the ill-treatment of another.

When introduced over 30 years ago, the Children Act 1989 aimed to achieve a balance between providing help and support to families (largely found in Part III and specifically under s17, CA89) and providing powers and duties to compulsorily intervene in family life when there is a risk of significant harm to the child (largely found in Part IV and V). It could be argued that the legal powers and duties placed on the state to safeguard and protect children are also consistent with an early help ethos – that children and their families should receive support in a timely manner, to prevent harm and not only at the point of crisis or after a child has experienced harm.

When examining the impact of the Children Act 1989 over the last 30 years, a recent report (Elvin et al., 2019: nd) concluded that there has been a policy shift away from an original 'emphasis on helping families to a greater emphasis on protective intervention The shift results not from the act itself but from much reduced funding alongside greater numbers needing services'.

It has been argued that the aim of a balance in the Children Act 1989 between preventative family support and proactive child protection is currently out of kilter. In an extended period of limited funding and resources to local authorities and the third sector, it has been claimed that services have become increasingly dominated by the need to take proactive protective intervention using statutory powers to safeguard children, as opposed to working in a more preventative, supportive way with families based on partnership and co-production. According to Elvin et al. (2019), this has been accompanied by a move towards more 'risk averse' practice as a response to media reporting of high profile child deaths.

Bywaters and Webb (2018) analysed the expenditure of Local Authorities on Children's Social Care in England (via their returns to the DfE). This showed a total reduction in expenditure per child on Children's and Young People's Services of 14% between 2010 and 2015, with the most deprived third of Local Authorities being cut by 21% compared with 7% in the least deprived third. Bywaters and Webb (2018) claim that the heaviest burden of these cuts was shown to have fallen on early years and early help services. However, the findings of the House of Lords Library (2022) suggests that in terms of Children's Social Care, expenditure has been protected from 2014/5 to 2019/20 'during a period in which government funding for local authorities has fallen in real terms'. This may have protected the provision of statutory child safeguarding intervention by local authorities (as detailed above) but perhaps at the cost of funding to early help services.

Challenges Within Safeguarding Practice

Although legislation, policies and procedures clearly set out that services should be provided to support families where a child is 'in need' or make enquiries if a child may be at risk of significant harm, it is also evident that, in practice, providing the right type of intervention at the right time remains challenging, subject to complex decision-making and is often dependent on effective multi-agency working. Key challenges to the delivery of effective safeguarding and child protection services have been explored over decades. Monro's (2008: 1) highly regarded examination of our child protection systems states:

> Child protection work inevitably involves uncertainty, ambiguity, and fallibility. The knowledge base is limited, predictions about the child's future welfare are imperfect, and there is no definitive way of balancing the conflicting rights of

> parents and children. The public rightly expect high standards from child protection workers in safeguarding children but achieving them is proving problematic.

This quote highlights that the safeguarding and protection of children is an intrinsically complex and challenging aspect of work with children and families. It requires a questioning and curious approach from all practitioners in contact with children. Often, detailed information about the child maybe unknown, or contradictory, or not known by all practitioners in contact with the child. Parents may not want to reveal what is happening within the family home. Professional intrusion into family life, to understand the daily lived experience of the child, can be resisted by parents/carers and judgements about whether a child is at risk of harm are often not clear cut.

Challenges in relation to information sharing is critical to effective safeguarding, as highlighted by the Review in the deaths of Arthur Labinjo-Huges and Star Hobson, which identified 'weaknesses in information sharing and seeking within and between agencies' (The Child Safeguarding Practice Review Panel, 2022: 9). Such findings echo those identified in many previous enquiries into child deaths, including those of Victoria Climbie in 2000 and Peter Connelly in 2007. It is evident that professionals continue to face significant challenges in safeguarding and protecting children at risk. However, Munro (2011: 10) reminds us that it is:

> ...not easy to identify abuse and neglect. Signs and symptoms are often ambiguous and so it is important that those working with children, young people and adults have ready access to social work expertise to discuss concerns and decide whether a referral to children's social care is needed.

Point of Reflection

- Can you identify any additional barriers to effective safeguarding of young children?

What can Practitioners Do to Safeguard Children?

All children and families benefit from involvement with universal services. Universal services are those that all children should access to support their health, learning and development. For young children, these would include health services such as a general practitioner (GP) and Health Visitor and early years services. Some children and families may need additional support in addition to universal services. Any family can experience times of additional stress or face challenges that require the help of others to overcome. Sometimes that help will come from relatives and friends, but some families will need more coordinated support from a range of different agencies.

Identification and Referral

All practitioners who work with children and families have a role in **identifying** and responding to safeguarding concerns. Their interaction with, and knowledge of, the child and family enables them to identify potential indicators of abuse or neglect. Practitioners are required to undertake regular safeguarding training. This will familiarise them with the main categories of abuse and neglect: physical abuse, emotional abuse, sexual abuse and neglect, and the signs and indicators of each of these categories of abuse. These different types of abuse are detailed within Working Together to Safeguard Children (DfE, 2023b) and are included within local Child Protection and Safeguarding Procedures. Practitioners not only need to be aware of the different categories of abuse and neglect, to help aide identification, but also be mindful that children can experience multiple risks in relation to different forms of abuse. Being familiar with the signs and indicators of abuse and neglect enable practitioners not only to identify safeguarding concerns but also to share these at the earliest opportunity, in the first instance, with their Designated Safeguarding Lead (DSL) within their early years setting or school. A referral to Children's Social Care can prompt timely, multi-agency intervention to safeguard the child or provide expert advice and guidance on next steps. Referral criteria for practitioners will be set out in local Child Protection and Safeguarding Procedures and details of how to access these procedures should be available on the Local Safeguarding Children Partnership websites, along with details of the referral process.

Sharing information regarding concerns about a child is key to effective safeguarding and can help inform complex judgements about a child's safety and well-being. Referrals to Local Authority Children's Social Care Services are often made via a single point of access within each local authority (this may be known locally as the Multi-Agency Safeguarding Hub [MASH], Integrated Front Door [IFD], Children – Single Point of Access). Here, the referral will be triaged in order for next steps to be decided. The next step could be a statutory assessment led by a social worker (under s17 or s47, Children Act 1989 – as detailed previously) or early help support provided by the local authority and partner agencies, or an onward referral.

Working as Part of a Multidisciplinary Team to Safeguard Children in Partnership With Children and Families

Where it has been identified that a child and family would benefit from joined up multi-agency support, there are different levels of intervention that can be accessed or provided to the child and family. To help ensure children and families receive the appropriate level of support, at the right time, the key safeguarding partner agencies in each local area are required to publish the local criteria for different levels of help and assessment for children and families. This is often referred to as a 'threshold document' and is often represented visually in the shape of a half circle with four sections, representing a 'continuum of needs'.

Generally, this threshold document outlines support for children and families at four different levels as follows:

- Level 1 Universal refers to the universal services that all children and families should access, for example a GP.
- Level 2 Early support/additional services may be where a child requires additional support from a particular service, for example speech and language therapy.
- Level 3 Targeted Early Help may be where a range of services need to be involved to safeguard the child and support the family, when a family may be experiencing multiple challenges. These may include services like parenting support, mental health support and housing services. It is a voluntary approach and the family would need to consent to work with the different services. Where the family and child are involved with multiple services it is important that work with the family is coordinated and reviewed by a lead professional.
- Level 4 Specialist Services includes support to children and families where there are child protection concerns and specialist interventions for children and families such as Child and Adolescent Mental Health Services (CAMHS).

Early Help – Development, Impact and Current Role Within the Safeguarding of Children

Services for children and families that reflect an early help ethos were being developed as far back as the 1970s, as part of the Children's Centre Movement (Warren-Adamson, 2006). Key aims were to address divisions between education, health and social care provision (an early recognition of how children can 'fall between the gaps' in services). The first Children Centres were 'multipurpose centres' to meet the diverse needs of young children and respond to growing concerns about child poverty, also a key concern in the 1970s (House of Commons Education Committee [HCEC], 2013). Services for children and families were mandated by the Children Act 1989 CA89 (Schedule 2, para 9 [1] [2]) as places where a range of services could be accessed under one roof. A review of the literature on Children Centres over 25 years, pre and post the Children Act 1989, explored how 'centre-based practice' embraced the whole spectrum of the needs of children and families (Warren-Adamson, 2006) but had an emphasis on the needs of vulnerable children and children in need.

The term 'Early help' began to gain traction within the children's workforce following the Government Green Paper, Every Child Matters in 2003, and the subsequent introduction of the Children Act 2004. The early 2000s were also a time of significant expansion and additional government funding for 'early help' provision. The labour government's flagship Sure Start programme saw investment rise from £500 million in 2000–2001 to £1.7 billion in 2009–2010 (Kelly et al., 2018: 54).

Sure Start aimed to deliver centre-based, integrated, multi-agency support in every community for young children and their parents/carers. It was a universal service funded by Local Authorities. A key aim was to reduce the attainment gap between the outcomes of children from disadvantaged backgrounds and those from more affluent backgrounds. With the change in government in 2010, came an end to the high levels of spending on centre-based, early help services. Since then, funding has reduced considerably, across the public sector in general and significantly within the area of centre-based early help, with numerous examples of the closure of Sure Start/Children's Centres within local authorities. Expenditure on early help services is now significantly lower than previously, with analysis showing that areas of higher deprivation have been disproportionately impacted (Bywaters and Webb, 2018).

Concurrently with the onset of reduced investment in centre-based early help provision, the term 'early help' was being adopted by Munro in her reviews of Child Protection, commissioned by the incoming Coalition government in 2010, in the wake of the death of Peter Connelly in 2007. Munro (2010: 21) adopted the term 'early help' as it 'carries a stronger connotation of working with families and supporting their aims and efforts to change'. The death of Peter Connelly in 2007 led to widespread public outcry and political concern about the failures by key agencies. It also became evident that referrals to Children's Social Care, most notably child protection referrals, were beginning to significantly increase. According to a Parliamentary Research Briefing (2021), the years between 2010 and 2020 saw a modest increase of 4% in relation to children identified as 'in need' but a 125% increase in child protection enquiries and a 32% increase in children on child protection plans. What is striking from these statistics is the dramatic increase in child protection investigations and children subject to a child protection plan. This may leave practitioners and others to question a possible link between the reduction in the provision of 'centre-based' early help provision for children and families and the increased numbers of children subject to child protection plans. The most recent data published by the Department for Education (2022) identifies that current referrals to Children's Social Care are at their highest since 2018, with 404,310 children identified as being 'in need', which equates to about 1 in every 30 children in England.

Early Help in the 2020s

The current DfE statutory guidance, 'Working Together to Safeguard Children' (DfE, 2023b: 41) states that:

> Early help is support for children of all ages that improves a families resilience and outcomes or reduces the chance of a problem getting worse.

Early help can now include a wide range of different services that support children and families when issues are emerging that could negatively impact the child. The Early Intervention Foundation (2019) states that early intervention consists of many different types of support for children and families, delivered in many different ways and settings. These can range from home visiting programmes to support parents, school-based programmes and mentoring schemes.

Early help services can be universal or targeted and they tend to fall between universal and statutory services (Early Intervention Foundation, 2019). Early help services tend to be non-statutory (i.e. services that are not a legal requirement) and it can be down to the discretion of local areas to determine what services are provided, and who can access these services. This can make early help more vulnerable to cuts when funding is limited, and provision may vary geographically.

Nonetheless, early help services form an important part of the 'continuum of support' that can be offered to children and families if they require additional support. This can be at different points in a child's life, for different periods of time and can be for a wide variety of reasons. However, the fundamental aim of early help remains to enable the child to reach their potential and support the family in this aim. It is a type of support provided before the point of statutory safeguarding interventions and child protection. Within Local Authorities, Children's Social Care support and intervention for children and families may be provided by Early Help Teams staffed by specialist early help practitioners. The provision of a continuum of support, help and protection for children and their families, from engagement with universal services accessed by all children, through early help, targeted support and ultimately protective/specialist interventions, has been a long-standing objective of both national and local safeguarding policy. However, the Independent Review of Children's Social (MacAlister, 2022) notes that the continuum of help and protection for children and families continues to challenge services providers. In part this may be due to tensions between the requirement on Local Authorities to fund statutory services, notably child protection, and the impact this has on the funding that remains for non-statutory early help services. This can be viewed within the context of funding cuts over many years to local authorities' public services.

The Current Agenda for Change

In 2022, a major review of Children's Social was published, calling for a 'reset' of Children's Social Care (MacAlister, 2022). It called for a 'revolution in Family Help' whereby families who need help from a range of professionals receive 'more responsive, respectful and effective support' (MacAlister, 2022: 29). It called for 'a shift from remote services to ones which build deep relationships with families and the communities they live in' (MacAlister, 2022: 30). It recommends the bringing together of the support currently being offered to families via 'targeted early help' and work under s17, CA89, to 'form a new single offer of Family Help' with the aim of supporting and keeping families together (MacAlister, 2022: 30).

In February 2023, the government published its response to both the MacAlister Review (2022) and the Report into the deaths Arthur Labinjo-Hughes and Star Hobson. This report, entitled 'Stable Homes. Built on Love' (DfE, 2023a) indicates that our safeguarding systems are likely to be subject to significant reform. A key theme of the government's response to the review is the call for Family Help to provide the right support at the right time so that children can thrive with their families (DfE, 2023a). It requests 'much more support' for families who need extra help and welcome the notion of multidisciplinary Family Help services. The report calls for the need to 'rebalance children's social care away from costly crisis intervention to more meaningful and effective help for families' (DfE, 2023a: 16). Part of the proposed plans to deliver change is for 'every area in England to provide families with supportive and welcoming Family Help services, delivered by a skilled multidisciplinary workforce' (DfE, 2023a: 17).

Following the commitments set out the Government report 'The best start in life: a vision for the 1,001 critical days' (HM Government, 2021) eligible local authorities are taking part in the establishment of Family Hubs. Family hubs aim to provide:

> families with the integrated support they need to care for their children from conception, throughout the early years and into the start of adulthood (HM Government, 2022: 1).

The intension is that these multi-agency hubs will support families to establish the positive foundations to promote positive child development.

Finally, in 2023, the House of Commons Education Committee (HCEC) published its report on support for childcare and the early years which identifies that safeguarding issues are less likely to be identified when a child does not attend an early years setting. This would therefore support the importance of the early years sector in the safeguarding of young children. However, with current concerns regarding a lack of available early years places for all children who need them this may limit opportunities for the most vulnerable children to be referred to additional services when required. Within this current policy agenda, it is therefore timely to review current safeguarding interventions and ask whether providing earlier help to children and their families – before a point of crisis – should be a priority, as indicated within the above government plans.

Case Study: Early Help Plan

Kirsty and her partner Elias have been married for 6 years and have 2 children, Esme aged 4 and Sky aged 2. Kirsty is 26-years old and identifies as white British and Elias is 30-years old and identifies as Black British. The family live in a two-bedroom social housing flat on the South Coast of England. Elias currently receives statutory sick pay following an accident at work two months ago. Karen works part time at a local café. The family is experiencing severe financial pressures and find it hard to cover everyday living costs, especially as their gas and electric bills have gone up so much recently. Kirsty is regularly missing meals to ensure that her daughters have enough to eat. Since being off work Elias has been smoking cannabis on a regular basis – he says that it helps with the pain from his accident. One month ago, the children's health visitor initiated an Early Help Plan, in agreement with the parents, to provide additional family support due to concerns about missed health and development checks for both children and a general concern that Kirsty and Elias were finding it hard to cope with

(Continued)

(Continued)

the day-to-day care of the children. Following this, Esme and Sky have started attending a local nursery on a part-time basis. Both children present as very quiet and reluctant to engage in any group activities. There are concerns about Esme's speech development and Sky is not reaching expected developmental milestones. Esme has begun to form a positive attachment with her key person at the nursery.

- How could this family be supported by the early years setting and wider professional networks?
- How could early help support the development of the children in this family?
- What may be the impact on the children if they do not receive help and support at this point?

Chapter Summary

In relation to ongoing initiatives to improve child safeguarding, a key question is whether earlier intervention in children's lives, especially for those younger children where there are indicators of vulnerability and need, should be funded and resourced to a higher degree than currently. Additionally, should the delivery and availability of early help services for young children and families be reformed and are Family Hubs going to adopt an early help agenda. Effective early help provided to children and their families 'in need' has the potential to make changes early in the child's life that can be highly significant in enabling more children to avoid living with risk and harm, to enable children to form positive primary attachments, to have their physical and well-being needs met to promote good health and to grow up in a family environment where they are safe – all factors that can be highly significant in terms of the child's future well-being and development.

Key Points

- Practitioners play a critical role in the recognition and referral of safeguarding concerns in relation to younger children.
- It is essential that help is provided to young children as soon as safeguarding concerns begin to emerge.
- Younger children are more vulnerable to safeguarding risks.

Further Reading

Department for Education [DfE] (2023a) *Stable homes, built on love: implementation strategy and consultation: Children's social care reform 2023.* Available at: https://webarchive.nationalarchives.gov.uk/ukgwa/20230308171142/https://www.gov.uk/government/consultations/childrens-social-care-stable-homes-built-on-love (accessed 11.1.24).

Department for Education [DfE] (2023b) *Working together to Safeguard children: Statutory Guidance.* Available at: https://assets.publishing.service.gov.uk/media/65803fe31c0c2a000d18cf40/Working_together_to_safeguard_children_2023_-_statutory_guidance.pdf (accessed 11.1.24).

NSPCC Learning (2023) *Infants: learning from case reviews.* Available at: https://learning.nspcc.org.uk/media/3148/learning-from-case-reviews_infants.pdf (accessed 11.1.24).

References

Brofenbrenner, U. (1979) *The Ecology of Human Development: Experiments by Nature and Design.* Cambridge, MA: Harvard University Press.

Bywaters, P. and Webb, C. (2018) Austerity, rationing and inequity: Trends in children's and young peoples services expenditure in England between 2010 and 2015. *Local Government Studies*, 44(3): 391–415.

Children's Commissioner (2019) *Childhood Vulnerability in England.* Available at: https://www.childrenscommissioner.gov.uk/resource/childhood-vulnerability-in-england (accessed 11.1.24).

Children's Commissioner (2020) *Childhood in the time of Covid.* Available at: https://assets.childrenscommissioner.gov.uk/wpuploads/2020/09/cco-childhood-in-the-time-of-covid.pdf (accessed 11.1.24).

Department for Education [DfE] (2023a) *Stable homes, built on love: implementation strategy and consultation: Children's social care reform 2023.* Available at: https://webarchive.nationalarchives.gov.uk/ukgwa/20230308171142/https://www.gov.uk/government/consultations/childrens-social-care-stable-homes-built-on-love (accessed 11.1.24).

Department for Education [DfE] (2023b) *Working together to Safeguard children: Statutory Guidance.* Available at: https://assets.publishing.service.gov.uk/media/65803fe31c0c2a000d18cf40/Working_together_to_safeguard_children_2023_-_statutory_guidance.pdf (accessed 11.1.24).

Early Intervention Foundation (2019) *What is early intervention?* Available at: https://www.eif.org.uk/about/who-is-eif#what-is-early-intervention (accessed 22.5.24).

Elvin, A., Evans, K., Feuchtwang, A., Jones, R., Thoburn, J. and Willow, C. (2019) *The Children act 30 years on.* Available at: https://www.cypnow.co.uk/features/article/the-children-act-1989-30-years-on (accessed 11.1.24).

HM Government (2021) *The best start for life: A vision for the 1,001 critical days: The early years healthy development review report.* Available at: https://assets.publishing.service.gov.uk/media/605c5e61d3bf7f2f0d94183a/The_best_start_for_life_a_vision_for_the_1_001_critical_days.pdf (accessed 11.1.24).

HM Government (2022) *Family hubs and start for life programme guide.* Available at: https://assets.publishing.service.gov.uk/media/62f0ef83e90e07142da01845/Family_Hubs_and_Start_for_Life_programme_guide.pdf (accessed 11.1.24).

House of Commons Education Committee [HCEC] (2013) *Foundation Years: Sure start children's centres, fifth report of session 2013–2014.* Available at: https://publications.parliament.uk/pa/cm201314/cmselect/cmeduc/364/364.pdf (accessed 11.1.24).

House of Commons Education Committee [HCEC] (2023) *Support for childcare and the early years*. Available at: https://committees.parliament.uk/publications/41066/documents/200023/default/ (accessed 11.1.24).

House of Lords Library (2022) *Independent review of children's social care*. Available at: https://lordslibrary.parliament.uk/independent-review-of-childrens-social-care/#heading-1 (accessed 22.5.24).

Kelly, E., Lee, T., Sibieta, L. and Waters, T. (2018) *Children's Commissioner: Public spending on children in England: 2000 to 2020*. Available at: https://assets.childrenscommissioner.gov.uk/wpuploads/2018/06/Public-Spending-on-Children-in-England-CCO-JUNE-2018.pdf (accessed 12.1.24).

MacAlister, J. (2022) *The independent review of children's social care: Final report*. Available at: https://webarchive.nationalarchives.gov.uk/ukgwa/20230308122449/https://childrenssocialcare.independent-review.uk/final-report/ (accessed 11.1.24).

Munro, E. (2011) *The Munro Review of child protection: Final report: A child-centred system*. Available at: https://www.gov.uk/government/publications/munro-reviewof-child-protection-final-report-a-child-centred-system (accessed 11.1.24).

NSPCC Learning (2023) *Infants: learning from case reviews*. Available at: https://learning.nspcc.org.uk/media/3148/learning-from-case-reviews_infants.pdf (accessed 11.1.24).

The Child Safeguarding Practice Review Panel (2022) *Child Protection in England: National review into the murders of Arthur Labinjo-Hughes and Star Hobson*. Available at: https://assets.publishing.service.gov.uk/media/628e262d8fa8f556203eb4f8/ALH_SH_National_Review_26-5-22.pdf (accessed 11.1.24).

UNCRC (1989) *The United Nations Convention on the Rights of the Child*. Available at: https://www.unicef.org.uk/wp-content/uploads/2016/08/unicef-convention-rights-child-uncrc.pdf (accessed 11.1.24).

Warren-Adamson, C. (2006) Research review: Family centres: A review of the literature. *Child and Family Social Work*, 11(2): 171–182.

7

Global Refugee Crisis: Focus on the Child

Linda Cooper and Debra Laxton

After reading this chapter, readers will be able to:

- Define and identify causes of humanitarian crisis.
- Consider the short and long-term consequences of a disrupted childhood.
- Explore a case study of the lived experiences of a child refugee in Bangladesh.

Introduction

From a European perspective, it could be easy to assume childhood as a stable and calm period of life. However, in contrast to romanticised notions of childhood as an idyllic stage in a person's life, characterised by playfulness and innocence, for many children the reality is impacted by complex social, economic and political factors. The experience of refugee children often disrupts lives, sometimes with devastating consequences. This chapter considers the causes and impact of disrupted childhoods, the tangled issue of international responsibilities and displacement and the significance of education. Complex issues of humanitarian crisis impact on countries across the globe and are a key determinant for population movement. For many interconnected and complex reasons families are forced to flee their countries in order to survive and protect their children.

Causes of Population Movement

Cultural, Political and Religion Persecution

Throughout the long arc of history, people have been forced to flee their homelands due to societal, political or religious differences and this continues today. Intolerance of diversity results in serious disruption to lives including the forced migration of populations. One of the largest recent movement of people occurred in Myanmar where many Rohingya people escaped persecution and violence by fleeing their home country to relative safety in Bangladesh. The Rohingya is a Muslim ethnic minority group, many generations of whom have lived in Myanmar. Despite this, the Rohingya community has never been recognised by the Myanmar Government and is consequently considered a stateless population. This lack of recognition has resulted in limited opportunities and access to services (Concern Worldwide, 2022). Violence aimed at the Rohingya people in Myanmar has been happening for decades and during this time many families have been forced to leave their home. However, in 2017 the violence escalated and resulted in renewed and significantly increased population migration. Recent figures (UNFPA, 2002) show that 902,947 Rohingya people, 52% of whom are women and girls, have fled Myanmar and the majority now live in one of 34 refugee camps in the Cox's Bazar district within the south-east coastal plain of Bangladesh.

War

Many refugees are a direct or indirect product of war. War and other violent conflicts lead to economic crisis, hunger and risk to life, causing mass movement of populations. More recently, Ukraine, Afghanistan, South Sudan and the Syria Arab Republic have been devastated by war. War and oppression in these regions have forced families to flee their homes. National Geographic (2022) notes that approximately 2.6 million people from Afghanistan have relocated to 69 different asylum countries, and half have been forced to flee more than once. Furthermore, the UNHCR (2002) states that Syria remains the world's largest displacement crisis with more than 13 million people leaving their host country or being made homeless within its borders, and most are condemned to live in poverty.

While some wars have appeared a more distant problem disconnected to childhood in the United Kingdom, the most recent war in Ukraine has radically changed this perception. The Russian challenge to Ukraine resulted in the sudden mass movement of a European population, many of whom have sought sanctuary in other European countries including the United Kingdom. According to Government statistics (Gov.uk, 2022), 104,000 Ukrainians had arrived in the United Kingdom by 2022; 31,300 came under the Ukraine Family Scheme and 72,700 through the Ukraine Sponsorship Scheme.

The refugees from Ukraine include a significant number of children who have found temporary homes with host families or relatives. Statistics reveal that 9,900 Ukrainian children have been offered school places in England, out of the 11,400 that applied (Good Law Project, 2002). While these children have found sanctuary from the dangers of war they are now faced with complex issues related to the loss of leaving their host country, friends and family. Children attending school are required to learn English as an Additional Language (EAL) to access the curriculum and socialise. Not only do families have to adapt to the norms of schooling in a different country, but it is also necessary to acclimatise to the expectations of their host families.

Climate Migration

The number of people relocating due to slow, on-set changes in the climate is increasing and is set to become an ever-increasing issue in the future. Hoffman et al. (2022) suggest that since 2008, an average of twenty million people per year have been displaced by the consequences of extreme weather. The impact of these changes on populations includes countries becoming too arid to sustain crops, too hot to be inhabited, desertification and salinisation of the soil.

Concurrently populations are also being impacted by an inundation of water. In many places across the globe flooding is caused by rising sea levels, but changing weather patterns are also causing the erosion of environmental features that previously prevented flooding. Those living in areas already subject to flooding are particularly vulnerable. For example populations who might traditionally move seasonally to avoid flooding find that areas which were previously safe havens have become flooded themselves. Climate change and the consequences of this will become an unavoidable feature of life for children of the 21st century.

Displaced People

The number of displaced people continues to increase and statistics relating to forcibly displaced populations demonstrate the scale of this daunting problem. According to the United Nations Refugee Agency [UNHCR] (2023), there are an estimated 103 million forcibly displaced people across the globe. The figures include those who are internally displaced, asylum seekers and refugees. The UNHCR (2023) states that more than seven out of ten refugees originate from just five countries; the Syrian Arab Republic, Venezuela, Ukraine, Afghanistan and South Sudan. Of the estimated 103 million displaced people, 36.5 million are children (UNHCR, 2023). Current figures suggest that 1.5 million children were born as refugees between 2018 and 2021; approximately 350,000 and 400,000 children per year (UNHCR, 2023). Moreover, children in countries affected by humanitarian crisis account for nearly half of all deaths of children under the age of five.

Definitions

The terminology used to describe displaced people can be confusing. Baauw et al. (2019) argue that the word 'refugee' encompasses different groups of people and they offer the following definitions that will be used in this chapter to discuss the entire population of refugee children.

Asylum seeker: An individual who has left their home country and calls on the protection of another country and whose request for sanctuary has yet to be processed.

Unaccompanied minor or unaccompanied minor refugee: An individual under the age of 18 applying for asylum without a relative older than 18 years of age.

Refugee: An asylum seeker that has fled their home country and has a 'well-founded fear of persecution' if they return home. Refugee status is granted when an asylum seeker has been acknowledged as a refugee according to the United Nations Refugee Convention. A refugee has completed the asylum process when they have been granted a residence permit.

Internally Displaced Persons: The UNHCR (2023) identify this as an additional category of people forced to move from their home. This heading relates to people who are homeless but have not crossed the border of their home country and are still under the protection of their own government. The UNHCR (2023) explain that these people are not protected by international refugee laws so they can be very difficult to help including them among the most vulnerable groups in the world.

Whose Responsibility?

Children and their families arriving in another country seeking asylum face a complex social and political landscape. Moreover, this is a landscape that is frequently shifting and ambiguous in nature. Questions about who should be responsible for people compelled to leave their homelands is fraught with difficulty and has created a political dilemma for governments in many of the countries who receive them.

Pijnenburg (2022) notes that most refugees are hosted in the Global South with relatively few managing to travel to wealthier countries in the Global North. One of the reasons for this is due to externalisation policies of some regions, such as Europe, Australia and United States that stop refugees from ever reaching their borders. Pijnenburg (2022) explains that externalisation policies also include destination countries negotiating with their neighbours to prevent refugees from arriving and the expelling of individuals who evade such measures, by either returning them to their place of origin or 'transferring' them to another country.

One example of an externalisation policy can be illustrated by the case of the United Kingdom's [UK] 2022 agreement with Rwanda, arranging for refugees to be transferred to that country without a right to return to the United Kingdom. However, the first planned deportation flight was cancelled due to legal challenges. Refugees in the United Kingdom are often confronted with challenging environments. It is easy to think of successful stories like that of Sir Mo Farah, gold medal Olympic athlete, as indicative of a caring asylum system. However, even though he has enjoyed international acclaim, his entrance into this country was complex. In 2022, Mo Farah revealed he had been trafficked into London from Djibouti under a false identity and endured a period of forced child labour before being adopted and becoming a British Citizen.

For families that have come to this country without passports or proper entrance permissions, their experience on arrival can be varied and often traumatic. Many people are housed in temporary hotels and their situation is fragile as they are dependent on the state; families cannot work or study until asylum applications have been decided. Some families might be held in 'detention centres' and subject to challenging living conditions. In 2022 short-term holding facilities in Kent, South-East England were established to accommodate up to 1,500 people who had crossed the English Channel in small boats. The population, including families and children, within the facility quickly rose to over 4,000 people and it was reported that hundreds of people appeared to have been detained beyond the legal limit

(Gentleman, 2023). The overcrowding at the centre and limited sanitary conditions resulted in disease outbreaks including life-threatening conditions like diphtheria, rarely seen in the United Kingdom.

The situation of refugees in the United Kingdom is further complicated by the seemingly different treatment of people depending on their country of origin. Refugees from the Ukraine have been generally welcomed with empathy and many have been accommodated voluntarily by host families. Others, who have come from similar plights, in other parts of the world are often treated very differently. A recent YouGov survey (2022) on the public perception of different refugee groups sheds further light on this issue. The survey concluded that the indigenous population's opinion towards Ukrainian refugees is warmer than towards those fleeing war zones in Afghanistan, Syria and Somalia. Children of different nationalities could therefore face different attitudes depending on their country of origin and race.

The public perception and experience of refugees are compounded by the way in which the media manages their stories and the wider issues of migration and displacement. The language and images used by the media often portray displaced people as both victims and villains, which can significantly impact on how refugees are viewed by the public. Humanitarian stories of helpless victims tend to focus on the lived experience of women and children, often eliciting public sympathy and empathy. However, the media also present the same people as 'villains' that threaten economic and national security, highlighting the need for greater border control (Georgiou & Zaborowski, 2017; Cooper et al., 2020). Issues related to border control have dominated the headlines in the UK media with stakeholders concerned with 'taking back control' of its borders. Media attention is regularly given to small boat crossings. Different portrayals of refugees in any capacity serve to marginalise the identity of refugees themselves who are usually discussed in the third person. Much of the context and background information on their lives and culture is lost (Georgiou & Zaborowski, 2017). It is into this maelstrom of opinion that families and their children enter the United Kingdom.

Point of Reflection

- Whose responsibility are refugees and why? What are their responsibilities?

Physical and Mental Well-being

Refugee children are some of the most vulnerable populations across the globe with physical and mental health a significant potential threat. Displaced from homes, often in low-income countries, many refugee children have been exposed to violence and trauma and for some their lives are, or have been, threatened. Forced to leave their country of origin, both unaccompanied children and children with families regularly find themselves in holding spaces, like refugee camps, for prolonged periods. All too frequently, conditions in refugee camps fail to meet basic human needs and children's rights are constantly violated (Laxton et al., 2021). Despite the United Nations Convention on the Rights of the Child (1989), enshrining rights to equality, education, health, a safe and clean environment to live and protection from harm, the socio-economic position and status of child refugees and their reliance on others renders them powerless and at the mercy of the country they find themselves in to protect and care for them.

Refugees are at risk of trauma at all stages of their journey; from the initial war or persecution in their country of origin, to the often long and arduous journey to find a place of safety, to the time spent within refugee camps (often years) and finally during resettlement. Rizkalla et al. (2020: 1) explains the significance of time spent in refugee camps by highlighting the term 'unchilding' as the loss of children's innocence and access to a normal childhood due to their 'captivity' in camps. Resettlement conditions are said to be the strongest influence on health and well-being (Dangman et al., 2022). Syrian refugee children, exposed to war, provide an example of how resettlement impacts on children's mental health; including high rates of anxiety, depression and post-traumatic stress disorder (Rizkalla et al., 2020).

The physical health of refugee children is impeded in multiple ways but the lack of health care access during long journeys and insufficient health services in refugee camps, including assessments of need on arrival, are significant factors. Infectious diseases can be prevalent. For some children this may manifest in a minor illness but for others chronic infections may require hospital admissions. Children who have not been immunised become at risk to vaccine preventable diseases, e.g. measles, typhoid, malaria, tuberculosis and this can have devastating consequences. As stated, refugee children and families face hardships along their journeys and in refugee camps, and one consequence is that children are often undernourished. Conversely, research has found that on resettlement children can become at risk to obesity. The reasons cited are related to families' usual dietary habits being forced to change to less healthy options and issues of stress (WHO, 2018).

Social Justice

It is important to highlight that refugees are not a homogeneous group and subsequently factors affect individuals and groups of individuals in different ways. Refugee children come from a wide range of countries and diverse backgrounds with varying socio-economic status. Research has shown that the higher the socio-economic status in the country of origin the more protection individuals have from adverse health effects during travel and the first years of migration (Bauer et al., 2020). Furthermore, the wealthier the nation of resettlement the more likely refugee children are to receive health promotion and prevention as a matter of course.

The gendered experiences of child refugees also differ. One example relates to daily life in some refugee camps where cultural gender roles often result in girls being expected to carry out burdensome domestic chores, for example fetching and carrying water, caring for other family members. Engaging in such mentally and physically strenuous activities can impact on physical health and caring for others impacts mental well-being. The experience of refugee girls is also more perilous than boys in relation to exposure to gender-based violence, persecution and sexual exploitation. While walking to collect necessary resources, women and girls can be unprotected and find themselves exposed to sexual violence.

Risk and Protective Factors

Risk factors that impact on the physical and mental health of child refugees are explained by Reed et al. (2011) as the personal, social and environmental influences that negatively impact on psychological and emotional development. Children can be impacted by several and cumulative risks. Protective factors are the factors that enable more positive outcomes despite adversity. These are listed in Table 7.1:

Table 7.1 Protective and Risk Factors

Protective Factors	Risk Factors
Secure attachments/Family connectedness	PTSD in either parent or the child
Culturally competent services	Trauma exposure
Self-efficacy & resilience	Intergenerational transmission of trauma
Health care availability & access	Maternal depression
Safe spaces to live	Loss of parents & bereavement
Trauma informed treatment for families	Separation from parent
Community social support networks	Being a carer
Emotional regulation	Disempowered/dependent parents
Younger children (under 12)	Toxic stress
Pre-school & school access and attendance	Length of time in refugee camp
Resettlement conditions	Cultural isolation
Country of resettlement e.g.	Number of transitions to resettlement
Higher socio-economic status	Malnutrition
	Perceived host Country discrimination
	Socio-economic status
	Unaccompanied children
	Parental employment

Source: Developed and adapted from (Fazel and Stein, 2002).

Whilst resilience is viewed as a protective factor it should be noted that resilience is not a fixed state but rather a process that develops responsively in the face of adverse challenges. Thus, some children who encounter high-risk situations might show resilience because they draw on sufficient protective factors to buffer them against adversity. Children could be seen as resilient in one situation and not in another based on previous experiences and responses. As complex causal chains and accumulation of traumatic exposure increases so can the negative impact on resilience putting children at greater risk of mental health in the short and long term. Education is vital to provide a safe place, opportunity and choice for refugee children in the short and long term.

Point of Reflection

- Consider the many complex issues that cause people to flee their homes and reflect on how a child may feel at the various stages of a journey to find safety and security.

Education and Fragility

The education of refugees is important and can be transformative; knowledge and skills are gained, children's aspirations raised and opportunities and life chances improved (Mason and Orcutt, 2018). UNESCO (2018: 17) states that, 'limited access to education can have the effect of entrenching vulnerability and undermining participation in other areas of life, such as employment or income generation'. The United Nation reinforces a commitment to global development and specifically education by adopting the '2030 Agenda for Sustainable Development' (United Nations, 2015). Sustainable Development Goal (SDG) 4 is ambitious and commits each country to 'ensure inclusive and equitable quality education and promote lifelong learning opportunities for all' (United Nations, 2015).

Data on refugee education is limited and accurate data is even harder to source for several reasons including the continuous movement of refugees, discrimination by host countries towards refugees and inadequate educational systems (OECD and European Union, 2018; Cerna, 2019). Furthermore, there is a serious lack of funding for refugee education globally. Despite a lack of reliable statistics, it is known that refugee school enrolment figures are woeful. According to the UNHCR (2023), there are currently 7.9 million refugee children of school age and almost half (48%) do not attend school even though every child has a right to primary and secondary education (United Nations, 1989). Only 42% of children enrol in early childhood education services, despite global recognition of its significance and importance; positive impact on child development, the opportunity to explore trauma through play and the promotion of school readiness. Primary school is better attended but 63% is still well below the global school attendance figure of 91%. At secondary school, attendance falls dramatically to 37% (European Union for Fundamental Rights, 2017; Cerna, 2019; UNHCR, 2023).

Where primary and secondary schools do exist, other difficulties are faced. Recruiting teachers in fragile contexts, like refugee camps, is a real challenge especially during the current global shortage of teachers (Ring and West, 2015). UNESCO (2022) report a shortage of teachers in all world regions and reiterate its 2016 projection that a further 69 million teachers are needed to achieve universal primary and secondary education.

Teachers are the richest resource in largely under-resourced schools in crisis settings and it is therefore vital that teachers have the knowledge, skills and attitude to deliver quality education. Unfortunately, the opposite is often the reality and many teachers working with refugees in low-income countries are either unqualified or have minimal qualifications. Teachers in refugee camps are generally sourced in two ways; refugees who are teachers working in the host country and national teachers teaching refugee populations. The INEE (2022) provide an example from Kakuma Refugee camp in the North Western region of Kenya. Here, 85% of teachers are refugees themselves and have no teaching qualifications. Fifty four percent have received relevant training, leaving 46% who have not received any. With no fault to the teachers, this must impact on the learning environments provided, the quality of the curriculum and delivery and ultimately the pupil experience and outcomes.

The concept of incentives is important to clarify. Teachers who are refugees themselves are often unable to be paid a salary due to their legal status in the host country and instead may be compensated by non-government organisations (NGOs) through incentives which are payments often significantly below the national rate. This unequal pay is clearly unfair and can create tensions between national and refugee teachers who are carrying out similar roles.

Early Childhood Care and Education (ECCE)

Alongside the assertion of children's rights through the UNCRC (United Nations, 1989), scientific evidence highlights the criticality of the early years in a child's life for laying down the foundations for future learning, health and behaviours (Gov.UK, 2021). During this time the impact of malnutrition, poor nutrition and emotional trauma can have a long-lasting impact. With global acceptance and acknowledgement of the importance of Early Childhood Care and Education (ECCE), an emphasis on provision in fragile environments, such as refugee camps, is developing. Again, the United Nations has played a role in raising expectations and influences legislation, policy and practice; for example SDG target 4.2 aims to ensure that all children have access to quality pre-primary education (United Nations, 2015).

ECCE provision in fragile states can enable children's basic needs to be met, for example food, shelter, health care and psychosocial support. ECCE can provide refugee children with a sense of comfort and stability through routine and familiarity which can be invaluable when they are living in circumstances where they may feel unsafe and witness violence. The value and importance of play is widely recognised and as such quality ECCE provision aims to provide play-based learning. Through play children make sense of their world; they can explore, express and process experiences and emotions. By leading their own play agenda, children have an element of control and can make decisions in a world where they have very limited agency. Play provides mental and physical stimulation and promotes holistic development including the opportunity to play with peers and become socially competent (UNICEF, 2018). Furthermore, play can enable children to be in the moment and process or even forget their worries for that time with opportunities to relax in a safe space with caring adults.

With a drive to increase ECCE provision for young refugee children (3–6 years) there are many challenges. Availability of safe spaces to play and therefore access to ECCE is very limited and yet this is a period of life when a nurturing and stimulating environment is essential for children to grow and thrive. A safe space could be a tented home, a fenced or unfenced outdoor space or a community building. Where safe spaces are created the challenges of teacher recruitment and qualification are even more extensive in the early years than those identified previously in relation to primary and secondary education.

An understanding of child development and early years teaching and learning, including play pedagogy, is vital in any ECCE setting but the challenges to educators are seriously increased within the context and vulnerabilities of refugee children (Jalbout and Bullard, 2021). Other key principles educators need to understand are the importance of, and how to promote, quality interactions, how to be a responsive practitioner who promotes positive relationships and resilience and how to create safe and stimulating child-centred environments. The need for qualified teachers is clear.

Inclusive Education

As we have already explored in this chapter, refugee girls are often discriminated against and exploitation is commonplace despite SDG 5 'to achieve gender equality and empower all women and girls' (United Nations, 2015). Education is another area where there is a lack of equity. Girls are less likely to attend school than boys at all stages of education and although this gap has narrowed in recent years, the divide widens as children become older. The UNCHR (2023) explain further:

> At global level, for every ten refugee boys in primary school there are fewer than eight refugee girls; at secondary school the figure is worse, with fewer than seven refugee girls for every ten refugee boys. Among populations where there are significant cultural barriers to girls' education, the difference is stark. In Pakistan, for example, 47 per cent of Afghan boys are enrolled at primary school, compared with 23 per cent of girls.

Education to secondary level is vital in broadening life opportunities and choices for girls and young women. UNESCO (2013) report that with education, child marriage could fall by 'almost two thirds' and 59% fewer girls in sub-Saharan Africa and South and West Asia would become pregnant. Educated girls gain community respect and are empowered to use their voices. Furthermore, on becoming parents, educated mothers have healthier and better educated children themselves improving the life chances of the next generation and beyond. With less secondary schools in refugee camps than other contexts the challenge to social change is even greater for refugee girls.

Despite the challenges, a somewhat improving picture is evident in the journey towards global gender equality education for refugee children. However, the barriers to education for refugee children with disabilities remain significant. Despite human rights frameworks like the UNCRC (1989) and the SDGs calling for education for all children (United Nations, 2015) access remains extremely limited. UNESCO explain that with 85% of refugees seeking refuge in poor countries and often over-populated refugee camps, countries already struggle to educate host nation children and the scale of educating refugee children in addition is a real and complex challenge. The implementation of inclusive education for children with disabilities arguably adds another layer of complexity and consequently is inadequate and commonly not even on the agenda. Perhaps unsurprisingly, data related to education and refugee children with disabilities is often non-existent and consequently the scale of the problem remains hidden.

Point of Reflection

- Education is key to supporting the long-term and short-term outcomes for children, their communities and wider societies. Why do you think is this?

Case Study: Ahmed

The Power of Education: An Anonymised Case Study From Bhasan Char Island

Ahmed is a 13-year-old Rohingya refugee who has lived on Bhasan Char Island, off the coast of Bangladesh, since February 2022. He fled his home country of Myanmar with his family during the August 2017 genocide and, along with over 800,000 other Rohingya refugees, arrived at the crowded Kutupalong 'mega camp'. Kutupalong is located in the coastal district of Cox's Bazar, Bangladesh, and is currently the largest refugee camp in the world.

To ease huge congestion and overcrowding in the Kutupalong refugee camp, the Bangladesh Government has been relocating tens of thousands of Rohingya refugees to Bhasan Char Island in the Bay of Bengal. The move is undoubtedly controversial with reports of forced relocations, restrictions on freedom of movement and concerns over the safety of the silt, cyclone-prone island.

There is a serious lack of learning facilities on the island, and education has been one of the top requests from the Rohingya refugee community since they arrived. Children on the Edge, a non-profit charitable children's rights organisation working globally in fragile states, already had experience working with communities in the Kutupalong camp. The charity had been providing high-quality learning centres for over a decade, and on the request of the Bangladesh Government, Children on the Edge set up ten model classrooms on Bhasan Char island in 2022.

(Continued)

(Continued)

Ahmed is one of the students on Bhasan Char Island and like many he has a remarkable narrative to share. Having fled his home country, Ahmed experienced significant trauma and upheaval as he was moved from place to place in search of safety, security and a home. Ahmed has faced further harrowing events since arriving on the island. His mother died suddenly of a stroke in March 2022 and his father escaped Bhasan Char Island shortly after her death to remarry. His father is now living near Cox's Bazar with a new wife and is no longer in contact with Ahmed. Ahmed and his siblings have been looked after by their grandmother since his father left. The family is isolated on an island without parents.

Access to education by attending school with his friends each day has provided Ahmed with vital care, stability and focus. Here he enjoys a varied curriculum, with multiple avenues for self-expression including art, singing, dance and drama. He takes part in sports, enjoys taking care of the gardens that surround the classroom and benefits from health education and interventions. Ahmed says, 'I am very happy to have been given a new uniform, a school bag, colouring pencils, a pen, a pencil and other learning materials – my grandmother would not be able to afford any of these items'.

One of his favourite things about school is the digital lessons provided by Children on the Edge. Ahmed says, 'I love coming to school every day and especially love watching the cartoons on the projector screen'. The Rohingya refugee children in Bangladesh are only permitted by the government to learn in Burmese – a language they do not understand – and the Rohingya dialect itself has no universally accepted script. To address language barriers, the entire curriculum has been translated into video lessons that employ verbal teaching, dubbed media and visual learning aids including cartoons and puppets. Child after child has expressed joy and disbelief to be able to finally understand the lessons being presented, resulting in a surge in school attendance and pupil progress.

The digital curriculum uses visual media from around the world to give children experiences of natural wonders, wildlife, culture, sports and news. The online newsletter platform 'Moja Kids' enables children to create their own fun-packed videos, using green screen technology and visual effects to express their ideas in any environment they can imagine. Their creations are compiled and shared across hundreds of classrooms each week, from the camps to the island, across slum and enclave communities in mainland Bangladesh and as far as India and Uganda.

Ahmed's teachers have reported how quickly the children have progressed in maths and English and how much they love the digital lessons. Parents on the island are particularly enthusiastic since the introduction of the Myanmar curriculum in 2022, as they feel it could pave the way for a return home. Having previously been denied access to education, children like Ahmed now feel they are gaining the tools to change their futures. Ahmed says, 'When I am older I will do everything I can to help my brothers and sister to improve their futures too' and his grandmother said 'I am so pleased to see Ahmed in school, he has had a difficult childhood. If he learns maths well enough to do accounting, I will set up a shop for him near our home'.

(Continued)

In a situation where refugee children have only known persecution and statelessness, they need the opportunity to develop confidence, self-esteem and social skills alongside curriculum knowledge. The digital education innovation from Children on the Edge not only creates access to quality primary education, but enables creativity, self-expression and connection for refugee children beyond the confines of both the camps and the Bhasan Char Island.

Children on the Edge hope that their digital education model will be replicated across the Kutupalong camp, enabling thousands more children to learn more effectively and become better equipped for both their present circumstances and future lives.

Points of Reflection

- What were the risk factors for Ahmed?
- What are the protective factors?
- Should governments rely on charities to fund and manage educational provision? (Consider both sides of this argument).

Summary

This chapter has highlighted the complexities and fragilities of refugee crises and experiences. In order to lessen pressure on a few low-income countries, it is necessary for a more sustainable and invested global movement to work collaboratively to aid the plight of all refugees so that the variation in refugee treatment, including basic human rights to dignity, health and education, is not left to individual Governments to determine. A world where some refugees are welcomed whilst others are shunned is inequitable and refugees are frequently treated as homogenous groups rather than as individuals. NGOs provide essential resource in crisis situations around the world and they are relied upon by Governments and refugees to do this. Child refugees frequently have limited access to education and consequently their future chances and potential is often significantly affected. Furthermore, children miss out on the social aspect of being at school as well as the opportunity to develop a love of learning and ambition for a better future.

Key Points

- The experiences of children who are refugees are complex and multi-layered.
- A global governmental approach which is equitable and welcoming is necessary to address issues for children and families who are refugees.
- One of the major challenges for children and young people who are refugees is access to equitable and quality education.

Further Reading

UNHCR The UN Refugee Agency https://www.unhcr.org/media/missing-out-refugee-education-crisis

Children on the Edge https://www.childrenontheedge.org/

Laxton, D., Cooper, L., Shrestha, P. and Younie, S. (2020) Translational research to support early childhood education in crisis settings: A case study of collaborative working with Rohingya refugees in Cox's Bazar. *Education 3-13*, 49, 8, 901–919. doi: 10.1080/03004279.2020.1813186

References

Baauw, A., Kist-van Holthe, J., Slattery, B., Heymans, M., Chinapaw, M. and van Goudoever, H. (2019) Health needs of refugee children identified on arrival in reception countries: A systematic review and meta-analysis. *BMJ Paediatrics Open*, 3 (1). https://doi.org/10.1136/bmjpo-2019-000516

Bauer, J. M., Brand, T. and Zeeb, H. (2020) Pre-migration socioeconomic status and post-migration health satisfaction among Syrian refugees in Germany: A cross-sectional analysis. *Public Library of Science Medicine*, 17 (3).

Cerna, L. (2019) *Refugee Education: Integration Models and Practices in OECD Countries*. OECD Education Working Paper No. 203. Available at: http://www.oecd.org/officialdocuments/publicdisplaydocumentpdf/?cote=EDU/WKP(2019)11&doc Language=En (accessed on 23.2.23).

Concern Worldwide (2022) *The Rohingya Crisis Explained*. Available at: https://www.concern.org.uk/news/rohingya-crisis-explained-5-things-you-need-know (accessed 27.4.23).

Cooper, G., Blumell, L. and Bunce, M. (2020). Beyond the 'refugee crisis': How the UK news media represent asylum seekers across national boundaries. *International Communication Gazette*, 83, 3. https://doi.org/10.1177/1748048520913230 (accessed 28.4.23).

Dangmann, C., Dybdahl, R. and Solberg, O. (2022). Mental health in refugee children. *Current Opinion in Psychology*, 48, https://doi.org/10.1016/j.copsyc.2022.101460

European Union for Fundamental Rights (2017) *Current Migration Situation*. Luxembourg: European Union for Fundamental Rights.

Fazel, M. and Stein, A. (2002) The mental health of refugee children. *Archives of Disease in Childhood*, 87, 366–370.

Gentleman, A. (2023, March 25) You walked in and your heart sank: the shocking inside story of Manston detention centre. *The Guardian*. Available at: https://www.theguardian.com/uk-news/2023/mar/25/inside-story-of-manston-detention-centre (accessed 5.4.23).

Georgiou, M. and Zaborowski, R. (2017). *Media coverage of the 'refugee crisis': A cross-European perspective. Council of Europe report*. Strasbourg: Council of Europe. Available at: https://rm.coe.int/1680706b00 (accessed 28.4.23).

Good Law Project (2002) *Thousands of Ukrainian children are joining UK schools, but some face issues obtaining school places*. Available at: https://goodlawproject.org/ukrainian-children-school-places/#:~:text=The%20war%20in%20Ukraine%20has,with%20relatives%20or%20host%20families (accessed 15.2.23).

Gov.uk (2021) *The Best Start for Life a Vision for the 1,001 Critical Days the Early Years Healthy Development Review Report*. Available at: https://assets.publishing.service.gov.uk/government/uploads/system/uploads/attachment_data/file/973085/Early_Years_Report.pdf (accessed 8.8.21).

Gov.uk (2022) *100,000 Ukrainians welcomed to safety in the UK*. Available at: https://www.gov.uk/government/news/100000-ukrainians-welcomed-to-safety-in-the-uk (accessed 15.2.23).

Hoffman, D., Zimmerman, A., Castelyn, C. and Kaikini, S. (2022). Expanding the duty to rescue to climate migration. *Voices in Bioethics*, 8. https://doi.org/10.52214/vib.v8i.9680

INEE (2022) *The Challenges of Training Female Teachers In Refugee Camps*. Available at https://inee.org/blog/challenges-training-female-teachers-refugee-camps (accessed on 2.3.23).

Jalbout, M. and Bullard, K. (2021) *Ensuring Quality Early Childhood Education for Refugee Children: A New Approach to Teacher Professional Development*. Available at: https://reliefweb.int/report/world/ensuring-quality-early-childhood-education-refugee-children-new-approach-teacher (accessed on 2.3.23).

Laxton, D., Cooper, L., Shrestha, P. and Younie, S. (2021) Translational research to support early childhood education in crisis settings: A case study of collaborative working with Rohingya refugees in Cox's Bazar, *Education 3-13*, 49 (8), 901–919.

Mason, C. and Orcutt, S. (2018) *Hear It from the Teachers: Getting Refugee Children Back into Learning*. Washington: Save the Children.

National Geographic (2022) *Refugee*. Available at: https://education.nationalgeographic.org/resource/refugee (accessed 15.2.23).

OECD/European Union (2018). *Settling in 2018: Indicators of Immigrant Integration*. Paris: OECD.

Pijnenburg, A. (2022) *Externalisation and the Socio-economic Rights of Refugees: What Are the Obligations of Destination States?* Available at: https://rli.blogs.sas.ac.uk/2022/09/27/externalisation-and-the-socio-economic-rights-of-refugees-what-are-the-obligations-of-destination-states/ (accessed 5.4.23).

Reed, R., Fazel, M., Jones, L., Panter-Brick, C. and Stein, A. (2011) Mental health of displaced and refugee children resettled in low-income and middle-income countries: Risk and protective factors. *Lancet*, 379, 250–65.

Ring, A. and West, H. (2015) Under-resourced, undervalued, and underutilized: making the case for teachers in refugee and emergency contexts. *International Education Journal: Comparative Perspectives*, 14 (3), 150–164.

Rizkalla, N., Mallat, N. K., Arafa, R., Adi, S., Soudi, L. and Segal, S. P. (2020) Children are not children anymore; They are a lost generation: Adverse physical and mental health consequences on Syrian refugee children. *International Journal of Environmental Research and Public Health*, 17 (22), 8378.

UNCRC (1989) *United Nations Convention on the Rights of the Child*. Available at: https://www.unicef.org.uk/what-we-do/un-convention-child-rights/ (accessed 22.5.24).

UNESCO (2013) *Education Transforms Lives*. Paris: United Nations Educational.

UNESCO (2018) *Migration, displacement and education: Building Bridges, Not Walls*. Available at: https://unesdoc.unesco.org/ark:/48223/pf0000266058 (accessed on 1.3.23).

UNESCO (2022) *Transforming Education from Within: Current Trends in the Status and Development of Teachers*. Available at: https://unesdoc.unesco.org/ark:/48223/pf0000383002/PDF/383002eng.pdf.multi (accessed 21.2.23).

UNFPA (2002) *Cox's Bazar: A Displaced People Longing for a Sense of Home*. Available at: https://www.unfpa.org/coxs-bazar-displaced-people-longing-sense-home (accessed 15.2.23).

UNHCR (2023) *Refugee Data Finder*. Available at: https://www.unhcr.org/refugee-statistics/ (accessed 15.2.23).

UNICEF (2018) *Learning through Play*. Available at: https://www.unicef.org/sites/default/files/2018-12/UNICEF-Lego-Foundation-Learning-through-Play.pdf (accessed 8.9.21).

United Nations (1989) *Convention on the Rights of the Child*. London: UNICEF.

United Nations (2015) *Transforming our world: The 2030 Agenda for sustainable development*. Available at: https://sustainabledevelopment.un.org/post2015/transformingourworld/publication (accessed on 1.3.23).

WHO (2018) *Health of Refugee and Migrant Children*. Copenhagen: WHO.

YouGov (2022) *Are Attitudes to Ukrainian Refugees Unique?* Available at: https://yougov.co.uk/topics/politics/articles-reports/2022/07/12/are-attitudes-ukrainian-refugees-unique (accessed 27.4.23).

8

Special Educational Needs and Disability (SEND) – Breaking Down Barriers and Access to Learning

Becky Edwards and Heather Green

> I remember, one sports day when our son ran in the opposite direction to everyone else . . . this is the journey that you go on with a child with special needs, you always feel like you're running in a different direction. (Susan, a parent, cited in Green and Edwards, 2023: 106).

After reading this chapter, readers will be able to:

- Understand some of the challenges faced by children with SEND and their families.
- Be familiar with models of disability.
- Understand the importance of co-production in building effective partnerships between professionals and families.

Introduction

Despite a greater understanding of concepts of inclusion and a gradual changing of societal perceptions of disability, children with special educational needs and disabilities (SEND) continue to face many barriers to accessing education and to being included. This chapter will explore historical views of disability and how these have changed over time, while critically discussing the journey towards an equality and equity that has not yet been achieved. Key concepts and theories will be linked to relevant policy and legislation and the way in which these can effectively support partnership working between parents and professionals will be explored and analysed.

Historical Context

Historically children with SEND have been believed to be possessed by spirits or to be the physical incarnation of the past sins of their parents (Smith, 2014). Often excluded and perceived as a problem which needed to be cured or an aberration which needed to be ignored, children with SEND have *faced* a constant struggle to be accepted as worthwhile members of society (Pelka, 2011). Despite philanthropic interest in those with disabilities leading to the charitable funding of schools for the deaf, blind and crippled 17th and 18th centuries (Smith, 2014); educational progress halted with the advent of the industrial revolution in the 19th century which created a societal divide based on the utilitarian idea that people's worth was dependent on their economic usefulness to society (Finkelstein, 1980). From 1850 onwards children and adults with disabilities, often called feeble-minded, were not deemed as useful (Finkelstein, 1980) and were institutionalised, segregated, excluded and sometimes sterilised to avoid 'the degeneration of the human race' (Minister of Health, 1934). The growing acceptance of such eugenically motivated views reinforced the perception that those with disabilities were a burden, with Huxley (1934), secretary of the London Zoological Society and chairman of the Eugenics Society commenting:

> What are we going to do? Every defective ... child is a burden. Every defective is an extra body for the nation to feed and clothe but produces little or nothing in return.

This view was corroborated by the actions of the Nazi party in Germany during the Second World War when children with SEND were not considered to meet the criteria of 'a perfect child' and were killed or removed from their families and taken to concentration camps (Rowgow, 1998).

While such extreme actions did not take place in the United Kingdom, it was only with the return of soldiers from the war, disabled physically and emotionally by their injuries and experiences, that the societal perception of disability began to change. Those who were prepared to sacrifice their lives for their country, and were now disabled, were often heralded as heroes; society had a duty to support them, and disability could no longer be perceived as something that should be hidden away. For children with SEND this culminated in the 1944 Education Act which stated that all children had the right to an education 'suited to their age, aptitude and ability', and that local education authorities were obliged to provide special educational treatment for those who needed it based on their medical condition. This led to the creation of categories of handicap dividing children into two groups: the educable and the ineducable. Those who were blind, partially blind, deaf, partially deaf, delicate, diabetic, epileptic and physically handicapped, the maladjusted or those with a speech deficit were considered to be educable, while those who were labelled as educationally subnormal (ESN) or defective were considered ineducable (Barnes, 1994). Children fitting these categories were separated from their peers and were either educated in schools specific to their need or in institutions. This division remained until after the Warnock Report (Warnock Committee, 1978), which recommended that categories of handicap be removed and that the more inclusive term Special Educational Needs (SEN) be introduced. Predicated on the idea that all children should have access to mainstream education (with 'special', adaptations and support where necessary) the 1981 Education Act, based on the Warnock report, introduced the key concepts of multi-agency working, individualised learning and inclusive practice that have continued to dominate and shaped SEND practice, policy and legislation in the 21st century. In parallel with these changing laws in the United Kingdom, the Union of the Physically Impaired Against Segregation (UPIAS) (1972) was gaining a voice in South Africa and the United States. Their motto 'nothing about us, without us', led to the development of the social model of disability reflecting the view that it is society that disables those who are impaired by devaluing, demeaning and systemically and environmentally disempowering them, a concept which gained both influence and momentum throughout the end of the 20th and the beginning of the 21st century. Underpinning the social model is the understanding that parents of and children with SEND should play a pivotal role in any decisions that are made about them. This view was reflected in the Children and Families Act 2014 which replaced the idea of multi-agency working with co-produced Education, Health and Care Plans (EHCPs) which were designed to bring together agencies, children and families to create meaningful, person-centred plans focused on the needs of the child and families rather than on the priorities of the agencies involved.

As the 21st Century has progressed, views on children with SEND have changed. No longer perceived as 'damaged versions', of what is considered normal (Sinclair, 2013) they should be recognised as valuable members of society rather than as a burden; as young people with rights rather than as tragic victims (Oliver, 1990); and as having a voice rather than as a silent minority. As with all children they should have access to an inclusive, person-centred education system that allows them to reach their potential. This view is supported both legally through the Equality Act 2010 and the Children and Families Act 2014 – and ideologically as formalised in the Convention on the Rights of Persons with Disabilities (CRPD) (United Nations, 2006). Yet parents of children with SEND still feel, as reflected in the quotation at the beginning of this chapter, that they and their children are running in a different direction from everyone else. The rest of this chapter will explore why this is still the case and provide an overview of the concepts and frameworks that simultaneously create barriers and help to overcome prejudice.

Point of Reflection

- What have we learnt from the historical context of disability and how has this influenced attitudes and legislation in the 21st century?

Models of Disability

Understanding models of disability is crucial if the barriers facing many children with SEND and their families are to be overcome. Disability models are frameworks of ideas that help make sense of experiences in our social worlds (Cameron, 2014). The medical and the social models reflect a societal and professional dichotomy in the understanding of difference and disability. The medical model of disability, which focuses on an individual's impairment or diagnosis as the reason for their experiences in society, was initially dominated by societal perceptions of disability (Oliver, 1990). The social model of disability, which focuses on the social world as the source of the structural oppression and disadvantage faced by disabled people (Barnes, 2018) originated in the civil rights and emancipatory movements of the 1960s. Both models continue to underpin inclusive methods and approaches today.

The Medical Model

The medical model views disability through a scientific and medical lens, categorising any behavioural variations from the norm as a condition or disorder, and viewing the cause of disability as an individual problem within the person themselves (Sewell and Smith, 2021). Scientific observation and measurement were used to generate categories of disability. Within these categories resources were employed to provide a 'cure' or ameliorate against an individual's impairment (Sewell and Smith, 2021). Those with impairments were generally perceived to be powerless and 'tragic', individuals, often dependent on others to survive.

The Personal Tragedy Model

The personal tragedy model is closely linked to the medical model where those who are disabled are perceived as tragic victims, lacking agency and in need of sympathy rather than support. As a model, it reinforces the cultural belief that being able-bodied is valued, while individuals with impairments are viewed as unfortunate (Cameron, 2014). The pitiful emotional response encouraged by this model reinforces societal pressure on disabled individuals to conform to normative behaviour. This has acted as a barrier to acceptance of the differently abled and has fuelled the Huxleyan view (Huxley, 1934) of disability as a societal burden. This view has been challenged by the affirmative model.

The Affirmative Model

According to Swain and French (2008) disabled individuals' narratives offer a more diverse and positive portrayal of disability compared to the tragedy-focused perspective presented in able-bodied narratives. The affirmative model challenges assumptions about the experiences and identities of people with impairments (Goldiner, 2022) promoting a non-tragic view of disability rooted in the lifestyle and life experience benefits of being impaired (Sewell and Smith, 2021). The affirmation model asserts that impairment is a common and ordinary part of human life and can help disabled individuals resist societal expectations. Cameron (2014) argues that it is not the impairment experience that is negative, but rather society's response to it. By promoting a respectful stance towards disabled individuals' physicality, the affirmation model can positively impact their psychological well-being.

The Social Model

The social model recognises disability as a consequence of environmental barriers and political and social issues and aims to challenge harmful perceptions based on the understanding that impairment only becomes a disability when perceived as such by society, which creates environmental and attitudinal barriers to inclusion and acceptance (Hodkinson, 2016). The Disabled People's International extended the model in 1981 to include people with sensory, emotional and cognitive impairments (Barnes, 1994). The model provides a foundation for disabled individuals to advocate for equality and challenge prejudice which has shaped SEND policy and legislation in the 21st century. While the social model provides a useful tool for making sense of the experience of impairment in a disabling society, it is important to recognise the impact of intersecting factors of inequality to avoid exaggerating the commonality of different impairment groups.

Variations in Approach

Both medical and social models of disability are utilised in planning processes to meet children's needs, but variations in philosophy, policy and methodology exist within Education, Health and Social Care. Divergent priorities, both locally and nationally, make inter-professional collaboration problematic and relocation difficult for families (Gray et al., 2015; Crane et al., 2016). There is also a discrepancy in service provision dependent on location, with certain areas providing greater support and attracting professionals from diverse backgrounds, bringing knowledge and expertise. This was reflected in the findings of the Lamb Inquiry (2009) where the dissonant experiences of parents living under the same system, some feeling happy and well supported, others feeling angry and isolated, highlighted the need for a more coordinated and holistic approach. The resultant Children and Families Act 2014 and SEND Code of Practice (DfE and DoH, 2015) were an effort to homogenise and streamline support through the introduction of co-produced Education, Health and Care Plans (EHCPs) and the Local Offer which provided information from Local Authorities on the support services available for children with SEND in their area. The efforts to create greater national consistency for children and families with SEND continued in 2022 through 'Right Support, Right Place, Right Time' (DfE and DHSC, 2022), the SEND review which promised to streamline the EHCP process, strengthen partnerships between families and professionals and ensure that parents were able to make informed choices with and for their children. Almost a decade after the introduction of the Children and Families Act

2014 the aim of this review seems to be to fix the problems with the system, rather than to learn from mistakes. If a system based on equity, inclusion and acceptance is to be created, control of the future of disabled people needs to rest with disabled people and their families.

Point of Reflection

- Should the social model of disability be the dominant model or are both the social and medical models needed in an inclusive society?

Community – The Power of Informal Networks

Aligned with the social model of disability, diverse groups and organisations have formed to ensure that children with SEND and their families have a voice. While this has been formalised through legislation and partnership working with professionals, it is those with lived experience who are best placed to ensure that changes in legislation and policy provide equal opportunity for all. It is frameworks and models that help people to make sense of experiences in their social worlds (Cameron, 2014) and communities can be considered to be a metaphorical 'framework' where individuals come together, helping one another to make sense of their experiences, linked by the commonalities of their situations, for example parents of children with SEND forming support groups. Informal communities created for parents and for those with disabilities are as important as formal collective coalitions and organisations. Much has been achieved in terms of information, resourcing and modelling through sharing information. This reflects the social model ethos where those with SEND gain agency based on vocalisation of shared experience which creates a sense of belonging and societal acceptance. The value and importance of such collaborative working for children with SEND and their families was formally recognised through the inclusion of co-productive practice in the Children and Families Act 2014 and the Care Act 2014. Designed to ensure that decisions about their services and resources are made by, for and (most importantly) with service users, effective co-production has become an essential building block to the creation of effective partnerships between professionals and those with SEND and their families.

The Benefits of Effective Partnership Working and Co-production

Co-production is a person-centred approach to partnership working where everyone involved, including those with disabilities and their families, agree on desired outcomes and recommendations and actions are produced collectively. Despite the investment in time and effort necessary to develop successful co-productive partnerships, it is widely acknowledged that there are multiple benefits to individuals and professionals, including improved outcomes for children with SEND. Effective co-production generates agency, deconstructing the personal tragedy theory (Oliver, 1990) changing perceptions of those with SEND as helpless victims or 'bundles of need' (Boyle and Harris, 2013) to the view that they are active participants in society and agents of their own outcomes. The understanding that parents know their children best and that this knowledge elevates them to the role of expert raises their acknowledged status within the professional/parent relationship and inspires confidence that their views will be heard and valued (Dyson, 2004). This represents a cultural shift within organisations, where the professionals transition from being fixers of problems to facilitators of shared solutions (Boyle and Harris, 2013) and parents, children and young people transition from being passive recipients to empowered decision-makers.

Being a Parent of a Child With SEND

Despite the growing understanding that parents know their children best and that their input is integral to decision-making processes (Dyson, 2004), it is important to acknowledge the challenges they face daily. The emotional and physical exhaustion they experience in their role as primary carers for their children is exacerbated by the sense they are in a constant battle with the systems designed to support them (Rix, 2020). The cumulative stress caused by these battles, the exhaustion of being carers as well as parents and the prevalence of concerns about their child's future are exacerbated by their experience of chronic sorrow, an often unacknowledged form of grief.

Understanding Chronic Sorrow

Chronic sorrow is a periodically recurring, progressive form of grief with no predictable end (Eakes et al., 1998). It begins with the birth of a child with SEND or with a diagnosis of impairment and continues throughout the life course of the child or parent. It is experienced cyclically as the result of trigger events which cause families to re-live the grief they experience at the initial diagnosis. The sorrow experienced is neither time limited nor finite (Olshansky, 1962; Roos, 2017). Instead, it is an ambiguous, cumulative and living loss (Roos, 2017) which re-occurs every time parents are reminded of what their children have not achieved compared to other children of the same age, such as walking, talking or as the result of missed milestones and rites of passage such as learning to drive, moving out and meeting a partner.

Double Grief

Unique to chronic sorrow is the double grief experienced by parents:

- Grief for the loss of their 'dreamt of child' (Roos, 2017);
- Grief for the future their child will now never have (Olshansky, 1962).

The duality of this parallel grief creates a depth of sorrow that often intensifies as the child grows and the awareness of the loss of the 'normal' life that neither they nor their child will now experience deepens. This loss incubates, constantly re-emerging throughout the life course, as the discrepancy widens between the lived experiences of their child compared to other children of the same age (Roos, 2017). With each re-experiencing of the loss, hope is depleted and sorrow grows.

Why Knowing About Chronic Sorrow Matters

Understanding the theory of chronic sorrow can help both parents and professionals. Many parents are unaware of the concept and often feel guilty at the sadness they feel (Wikler et al., 1981). Knowing that their response is normal can mitigate against feelings of otherness and guilt while knowledge of chronic sorrow can help professionals to 'be wise' (Olshansky, 1962), enabling them to better understand and empathise with parents. It is only when there is better understanding of such concepts and of the challenges faced by children with SEND that a society based on acceptance and inclusion can begin to emerge.

Inclusion

The term inclusion can mean different things to different people (Hornby, 2015). This is especially true in relation to the education and lived experience of children with SEND. While inclusive education gives children with SEND the right to learn in mainstream settings, ratified in the UN Convention on the Rights of Persons with Disabilities UNCRPD (2006) (United Nations, 2006), the concept of inclusion cannot be defined purely in terms of the school, college or setting in which a child or a person with a disability is placed (Hodkinson, 2016). Instead, inclusion must be viewed as a continuous journey throughout the life course. This engenders a change in mindset and societal values. Successful inclusion involves intentional, ongoing effort to ensure that every individual is able to fully participate in society through the creation of equality of opportunity and greater economic and educational equity. Blunkett (2000, cited in Judge, 2003: 163) stated that, 'the education of children with special educational needs... is vital to the creation of a fully inclusive society'. However, in education, the concepts of justice, equity and equality are often interpreted as meaning sameness – the same school, class or curriculum as every other child (Imray and Colley, 2017: 16). An approach based on achieving 'sameness' does not remove disabling barriers to education. Educational settings must have inclusive provision to fulfil the individual's right to education and to ensure that they can reach their potential; adaptations and support are needed to make access to the same curriculum possible (Cartagena and Pike, 2020). Inclusive settings may struggle to meet a child's needs if resources are inadequate (Hoskin, 2019; Paseka and Schwab, 2020). As the 21st century has progressed, adaptations have increasingly included assistive technology, to ensure and enhance accessibility for individuals with disabilities. This encompasses physical accessibility within school premises as well as access to learning through adaptations embedded within the curriculum's design. The Disability Discrimination Act 1995 and the Equality Act 2010 underpin the notion of 'reasonable adjustments' that must be instituted if inclusion is to be successful. Schools must consider the support provided under SEN legislation when determining the necessity of additional 'reasonable adjustments' for students. Some may already receive adequate assistance, eliminating the need for further adjustments, while others may require both reasonable adjustments and SEN provision. The level of SEN support necessary and put in place is determined by the school under the guidance of policy and frameworks. In summary, the level of SEN support is a key factor in determining the reasonableness of additional actions for schools. Therefore, what is deemed to be a necessary 'reasonable adjustment' in one setting may differ to another, arguably making reasonable adjustments an ambiguous term.

The Future of SEND Support and Assistive Technology

Assistive technology can be fundamental in aiding people with SEND to access daily living and educational opportunities (Sewell and Smith, 2021: 95), and is used widely to support learners and people with disabilities in overcoming barriers. The sociologist, Bain (1937), defines technology as any item produced and utilised by a human being. This includes 'tools, machines, utensils, weapons, instruments, housing, clothing, communicating and transport devices' (Bain, 1937, cited in Sewell and Smith, 2021: 94). The modern world is immersed in technology with roots founded in the historical invention and use of tools by humans. Assistive technology is defined more specifically as 'any item, piece of equipment, or product system, whether acquired commercially, modified, or customised, that is used to increase, maintain, or improve the functional capabilities of a child with a disability' (Edyburn, 2004, cited in Sewell and Smith, 2021: 94). The World Health Organisation (WHO) (2023) defines assistive technology as any technology that enables and promotes inclusion and participation, especially of persons with disabilities. The purpose of assistive products primarily is to promote independent, and dignified lives, and to participate in education and employment (WHO, 2023). Considering both definitions, assistive technology can be anything adaptive, modifying an aspect of individual experiences so they can perform daily life functions with the device, which they previously could not. In education, Kuo et al. (2021) suggest that assistive technology can facilitate participation, positively influencing educational experiences and increasing opportunities.

Assistive technologies can be classified by the level of assistance or category of assistance. For example a timetable to assist with organising learning would be considered no-technology due to the simplicity of its formation. In contrast, eye gaze tracking would be considered high-technology due to the complexity of its production. Eye gaze tracking is a sensor technology that monitors a person's gaze in real-time, converting eye movements into a data stream with details like pupil position, gaze vector and gaze point. Typically, an eye tracking system includes cameras, light sources and computer applications utilising algorithms and machine learning to process the camera feed into information. Levels of complexity of technology should not be confused with the impact of producing change for the individual user. 'No' and 'low-tech' can be just as impactful as 'high-tech'.

When exploring avenues to facilitate education for children and young individuals, it is essential to consider both the level of technology and its intended purpose. It is important to recognise that costly high-tech hardware may not always yield the most effective means of enhancing learning access. For instance, the successful utilisation of sophisticated eye gaze equipment necessitates the user's ability to control their eye and head movements with a certain degree of steadiness. For some individuals, there are several limitations as has been found by Bryan (2018) author of 'Eye Can Write', who has cerebral palsy and describes his journey about learning to communicate using his eyes.

Assistive technology serves as a bridge to overcome gaps and capitalises on a learner's strengths, thereby aiding students in independently engaging with the curriculum.

Mainstream assistive technology is increasingly integrated into school environments, encompassing devices like laptops, smartphones and tablets. These technologies effectively address some of the challenges learners might encounter. Notably, they come equipped with word processors and built-in proofreading software, and some even feature recording software, enabling the capture of notes or lectures (Seale et al., 2021). Additional technologies accessible to learners include text-to-speech and speech-to-text tools, mind-mapping software and reading pens. Despite commendable efforts to enhance educational accessibility for learners with dyslexia through assistive technology, outcomes remain varied in terms of their effectiveness (Seale et al., 2021). For instance, text-to-speak software can support the functionality of reading and writing. However, if the user has not reached an understanding of the relation between letters and sounds and how to combine them, it might be harder to improve their decoding after using the software application. Svensson et al. (2021) suggest it is therefore necessary to have acquired basic skills in reading as a fallback.

Research from McNicholl et al. (2021) reveals that the diversity of available technology, which might involve juggling various technologies, can be overwhelming. Implementation often necessitates training, and the suitability of equipment might not always align with learners' motivations or skill sets. Furthermore, issues related to technology quality and post-purchase support can arise, leading to low adoption rates or even abandonment of equipment (McNicholl et al., 2021).

Augmented and Alternative Communication (AAC)

Augmented and Alternative Communication (AAC) pertains to any assistive technology device that facilitates an individual's ability to communicate, enabling them to express their desires, needs and opinions to others. AACs can be categorised into three main types: unaided, non-electronic aided and electronic aided.

Unaided AAC encompasses communication methods that the user can perform independently, involving gestures and manual signs to convey messages. British Sign Language and Makaton are examples of unaided communication methods.

Non-electronic-aided AAC pertains to devices that are physically separate from the user and are not electronic in nature. The Picture Exchange Communication System (PECS) is an illustration of this category. In PECS, a picture on a card is associated with a specific item or activity. The user presents the card to convey their desire or requirement for a particular item or activity.

Electronic-aided AAC, often referred to as Speech Generating Devices (SGD) or Voice Output Communication Aids (VOCAs), constitutes devices that are distinct from the individual and fall under the high-tech classification. Examples of these are customisable devices and smartphone applications that can provide predicted texts and text-to-speech.

Artificial Intelligence (AI)

Artificial intelligence (AI), as defined by Tai (2020), refers to the collaboration of computers and machines to simulate human cognitive processes logically. This concept is particularly significant for individuals with disabilities who frequently utilise assistive technology functionalities, such as speech-to-text, on their smartphones and other technologically advanced devices to interact with their surroundings (Fernandez-Batanero et al., 2022).

AI's Impact on Learning for Students With Disabilities

Generative AI has the potential to revolutionise the learning experience for students with disabilities. AI-powered tutoring systems, exemplified by platforms like Tutorly (https://tutorly.ai), offer personalised instruction tailored to the pace of individual students with disabilities. This adaptability facilitates a more inclusive learning environment. Furthermore, AI-driven assessment systems, like those provided by Education Co-Pilot (https://educationcopilot.com), can furnish teachers with valuable support. These systems help educators pinpoint areas for enhancement, enabling them to fine-tune their teaching strategies accordingly, thereby benefiting students with disabilities.

Assistive Technologies Enhanced by AI

AI-driven assistive technologies also play a pivotal role in aiding students with disabilities. Text-to-speech software and voice recognition systems are examples of such technologies. These tools contribute to a more inclusive learning ecosystem by providing essential support to students who require alternative means of interaction with learning materials.

In summation, the synergy between AI and assistive technologies holds immense promise for students with disabilities, potentially reshaping the landscape of education to be more accessible, personalised and effective, and perhaps ensure that the barriers faced by those with disabilities can finally be overcome.

Are Barriers Being Broken Down? Can Those With SEND Access Learning?

Despite changing attitudes to and understanding of the way in which disability is viewed, there are few parents, professionals or people with SEND who would argue that barriers and access to learning have been overcome. The emergence of the Social Model of disability at the end of the 20th Century has led to changing concepts of disability and the perception that it is a societal construct, rather than a personal tragedy. The legislation in the first part of the 21st century reflects these changing views through the introduction of co-productive working placing those with SEND and their families at the heart of all decisions made about them. Yet despite these changes, inclusion remains an elusive and often misunderstood concept and parents continue to feel that they face constant battles to access what should be the intrinsic rights of their children. Advances in assistive technologies should ensure that children with SEND can be better supported in all environments, that communication can be improved and that the voices of those who have historically been voiceless can be heard. And yet, families of children with SEND still feel that their children are running in a different direction from everyone else. Perhaps it is time for all us to change direction and start running with them.

Point of Reflection

- What creates barriers to inclusion and how can these be overcome?

Case Study: Sarah and Anna

Sarah wants to send her 4-year-old daughter, Anna, to the local state primary school. Her daughter, as a result of a disability, is not able to fully exercise control of her bowel movements and requires a hoist to access the toilet. The school has told Sarah that Anna cannot attend the school because the school's policy maintains that all children must be toilet trained. The school states that it is not refusing access to the school because Anna has a disability but is applying its toilet training policy equally to all children.

- Is the school right?
- What should Sarah do?
- Who else's views need to be considered?

Chapter Summary

Children with SEND and their families face an ongoing battle with prejudice, lack of understanding and a society that often prioritises the medical model over the social models. While the Equality Act 2010 states that disability is a protected characteristic and that those with SEND should not be discriminated against, both children and parents/carers struggle to feel included. Advances in assistive technology mean that children with SEND are better able to communicate and to access previously inaccessible activities. An increasingly holistic understanding of what is meant by inclusion ensures that new opportunities are increasingly being offered to those with disabilities. Understanding the potential impact of chronic sorrow on the health and well-being of parents might help professionals to have a better understanding of the parental experience and support the effective use of co-production to ensure that children and families are at the centre of and agency over the decisions made about them. But it is only when societal attitudes change that true acceptance can occur and those with SEND will consistently be able to reach their potential. Despite changes in legislation and policy, this goal continues to be elusive to too many.

Key Points

- Ensure that all professionals are kept up to date about advances in relevant technology;
- Support children with SEND to have a voice and agency;
- Challenge societal views that focus on the medical rather than the social model.

Key Resources

Green, H and Edwards, B. (2023) *True Partnerships in SEND. Working Together to Give Children, Professionals and Families a Voice*. London: NASEN Spotlight, Routledge.

Imray, P and Colley, A. (2017) *Inclusion is Dead. Long Live Inclusion*. Oxon: Routledge

Martin-Denham, S. (2022) *Co-Producing SMART Targets for Children with SEND: Capturing the Authentic Voice of Children, Young People and Their Caregivers*. Oxon: Routledge.

References

Bain, R. (1937). Technology and state government. *American Sociological Review*, 2(6), 860–874.

Barnes, C. (1994) *Disabled people in Britain and discrimination: A case for anti-discrimination legislation*. London: Hurst and Co. in association with BCODP.

Barnes, C. (2018) Theories of disability and the origins of the oppression of disabled people in western society. In *Disability and society* (pp. 43–60). London: Routledge.

Beckett, A. E. (2010). Challenging disabling attitudes and stereotypes. In *Transform-ing the role of the SENCO: Achieving the national award for SEN coordination*. Maidenhead: McGraw-Hill Education. (pp. 126–132).

Bryan, J. (2018) *Eye can write: A memoir of a child's silent soul emerging*. London: Lagom.

Bryant, B.R., Bryant, D.P., Shih, M. and Seok, S. (2010) Assistive technology and supports provision: A selective review of the literature and proposed areas of application. *Exceptionality*, 18(4), 203–213.

Cameron, C. (2014) *Disability Studies: A student's guide*. London: SAGE.

Care Act 2014c, 23. Available at: https://www.legislation.gov.uk/ukpga/2014/23/contents/enacted (Accessed 16 January 2024).

Cartagena, S. and Pike, L. (2020). Start with the end in mind: Frameworks for designing a socially inclusive school environment. *International Journal of Technology and Inclusive Education*, 9(2), 1559-1565.

Children and Families Act (2014) London: HMSO. Available at: https://www.legislation.gov.uk/ukpga/2014/6/contents/enacted (Accessed 8 January 2024).

Crane, L., Chester, J. W., Goddard, L., Henry, L. A. and Hill, E. (2016). Experiences of autism diagnosis: A survey of over 1000 parents in the United Kingdom. *Autism*, 20(2), 153–162.

Department for Education and Department of Health (2015) *Special educational needs and disability code of practice: 0 to 25 years*. Available at: https://www.gov.uk/government/publications/send-code-of-practice-0-to-25 (Accessed 6 January 2024).

Department for Education and Department of Health and Social Care (2022). *SEND review: right support, right place, right time*. London: HMSO. Available at: https://www.gov.uk/government/consultations/send-review-right-support-right-place-right-time (Accessed 8 January 2024).

Disability Discrimination Act 1995 c.50. Available at: https://www.legislation.gov.uk/ukpga/1995/50/contents (Accessed 16 January 2024).

Dobson-Waters, S. and Torgerson, C.J. (2021) Dyslexia in higher education: A systematic review of interventions used to promote learning. *Journal of Further and Higher Education*, 45(2), 226–256. doi:10.1080/0309877X.2020.1744545

Dyson, S. (2004) *Mental Handicap Dilemmas of Parent-Professional Relations*. New York: Croom Helm.

Eakes, G., Burke, M.H. & Hainsworth, M.A. (1998). Middle-range theory of chronic sorrow. *Journal of Nursing Scholarship*, 30, 179–184.

Education Act 1944. London: HMSO Available at: https://www.legislation.gov.uk/ukpga/Geo6/7-8/31/enacted (Accessed 8 January 2024).

Education Act 1981. London: HMSO Available at: https://www.legislation.gov.uk/ukpga/1981/60/enacted (Accessed 8 January 2024).

Equality Act 2010, c15. London: HMSO. Available at: https://www.legislation.gov.uk/ukpga/2010/15/contents (Accessed 17 January 24).

Fernández-Batanero, J.M., Montenegro-Rueda, M., Fernández-Cerero, J. & García-Martínez, I. (2022) Digital competences for teacher professional development. *Systematic review, European Journal of Teacher Education*, 45(4), 513–531, doi: 10.1080/02619768.2020.1827389

Franits, L. E. (2005). Nothing about us without us: Searching for the narrative of disability. *AJOT: American Journal of Occupational Therapy*, 59(5), 577–580.

Finkelstein, V. (1980) *Attitudes and disabled people: Issues for discussion*. New York: World Rehabilitation Fund.

Goldiner, A. (2022). Understanding "disability" as a cluster of disability models. *The Journal of Philosophy of Disability*, 2, 28–54.

Gray, L., Gibbs, J., Jolleff, N., Williams, J., McConachie, H. and Parr, J. R. (2015). Variable implementation of good practice recommendations for the assessment and management of UK children with neurodisability. *Child: Care, Health and Development*, 41(6), 938–946.

Hodkinson, A. (2016) *Key issues in special educational needs and inclusion*. London: SAGE.

Hornby, G. (2015) Inclusive special education: Development of a new theory for the education of children with special educational needs and disabilities. *British Journal of Special Education*, 42(3), 234–256.

Hoskin, J. (2019) Aspiration, austerity and ableism: to what extent are the 2014 SEND reforms supporting young people with a life-limiting impairment and their families to get the lives they want? *British Journal of Special Education*, 46(3), 265–291.

Huxley, J (1934) *Scientific research and social needs*. London, Watts.

Imray, P. and Colley, A. (2017) *Inclusion is dead: Long live inclusion*. Oxon: Routledge.

Judge, B. (2003) Inclusive Education: principles and practices In K. Crawford (Ed.) *Contemporary issues in education*. Dereham: Peter Francis.

Kuo, H.J., Sung, C., Newbutt, N., Politis, Y. and Robb, N. (2021) Current trends in technology and wellness for people with disabilities: an analysis of benefit and risk. In *Recent advances in technologies for inclusive well-being: Virtual patients, gamification and simulation* (pp. 353–371). doi: 10.1007/978-3-030-59608-8_19

Lamb, B. (2009) *Lamb Inquiry, Special Educational Needs and Parental Confidence*. London: DCFS.

McNicholl, A., Casey, H., Desmond, D. and Gallagher, P. (2021) The impact of assistive technology use for students with disabilities in higher education: a systematic review. *Disability and Rehabilitation: Assistive Technology*, 16(2), 130–143. doi: 10.1080/17483107.2019.1642395

Minister of Health (1934) *Report of the Departmental Committee on Sterilisation*. Great Britain. Board of Control. Committee on Sterilisation, London.

Oliver, M. (1990) *The politics of disablement*. Basingstoke: Palgrave Macmillan.

Oliver, M. (1996) *Understanding disability: From theory to practice*. Basingstoke: Palgrave Macmillan.

Olshansky, S. (1962). Chronic sorrow: A response to having a mentally defective child. *Social Casework*, 43(4), 190–193.

Paseka, A. and Schwab, S. (2020). Parents' attitudes towards inclusive education and their perceptions of inclusive teaching practices and resources. *European Journal of Special Needs Education*, 35(2), 254–272.

Pelka, F (2011). *What we have done: An oral history of the disability rights movement*. Amherst: University of Massachusetts Press. Available at: ProQuest Ebook Central. [12 August 2023].

Rix, J. (2020) Our need for certainty in an uncertain world: the difference between special education and inclusion? *British Journal of Special Education*, 47, 283–307. https://doi.org/10.1111/1467-8578.12326

Roos, S. (2017). *Chronic sorrow: A living loss* (2nd Edition) Taylor and Francis.

Rowgow, S.M. (1998) *Hitler's unwanted children: Children with disabilities, orphans, juvenile delinquents and non-conformist young people in Nazi Germany*. http://www.nizkor.org/ftp.cgi/people/r/rogow.sally/hitlers-unwanted-children (Accessed 15 September 2023).

Seale, J., Colwell, C., Coughlan, T., Heiman, T., Kaspi-Tsahor, D. and Olenik-Shemesh, D. (2021) 'Dreaming in colour': 'Disabled higher education students' perspectives on improving design practices that would enable them to benefit from their use of technologies. *Education and Information Technologies*, 26, 1687–1719.

Sewell, A. and Smith, J. (2021) *Introducton to special educational needs, disability and inclusion: A student's guide*. London: SAGE.

Sinclair, J. (2013) Why I dislike "Person First" language. *Autonomy, the Critical Journal of Interdisciplinary Autism Studies*, 1(2), 2–3.

Smith, P. (2014) *A short history of disability and diversity An introduction*. Dubuque: Kendall Hunt Publishing Company (pp 9–16).

Svensson, I., Nordström, T., Lindeblad, E., Gustafson, S., Björn, M., Sand, C., Almgren, G. and Nilsson, B and S. (2021) Effects of assistive technology for students with reading and writing disabilities, disability and rehabilitation: *Assistive Technology*, 16, (2), 196–208.

Swain, J. and French, S. (2008) *Disability on equal terms*. London: SAGE.

Tai, M. (2020). The impact of artificial intelligence on human society and bioethics. *Tzu Chi Medical Journal*, 32(4), 339–343.

United Nations Convention on the Rights of Persons with Disability (UNCRPD) (2006) Available at: https://www.un.org/development/desa/disabilities/convention-on-the-rights-of-persons-with-disabilities/convention-on-the-rights-of-persons-with-disabilities-2.html (Accessed 8 January 2024).

Union of the Physically Impaired Against Segregation (1976) *Fundamental principles of disability*. London: The Disability Alliance.

Warnock Committee (1978). *Special educational needs: The Warnock Report*. London: Department for Education and Science.

World Health Organisation [WHO] (2023) *Assistive technology*. Available at: https://www.who.int/health-topics/assistive-technology#tab=tab_1 (Accessed 9 April 2023).

Wikler, L., Wasow, M. and Hatfield, E. (1981) Chronic sorrow revisited: parent vs. professional depiction of the adjustment of parents of mentally retarded children. *American Journal of Orthopsychiatry*, 51(1), 63. http://www.gov.uk/government/uploads/system/uploads/attachment_data/file/398815/SEND_Code_of_Practice_January_2015.pdf

9

Health Inequalities and Well-being

Suzanna McGregor

After reading this chapter, readers will be able to:

- Identify the impact of inequalities on children's health and well-being.
- Critically evaluate the social determinants of children's health.
- Consider the global issues related to children's health and well-being.

Introduction

This chapter explores the link between social policy and children's health and well-being. It examines theories on social and cultural capital, making connections to health inequalities and the uneven distribution of access to health provision. It considers models of public health, the prevention agenda and the impact of national and local health policy and legislation which are assessed in terms of their contribution to the well-being of children. This chapter begins by taking an overview of health in the United Kingdom and the inequalities that arise within this complex area. As the social determinants of health are many, we consider the depth of social injustice and the inequalities experienced by children and their families from food banks usage to the impact of poverty. Lastly there will be a reflection on the global state of children's health, including the impact of the Covid-19 pandemic.

Inequalities and Children's Health and Well-being

Social and economic determinants are the factors that underpin children's health worldwide. From birth, throughout childhood and onto adolescence, morbidity, mortality, growth and development are socially determined (Marmot, 2017). This results in the most disadvantaged having the highest risk of poor health outcomes. Here in the United Kingdom local government and actions are shaped by national decisions and combine many factors from housing, communities, education, health and social care, crime and employment. Therefore, it is impossible to explore children's health in isolation as there are multiple factors that have a direct impact on children's lives,

Social Determinants of Children's Health

The social construction of health and illness refers to the ways our social world shapes the assessment, treatment and collective understanding of various diseases and health conditions (Mullan, 2017). Therefore, the way that children's health conditions and illnesses are socially constructed will impact on how society and medical institutions might treat conditions and construct public discourses about illness (Bilton, 2022; Conrad and Barker, 2010). Some illnesses are particularly embedded with cultural meaning, which is not directly derived from the nature of the condition but nevertheless shapes how society responds to those with the illness and the experience of that illness. For example measles or chicken pox are often associated with childhood and seen as a part of childhood.

Understanding the wider determinants or as they are sometimes referred to the social determinants of health provides the public health system and practitioners with intelligence to help improve population health and reduce health inequalities. The Marmot review in 2010 and again in 2020 raised the profile of social determinants of health by emphasising the link between social inequality and poor health outcomes. Further research by the Dame Black Review (Black, 2007) supports the correlation between socio-economic, cultural and environmental conditions, community networks and individual lifestyles. According to Marmot et al. (2020), child poverty in the United Kingdom has increased to 22% compared to 10% in Norway, Iceland and the Netherlands, the lowest in Europe. Furthermore, many Sure Start children centres and youth centres have closed, and funding for education has been cut (DfE, 2019). These key elements of community were for many families the safety net to sustainable health and well-being. From the Marmot 2010 and 2020 reviews, key messages can be considered:

- Good quality health and care services benefit not only early years but also the whole family, community and society and have long-term positive effects.
- Outcomes for disadvantaged children are strong and make a significant different. For example strong communication skills and the development of personal and social skills show higher levels of academic learning in later stages of childhood.
- Long-term, secure and well-paid employment has a positive impact on health outcomes.

The Marmot 2020 review's goals included:

- To reduce inequalities in the early development of children's health and well-being;
- To ensure high-quality maternity, parenting programmes and early years education;
- To build resilience and well-being in all children in society.

Not to achieve these ambitions seems illogical to constructing the foundation of a healthy society from the bottom up. Cuts in services for young children and their families are likely to have an impact on building a healthy society. Over the last decade key services such as Sure Start Children's Centres, established in the late 1990s to provide integrated targeted services for children and families, have fallen by over 30% from 3,620 in 2010 to 2,350 in 2019 (DfE, 2019). In the most disadvantaged areas, the rise in food bank usage can be over looked when considering the health and well-being of young children. However, during the Covid-19 pandemic the largest franchise of food banks, the Trussell Trust, reported an 89% increase in the need for emergency food parcels during April 2020 compared to the same month in the previous year, including a 107% rise in food parcels given to children. A coalition of charities, including the Trussell Trust, Child Poverty Action Group (CPAG), Children's Society, Joseph Rowntree Foundation (JRF), StepChange and Turn2us, is urging the government to act quickly in providing a stronger lifeline to families to prevent many from being swept into destitution. This increasing role of the voluntary sector providing street level welfare when child development in the early years is so significant in the long-term health of the population is of grave concern. While the voluntary sector is a sign of a healthy society, the growing use of emergency food parcels to families (or anyone) with young children is not. The concern is that so many families are now reliant on this type of philanthropy, and that food banks have taken on much of the welfare previously delivered by the state. Serious consideration must be given to the dilemma of who is responsible for the health and well-being of the nation's children. Caplan (2020) tackles the argument of food poverty by asking who is accountable for people going hungry. She challenges society to look beyond the discourse of food banks and bring to account those responsible for this injustice. Children's right to food should not be the concern of local churches and food banks but a universal right as defined by the United Nations (1989) in the Conventions on the Rights of the Child, Article 27. Riches (2018) and Caplan (2016; 2020) argue that everyone should have the right to choose and prepare their own food.

Some of the reasons as to why so many children and their families are receiving emergency food parcels include governmental changes to key policy. This fundamental approach is to pare down the welfare state and simplify the benefits regime. This has resulted in food poverty for many families as a result the voluntary sector is under increasing pressure to provide street level welfare for families. Some of the reasons as why food banks exist include fundamental changes to welfare, policy, and legislation. These include the following:

- The **Health and Social Care Welfare Act**, 2012, introduced extensive changes to the organisation, structure and delivery of health services. However, rather than improving services, the Act together with austerity and cuts to welfare has had a negative impact on low-income families including food poverty.
- **Universal Credit is** a single monthly payment for people in or out of work, merging some of the benefits and tax credits such as income-based job seekers allowance and support allowance, income support, child tax credit, working tax

credit and housing benefit. The minimum five week wait for Universal Credit has led to many families experiencing hardship as they often do not know how much or when they will receive their benefit.

- **Neo Liberalism** is an ideology which promotes a free market and non-interventionist state which emphasises the individual (Ledwith, 2006; Mullan, 2017). In recent years, a neoliberal government approach has resulted in long-term austerity and a reduction in welfare support, with those on the lowest incomes being impacted the most.

Child Development and Children's Health and Well-being

Children's development is impacted by a range of factors including breast feeding, childcare, family situation, communication pattern and the immediate wider environment. Bronfenbrenner's bio-ecological systems (1977) supports the supposition that a child is entirely shaped by their early environment. In 2006, Bronfenbrenner and Morris renamed the theory as bio-ecological systems recognising the importance of children's physical development over time, as well as the environmental systems that surround the child. From conception to birth and in the very early stages of development combined risk factors will continue to produce their effects throughout a lifetime (see Figure 9.1).

Inequalities surrounding children's health and well-being are deep rooted and complex. Further exploration and relevant theory is essential to unpick some of the fundamental issues in early childhood. It is essential to consider the complexities that surround a child's positive health and development and the interrelation connection of key elements such as housing, work, school, family, friends and government agencies play.

Case Study: Paul and Martha

Paul and Martha are young parents and have recently moved into the area, with two children under the age of five. Mum works part time and dad full time. You have contact with Martha via the general practitioner (GP) surgery where the family has registered. This takes place in a rural environment. Drawing on Bronfenbrenner and Morris' (2006) bio-ecological systems theory consider the following:

- How will the family access the levels of support needed to raise their child?
- What action could you take as a practitioner to help support the children's emotional and social development?

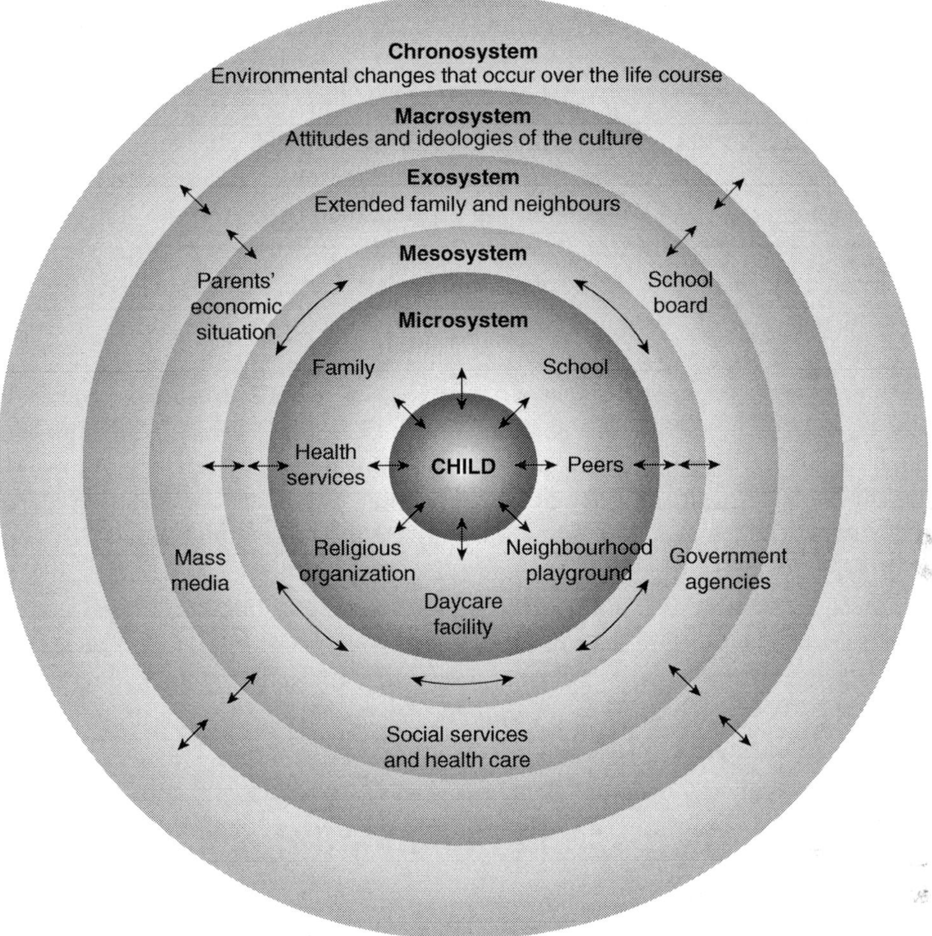

Figure 9.1 Bronfenbrenner and Morris' (2006) Bio-ecological Systems
Source: Bronfenbrenner and Morris (2006).

The Multi-dimensions of Health and Cultural Capital

Health is defined by the World Health Organisation (WHO) (2023) as a state of complete physical, mental and social well-being and not merely the absence of disease or infirmity. The WHO's (2023) set of principles include that the 'achievement of any State in the promotion and protection of health is of value to all'. In addition, these principles also declare that the healthy development of the child is of fundamental importance, and that the ability to live harmoniously in a changing environment is essential to such development. If the theory of Bronfenbrenner and Morris (2006) is applied further, then the development of good health should take into account physical, cognitive, language, emotional as well as the societal, environmental, moral and spiritual needs of the individual child. Essentially each system in a child's life, including their immediate and wider environments will influence their development (Bronfenbrenner and Morris, 2006). Children do not exist in isolation and the extent to which families can access the support they need is often determined by their level of social capital. Social capital and social networks are valuable source of information, support and care that exist in communities in many different forms (Mikiewicz and Cunha de Arujo, 2021). Social networks can take the form of parents, grandparents, other relatives and friends from play groups or mutual societies. Knowing who to go to and who has high levels of social and cultural capital can strengthen an awareness of the networks that are needed to enhance a child's health and well-being. This could be in the form of knowing where the children's lunch club is or when the baby clothes swap shop is open. Eriksson (2011) suggests that particularly in low-income communities social capital is critical to alleviate poverty and isolation, a key social determinant in health. In her work on social capital and health promotion, she declares that social capital can provide new ideas about the processes that influence human and community interaction. Access to high levels of social capital can account for the positive impact of informal care and support in cases of illness and other conditions.

A Holistic Approach to Childhood Health Development

Holistic health approaches consider the whole child in the development of health and well-being (see Figure 9.2).

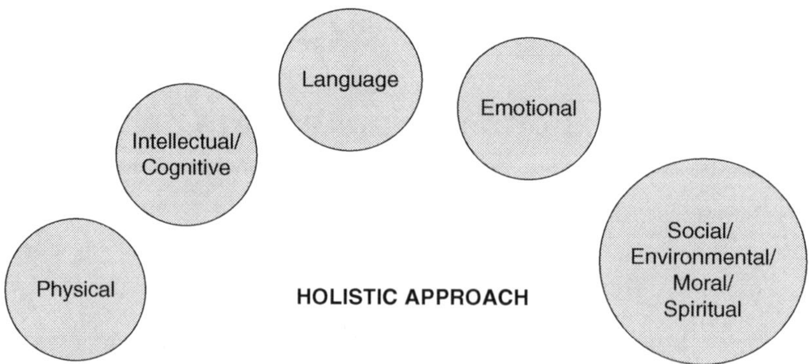

Figure 9.2 Holistic Approach to Childhood Health Development

Some of the key factors which support a holistic approach to children's health are considered below (NSPCC, 2023). These factors can affect a child's health including their educational attainment, relationships and physical well-being.

Emotional factors include:

- response to others and by others;
- communication and ability to express feelings;
- feeling special and loved;
- developing healthy dependence and independence, and self-care;
- forming attachments and relationships;
- family history and functioning;
- wider family, networks and support systems;
- development of behaviour;
- boundaries and stimulation;
- respect for others, culture, values and belief systems.

Psychological factors include:

- lifestyle;
- coping skills, temperament, adjusting and resilience;
- confidence;
- knowledge/ignorance;
- personality;
- self-sufficiency, self-esteem, self-image and presentation.

What Is Health Promotion?

Health promotion is crucial to improving the outcomes for children's health and well-being, enabling families to increase control over and improve their health. According to the WHO (2024), it is the process by which health determinants are addressed as they impact on individuals and communities. Health promotion has two fundamental directives: health education and illness prevention. These two principles focus on improving children's health so that everyone, irrespective of where they live or their circumstances, can expect to experience good health.

Government Priorities . . . Do They Match Personal Priorities?

It is important to know government priorities in tackling health promotion and the inequalities that exist. The oversight of public health comes under the Office for Health Improvement and Disparities (OHID) and works across the Department of Health and Social Care (DHSC). The OHID (2024) brings together expert advice, analysis and evidence with policy development and implementation to shape and drive health improvement and equalities priorities for government and have identified the following priorities:

- to identify and address health disparities, focusing on those groups and areas where health inequalities have greatest effect;
- to take action on the biggest preventable risk factors for ill health and premature death including tobacco, obesity and harmful use of alcohol and drugs;
- to work with the National Health Service (NHS) and local government to improve access to the services which detect and act on health risks and conditions as early as possible;
- to develop strong partnerships across government, communities, industry and employers, to act on the wider factors that contribute to people's health, such as work, housing and education;
- to drive innovation in health improvement, harnessing the best of technology, analytics and innovations in policy and delivery, to help deliver change where it is needed most.

Point of Reflection

- Consider the government health priorities listed above; do they match what is important to the families you work with?

There are many different approaches to health promotion depending on the audience and message portrayed:

- The Medical approach looks at illnesses through the causes and treatments of medical intervention, for example the human papillomavirus (HPV) vaccine protects girls from the strains of the HPV responsible for causing 70% of cervical cancers.
- A behavioural and educational change approach is based on the premise that people will modify their behaviour by their own choice. Urban Footsteps is a practical pedestrian training programme, developed for Key Stage 1 pupils in urban localities. It aims to influence children's attitudes towards good road use.
- A client centred approach has the person as the focus and meets their needs in a holistic way, for example a support group aimed at giving mothers help and advice on breast feeding.
- A social change approach aims to change the physical, social and economic environment to improve the health of families and children.
- A fear approach is arguably the least effective. This approach uses news stories and projections to scare people into stopping or taking up new behaviours, for example the dangers of smoking around children. However, change will only take place if people perceive the threat to their health as real and when the benefits of taking the recommended action outweigh the barriers.

Health promotion targeted at children in early years setting includes the following:

- The Integrated Review for two-year olds includes a health and education child development review when children are two years of age. Reviewing children at two-years old provides better and earlier intervention to support children's future outcomes and is a key point in development where the need for intervention may emerge (Blades et al., 2014).
- The Early Years Foundation Stage (EYFS) Progress Check (Blades et al., 2014) at age two brings together the Healthy Child Programme (HCP) 2–2½-year old health and development review (delivered by health visiting teams), where possible, in an Integrated Review.

However, health promotion will only work if a holistic approach is taken. Medical health professionals, families and early years practitioners bring different perspectives together and if working jointly they can have a holistic approach to improving children's health and well-being. The structures within the Department of Health and Social Care are complex, bound by bureaucracy, unfamiliar terminology and procedural rhetoric. It would therefore be a challenge for any family to successfully navigate these complexities.

Health Promotion, Prevention, Early Intervention and Care

There are three main principles of health promotion to consider:

- the process of enabling people, children and families to increase control over and to improve their health;
- the process by which health determinants are addressed and how they impact on individuals and communities;
- the factors that help people, children and families maintain the necessary stability to foster ongoing development.

Having these principles at the heart of a strategy helps to achieve a healthier nation. Health strategies operate at both a population and performance level and usually involve two approaches: health education and illness prevention (see Figure 9.3).

Health promotion can take a number of different approaches; however, the one thing they all have in common is **change.** Disease prevention through vaccination campaigns, early screening, awareness and education of ill health has been the backbone of success in public health promotion. Recent improvements to improve health strategies for children have included universal hearing tests for infants and meningitis vaccines (Underdown, 2007).

The concept of health promotion and well-being is not one of a fixed schedule of miles stones and related services but of a holistic approach to the individual child. Many of the health promotion strategies are now structured to provide core services and

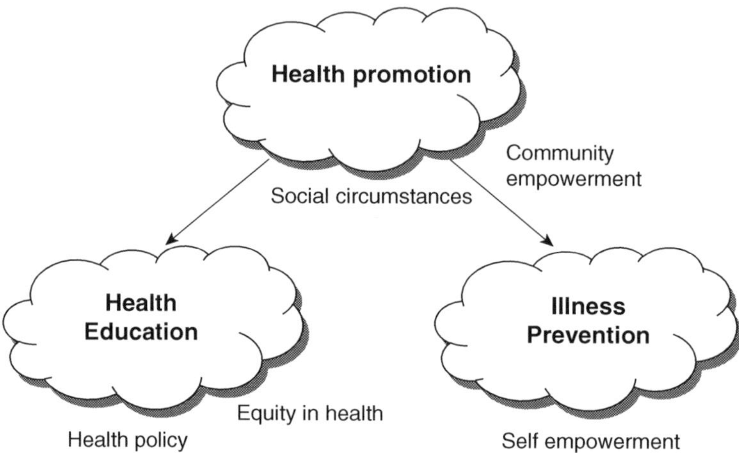

Figure 9.3 Health Promotion

check-ups for children, with additional provision targeted towards families needing extra support and help. This is regarded as 'proportionate universalism' a term coined by the Marmot review 2010. The role of the voluntary sector is imperative in children's health and well-being. Effective communication with parents and families is fundamental in building up good relationships. Charities and grassroot organisations (those that start with ordinary people) can offer support and mutual understanding of health conditions, circumstances or mutual interests.

Case Study: Signposting Families

Consider how you would prepare for the following challenging discussion. What organisations could you research that would be useful to signpost the families in the following scenarios?

- A family decision has been reached to try to explain to a two-year old that they have a serious health condition which is cardiovascular-related. The condition has implications for the level of activity the child can engage with in their early years setting.
- A mum receives news that she has been diagnosed as HIV positive.
- A new mum has post-natal depression and a one-month-old child.
- A dad's partner has recently died. He has two children under five and has given up his full-time job to care for his children. He has support from his family but both sets of grandparents are elderly and a little frail.

In addition to the depth of knowledge and support that non-for-profit groups can offer; the NHS has a free 111 phone service which was launched in 2014. This is a single point of access to urgent care with trained health professionals. Key to current discourse surrounding health and well-being is integrated services and collaboration. Health promotion strategies have always recognised the value and expertise that organisations can bring. Working together with local authorities, education provisions, the NHS and the voluntary sector can bring about joined-up thinking and integrated care reducing the obstacles that fragmented health and social care systems can bring (Corbin et al., 2017). Organisations like the British Heart Foundation, Children's Society and the NSPCC are examples of large voluntary sector organisations that provide specialist care and knowledge in areas within health and well-being. As practitioners is it fundamental to know where this specialist help exists, how it is structured and how to access it.

Early Intervention

Early intervention helps to provide timely support to parents and families and can increase protective factors and make a positive impact to a child's well-being by decreasing risk factors that impact negatively on a child and later as an adult. One example of early intervention is the government's approach to tackling eating disorders. At the beginning of 2020, the government set a net standard aiming for 95% of children (up to 19-years old) with eating disorders to receive treatment within a week for urgent cases, and four weeks for routine cases. In 2019, the NHS Long term Plan, delivered a £33.9 billion cash funding increase over five years to boost investment in children and young people's eating disorder services. The government also launched an initiative to ensure students in schools are aware of mental health issues and able to identify when they are struggling. Additionally, in other areas of the United Kingdom such as Wales, the Government has commissioned research to develop a new strategy for countering eating disorders.

Yet, despite these changes, access to treatment for eating disorders remains a significant challenge for families – and one that has been exacerbated by the Covid-19 pandemic. In 2019, the eating disorder charity, Beat, argued that a 'postcode lottery' existed for NHS eating disorder treatment in England, with children and young people in some areas experiencing much longer waiting times than others. It also found few improvements to provision had been despite recommendations made by the Parliamentary and Health Service Ombudsman (PHSO) (2017), which highlighted the disparity between services for adults compared to children, gaps in professionals' knowledge and the need for more education and training for non-specialists about how to respond to eating disorders. An inquest into five deaths in November 2020, accused the NHS treatment of anorexia patients as 'not a safe system' which 'risks future deaths' – only 50% of all eating disorder patients fully recover, according to Eddy et al. (2017). Furthermore, the standard of eating disorder care varies along socio-economic lines with what has been described as 'eating disorder inequality' disproportionally affecting those with SEND, pre-existing mental health conditions and those from black, Asian and ethnic minority groups. Therefore, a forum is needed for both practitioners and policymakers to consider key issues within the treatment of those experiencing eating disorders, and strategies to improve access to services and education to help raise awareness and ensure early intervention. For further information see the key sources at the end of the chapter.

Mental Health, Global Reflection, Race and the Scale of the Problem

Inequities have a profound impact on the health and development of children globally. While inequities are greatest in the world's poorest countries, even in richer nations poorer children have poorer health and developmental outcomes. From birth through childhood to adolescence, morbidity, mortality, growth and development are socially determined, resulting in the most disadvantaged having the highest risk of poor health outcomes (Spencer et al., 2019). The International Society for Social Paediatrics and Child Health (ISSOP) (2018) calls on governments, policymakers, paediatricians and professionals working with children and their organisations to act to reduce child health inequity as a priority. ISSOP recommends that governments act to reduce child poverty; ensure rights of all children to healthcare, education and welfare are protected; and that basic health determinants are available to all children.

The stigma attached to mental health is profound, but this is compounded for ethnic minority groups, who often experience other societal adversities such as poverty and discrimination. Possible solutions according to the WHO (2023) include anti stigma strategies combined with socially cultural sensitivity. Mental health influences a wide range of outcomes for individuals, children, families and communities. These include life span, being a productive member of a family unit and of wider society and progressing successfully from child to adulthood. With the increase in concerns about children's health and well-being there have been many more families in the United Kingdom needing support. At the same time services have been cut, which has resulted in remaining services being swamped with demand. Consequently, prevention has become a key driver for the government and in 2021 the Department of Health and Social Care published a mental health and well-being recovery plan which defines how the government will focus on prevention, mitigation and address the mental health impact of the Covid-19 pandemic. It also included action to improve child and adolescent mental health services. Furthermore, Public Health England (UK Gov, 2021) has published guidance on promoting children and young people's emotional health and well-being in schools and colleges. This prevention agenda priority is further demonstrated by the involvement of the voluntary sector. The National Autistic Society and Mind (2021) have produced a free practice guide to help professionals in the United Kingdom adapt talking therapies for autistic children and adults. This has focused on packaging cognitive behavioural therapy and training an army of 'psychological well-being practitioners' to support children and adults with depression and anxiety disorders.

Social Justice and Mental Health

Social justice is about ensuing that everyone has equal opportunity and access to health services and support; however, this is often not the case in the field of mental health. According to the charity Young Minds (2022), poor mental health can impact a child's self-worth, confidence, agency and evaluation of their abilities. Social injustices (unequal access and opportunity) create self-doubt despair and a sense of isolation in young children. Individual and collective good mental health is reliant on reducing the gap and inequalities between the richest and poorest (Anderson et al., 2020). More recently, this gap has been exacerbated by the Covid-19 pandemic and the increase in children needing mental health support (Longfield, 2012). One of the biggest challenges as reported by GPs in primary care is that children often do not fit a clear referral pathway because of the complexities of their needs. These are often compounded by multiple factors such as poverty, social isolation, discrimination and trauma (Marmot, 2017).

Global Problem

The WHO has been the platform for the establishment of the Commission on the Social Determinants of Health (WHO and CSDH, 2008). This work has identified the inequalities both within and between countries. The initiative hopes to add energy to the debate promoting good global health and establishing a global movement for action on health and mental health equity. The Commission proposes that an individual's position in the hierarchy of society will influence mental health. Social position also affects social constructs of identity which impacts on well-being. An example of this would be children coming into an early years setting hungry and without appropriate clothing for the season. They may feel shame, embarrassment and a sense of isolation from their peers (de Botton, 2004). According to the UNCRC Article 28 (UNCRC, 1989), children should have the right and freedom to attend their education without shame. Education is a key social and cultural right and has the potential to play a significant role in reducing poverty.

Adverse Childhood Experiences (ACEs) and Children's Mental Health Development

Adverse Childhood Experiences (ACEs) are traumatic experiences that children experience that can have lasting impacts on their physical and mental well-being. ACEs can affect the development of children's nervous system and the brain such as the hippocampus and amygdala (for more information see the work of McCrory et al., 2017). The risks for children from black and ethnic minorities are increased when compounded with ACEs (Lopez-Tamayo et al., 2022) and are found to have higher levels of the stress hormone cortisol and show faster biological ageing (Lee, 2018). This can create children who are constantly on red alert for potential danger and has a strong effect on their immune function and the ability to relax and recover. The healthy rest and digestive system can barely function if a child is constantly under threat (Lee, 2018).

Hearing the Child's Voice

The discourses surrounding children, their health and well-being has changed and developed with time. In line with adults health, there is a shift in paradigm to hearing the child voice and shared responsibility for action (Prout, 2005). Changing the cultural view of children and their ability to make informed decisions may take time; however, it is all about perceptions. Children who are more involved in the decisions about their lives are more likely to feel ownership and therefore make decisions which are appropriate for them. Many children in the home environment will be given choices about what they wear and eat (within reason) but within a corporate environment, a nursery or hospital where those providing care have a regime and purpose to consider their choices may be limited. There is often an acceptance that adults know best. School routines especially are based on the premise where adults hold most of the power and decision-making. However, the importance of the voice of the child is beginning to receive more recognition (Ofsted, 2010). Listening to the voice of children takes time, respectful decision-making and negotiation (Underdown, 2007). It often includes challenging the established protocols that exist in systems that are designed to protect and care for children with power and knowledge residing with adults. Decisions that are arrived with mutual dialogue and consensus may take a little more time but will undoubtedly result in a shared and open ownership that will reflect the rights of the child which are embedded within the UNCRC (1989). Changing perceptions initially needs a recognition that children are habitually excluded and that they are a passive recipients in their own care, health and well-being. If practitioners aim for a balance of power, shared decisions and an environment where children are empowered to be a sincere part of the decision-making, a more positive attitude to health and well-being may be achieved. The work by Cameron and Moss (2020) draw on research to develop holistic early childhood education and actively hear the voice of the child.

The health and well-being of children and their families is a complex multifaceted social dilemma of prevention, treatment, the role of state welfare, what role the voluntary sector plays and navigating difficult and challenging structure of bureaucracy and government departments. The following is a typical case study that will encourage you to consider the various elements, theories and issues in the health and well-being of children and their families.

Case Study: Susan

Susan is a single mum, living with her two teenage sons and twin three-years olds in a private rented house. The two older children are still in full-time education. The younger children have various long-term health conditions which require intensive support and regular hospital visits. The twins, a boy and a girl, both have chronic

(Continued)

asthma and diabetes type 1, requiring insulin injections. Susan separated from her partner four years ago, partly due to the stress of looking after their youngest twins. That is also when she gave up a good job in order to look after her children full time. Their home of the last seven years is in extremely poor condition; it is damp and cold, which has aggravated her children's medical problems. She has applied to go on the waiting list for social housing, as yet without success. Susan's house is in a very isolated location; this, along with no longer being in work, has contributed to her sense of loneliness. Nevertheless, she was coping until her Child Tax Credit was cut earlier this year without any warning, even though she had informed HMRC that her children were still in education. The cut in Child Tax Credit had a catastrophic impact on Susan's finances. Susan relied on her tax credits to pay for food and other daily necessities once all her regular bills were paid (electricity, bus fares for her older children, car insurance, telephone, insurance and debt repayment).

- As a practitioner, how could you support Susan to access help and support?
- How could the voluntary sector (for example food banks) support Susan and her family and what financial help is there available?
- Consider a holistic approach to the family's health; is there one element which is more significant than another or is a multidisciplined team approach needed?
- How could you involve the children in any decision-making?

Chapter Summary

This chapter has highlighted the complex area of children's health and well-being. There is an overview of the impact of health inequalities and how this directly affects a child mental and physical health. This chapter considers the global and national social determinants of health, health promotion and why this is important and relevant policy and legislation. These are complicated systems and relevant theory of social capital is discussed in detail and highlighted within the case studies.

Key Points

- Children's health and well-being is a complex area affected by multiple and interconnected factors, including inequality.
- Early intervention is essential to successfully supporting children's health and well-being.
- Taking a holistic approach ensures that all aspects of children's health and well-being are considered.

Further Reading

- The Kings Fund is an independent charitable organisation working to improve health and care in England https://www.kingsfund.org.uk/about-us
- The NSPCC is an invaluable source of publications, campaigns and repositories of relevant documents and research on children' health and well-being https://www.nspcc.org.uk/
- For information on the complicated health care systems see this audio video available from the Kings Fund: https://www.kingsfund.org.uk/audio-video/integrated-care-systems-health-and-care-act

References

Anderson, G., Frank, J.W., Naylor, C.D., Wodchis, W. and Feng, P. (2020) Using socioeconomics to counter health disparities arising from the Covid-19 pandemic. *BMJ*, 369, m2149. https://doi.org/10.1136/bmj.m2149

Black, C. (2007) *Review of the health of Britain's working age population.* https://assets.publishing.service.gov.uk/government/uploads/system/uploads/attachment_data/file/209784/hwwb-healthier-tomorrow-evidence-summary.pdf Accessed 21/08/23.

Blades, R., Greene, V. and Wallace, E. (2014) *Implementation study: Intergrated Review at 2-2 ½ Year the Early Years Foundation Stage Progress Check and the Healthy Child Programme health and development review.* Department of Education.

Bilton, T. (2022) *Introduction to sociology*. New York. Palgrave.

Bronfennbrenner, U. (1974) Developmental research, public policy and the ecology of childhood. *Child Development*, 45(1), 1–5.

Bronfenbrenner, U. and Morris, P. (2006) The bioecological model of human development. In R. M. Lerner and W. Damon (Eds.) *Handbook of child psychology: Theoretical models of human development* (pp. 793–828). New York: John Wiley and Sons, Inc.

Cameron, C. and Moss, P. (Eds.) (2020) *Transforming early childhood in England; Towards a democratic education.* London: UCL Press.

Caplan, P. (2016) Big Society or broken society? Food banks in the UK. *Anthropology Today*, 32(1), 5–9.

Caplan, P. (2020, June) Struggling for food in a time of crisis. *Anthropology Today*, 8–10.

Conrad, P. and Barker, K.K. (2010) The social construction of illness: Key insights and policy implications. *Journal of Health and Social Behavior*, 51(5), 567–579.

Corbin, J., et al. (2017) Health Promotion, partnerships and intersectoral action: Editorial. *Health Promotion International*, 32, 923–929.

De Botton (2004) *Status anxiety*. London, Hamilton.

Department for Education (DfE) (2019) *Number of children's centres, 2003 to 2019.* https://www.gov.uk/government/publications/number-of-childrens-centres-2003-to-2019 Accessed 29/8/23.

Eddy, K.T, Tabri, N., Thomas, J.J., Murray, H.B., Keshaviah, A., Hastings, E., Edkins, K., Krishna, M., Herzog, D.B., Keel, P.K. and Franko, D.L. (2017 February) Recovery from Anorexia Nervosa and Bulimia Nervosa at 22-year follow-up. *The Journal of Clinical Psychiatry*, 78(2), 184–189. https://doi.org/10.4088/JCP.15m10393

Eriksson, M. (2011) Social Capital and health implications for health promotion. *Global Health Action*, 4, 5611.

Gov (2021) *The best start for life: A vision for the 1001 critical days*. https://assets.publishing.service.gov.uk/government/uploads/system/uploads/attachment_data/file/973112/The_best_start_for_life_a_vision_for_the_1_001_critical_days.pdf Accessed 21/8/23.

Hubley, J., Coperman, J. and Woodall, J. (2021) *Practical health promotion*. Polity Press.

ISSOP (2018) *International Society for social pediatrics and child health (ISSOP) position statement 1 on child health inequities*. https://www.issop.org/cmdownloads/issop-position-statement-1-on-child-health-inequities-june-2018-update/ Accessed 13/5/2019.

Lee, D.B. (2018) Psychological pathways from racial discrimination to cortisol in African American males and females. *Journal of Behavioural Medicine*, 41(2), 208–220.

Ledwith, M. (2006) *Community development*. Bristol: Policy Press.

Longfield, A. (2012) *Damage to children's mental health caused by Covid crisis could last for years without a large scale increase for children's mental health services*. The Children's Commissioner. https://www.childrenscommissioner.gov.uk/news/damage-to-childrens-mental-health-caused-by-covid-crisis-could-last-for-years-without-a-large-scale-increase-for-childrens-mental-health-services/ Accessed 21/08/23.

Lopez-Tamayo, R., et al. (2022) The impact of adverse childhood experiences and community violence expose on a sample of anxious, treatment-seeking children. *Journal of Child & Adolescent Trauma*, 1081–1093.

Marmot, M. (2010) *Fair society, healthy lives: The Marmot Review: Strategic review of health inequalities in England post-2010*. https://www.parliament.uk/globalassets/documents/fair-society-healthy-lives-full-report.pdf

Marmot, M. (2017) Social injustice, epidemiology and health inequalities. *European Journal of Epidemiology*, 32(7), 537–546.

Marmot, M., Allen, J., Boyce, T., Goldblatt, P., Morrison, J. (2020) *Health equity in England: The Marmot Review 10 years on*. Institute of Health Equity. health.org.uk/publications/reports/the-marmot-review-10-years-on

McCrory, E. et al. (2017) Of Childhood maltreatment. In *The Wiley handbook of what works in childhood maltreatment; An evidence based approach to assessment and intervention in child protection*. New York: John Wiley & Sons.

Mikiewicz, P. and Cunha de Arujo, G.C. (2021) Social capital and education - AN attempt to synthesize conceptualisation arising from various theoretical origins. *Cogent Education*, 8, 1.

Mullan, B.P. (2017, April–June) The sociology of inequality and the rise of neo inequality *Sociological Focus*, 50, 2, 00380237.

National Autistic Society (2021) *Good practice guide: For professionals delivering talking therapies for autistic adults and children*. https://www.autism.org.uk/what-we-do/news/adapt-mental-health-talking-therapies Accessed 22/5/24.

NSPCC (2023). https://learning.nspcc.org.uk/child-health-development/child-mental-health Accessed 21/8/23.

NHS (nd) *Conditions*. https://www.nhs.uk/conditions/

Ofsted (2010) *The voice of the child: Learning lessons from serious case reviews*. https://assets.publishing.service.gov.uk/media/5a74a872ed915d0e8bf1a15f/The_voice_of_the_child.pdf Accessed 5/10/23.

OHID (2024) *About us: Priorities*. https://www.gov.uk/government/organisations/office-for-health-improvement-and-disparities/about Accessed 24/5/24.

PHSO (2017) *Ignoring the alarms: How NHS eating disorder services are failing patients*. https://www.ombudsman.org.uk/sites/default/files/page/ACCESSIBILE%20PDF%20-%20Anorexia%20Report.pdf Accessed 24/5/24.

Prout, A. (2005) *The future of childhood*. Oxford: Routledge.

Riches, G. (2018) *Food bank nations*. London: Routledge.

Spencer, N., Raman, S., O'Hare, B. and Tamburlini, G. (2019) Addressing inequities in child health and development: Towards social justice. *BMJ Paediatrics Open*, 2019(3), e000503.

The Health Foundation (2019) *What makes us healthy*. https://www.health.org.uk/publications/what-makes-us-healthy Accessed 07/09/2023.

Tillery, A.B. (2019, September) What kind of movement is Black lives matter? *Journal of Race and Ethnicity and Politics*, 4(2).

Treacher, M.H. (2016) The effects of childhood maltreatment in brain structure, function and connectivity. *Nature Reviews Neuroscience*, 17(10), 562–666.

Underdown, A. (2007) *Young children's health and well-being*. Open University Press.

UNCRC (1989) *Convention of children's rights*. https://www.unicef.org.uk/what-we-do/un-convention-child-rights/

UK Gov (2021) *Promoting children and young people's mental health and well being*. https://www.gov.uk/government/publications/promoting-children-and-young-peoples-emotional-health-and-wellbeing

WHO (2024) *Health promotion*. https://www.who.int/westernpacific/about/how-we-work/programmes/health-promotion Accessed 22/5/24.

WHO and CSDH (2008) *Closing the gap in a generation*. https://www.who.int/publications/i/item/WHO-IER-CSDH-08.1 Accessed 22/5/24.

World Health Organisation (2023) *Health and well-being*. https://www.who.int/data/gho/data/major-themes/health-and-well-being. Accessed 21/08/23.

Young Minds (2022) *Impact report*. https://www.youngminds.org.uk/about-us/reports-and-impact/impact-report-2022/highlight-tour/ Accessed 21/08/23.

10

Childhood, Loss and Bereavement

Marie Price

After reading this chapter, readers will be able to:

- Understand and explore children's grief within a developmental, societal and environmental context.
- Provide an overview of how children grieve including what behaviours to watch out for.
- Reflect on how families and practitioners can work together to support children who are experiencing loss and bereavement.

Introduction

This chapter is designed to give those of you who are working with children, in any setting, an overview of the experiences that children may have when they are facing the death of someone close to them, and how they might understand their grief. Although this chapter is aimed at people who work with children, the principles relating to these areas apply to anyone with a child in their life. The feelings that children may have, when they are faced with the loss of someone close to them will be explored, including how these may differ according to children's stage of development. This chapter also provides suggestions as to how to support children who are grieving and in turn looks at how adults, in these situations, can look after themselves in the process.

Understanding the Experiences of Loss and Bereavement in Children

Childhood bereavement is recognised as an Adverse Childhood Experience (ACE), and as such experiencing loss and bereavement in early life is generally equated with poorer mental health in adulthood. However, if handled well these experiences may also enable the child to build up some form of resilience or protective factors for future events. For a child knowing that they can survive something that at first appeared to be not survivable can temper some of the affects; however, what is not in dispute is that experiencing someone close to you dying is life changing:

> The journey to healing grief weaves throughout a child's developmental years. Sometimes a child's grief is obvious and visible. Sometimes it isn't. However, it is always in the background, influencing his or her emotions, behaviours, interactions, and communication (Di Ciacco, 2008: 15).

With reference to the quote above understanding the experiences of loss and bereavement in children is intertwined with all human experience of grief. Most of us, as adults, have a template of how loss was handled for us as children and, in turn, children are on the receiving end of those models and frameworks. Thankfully, as more is understood about children's development and understanding of the world around them, more and more ways of expressing grief are becoming known and accepted. With this has come the realisation that although children have similar experiences and feelings to adults, they are also influenced by the attitudes and understanding of the adults that they live with, or support them. It has long been recognised that adults in trying to protect their children from the pain of grief, in fact, often do the opposite. Even though adults may:

> want to spare children the difficult task of having to deal with the emotions and other issues that bereavement can raise. However this denies children the means to overcome their loss and the ability to overcome painful situations (Pennells and Smith, 1999: 10).

Children's grief is hard to witness and be supportive of – but it does not mean it does not occur. Sometimes the 'protection' of the child is a form of self-protection for the adults when they find the pain the child is experiencing too much to bear.

The following extract comes from Arnold's (2017) understanding of grief in children and adolescents and illustrates how a child's behaviour can be misinterpreted and thought of as inappropriate:

> Several years ago, a colleague told me a story about a ten year old boy, named Sam who had experienced the death of his best friend. At this young boy's wintry funeral, Sam was making a snowman. This activity was deemed "inappropriate" and "disrespectful" by many at the funeral and Sam was admonished for "playing" at such a sombre time. Sometime later, in the context of grief counselling, the therapist asked him why he was making a snowman at his best friend's funeral. Sam replied that one of the favourite activities for him and his friend was to make snowmen, and he wanted to leave a really good one at his friend's grave" (Arnold, 2017: 15).

This moving account of Sam's encounter at his friends' funeral, and his subsequent explanation, illustrates the fact that we need to watch and listen carefully to what children are telling us, with their behaviour, about their feelings and experiences, both verbally and non-verbally. These clues will both tell us something about the experiences of that child and what they need to do to express these experiences and feelings. This may vary depending on what sorts of death children might experience.

Points of Reflection

- Is grief the same for children and adults?
- How might children's grief differ from that of adults? Why?

Types of Death

The types of death children may encounter are not different from the types of death that adults may experience. These deaths can broadly be categorised into two different groups': deaths that are anticipated or expected and deaths that are not.

Expected – when a death is expected children can be helped to prepare for that impending death. They can be enabled to ask questions, say what they need to say to the person who is dying and, maybe, talk to the person about their relationship alongside working out ways to say their goodbyes. They can build memory boxes about the person. These are boxes, or repositories, of any shape, size or colour that can be used to 'hold' all the memories, photos or objects that represent the person that has died or have been created by the child to represent that person. These can be used alongside other creative methods to help them understand what they are thinking or feeling – they do not have to be expensive or prescriptive they can be of any materials and any colour of decoration the child would like and can also be done in conjunction with the person who is ill.

Case Study: Helena

I was introduced to Helena when she was admitted to a hospice that I was working in over a decade ago. She had a rapidly progressing neurological disorder that meant that she was likely to die within a few months. Helena also had two very small children that she was trying to leave some memories and messages for. The children were both under the age of three meaning that engaging them in many activities was difficult. However, one of Helena's concerns was that her children were not going to remember her voice as they got older and neither was she going to be able to attend any of their special occasions or transitions. She was unable to use her arms at this point so writing was not possible so we hit on the idea that she could record messages for her children for various points in their future, which is what she did. We set up a recorder in such a way that it balanced on her pillow and I left the room. At various agreed intervals I checked that the recorder had not slipped and that she was able to say what she wanted to say. By doing so the children would know she cared enough to provide them with the support she knew she would not be there to give herself.

(Continued)

(Continued)

Addendum – it does not mean that people who are not able to do this sort of recording do not care. It may not occur to them conversely or it may be too difficult for a variety of reasons.

- Why do you think it may be too difficult to embark on this course of action?
- What do you think you might need in order to support someone in this position?

Sudden deaths can, broadly speaking, be separated into three areas:

Suicide – When someone dies by suicide, it can be very difficult to talk about what has happened. Adults often want to protect children from the truth and may worry about explaining suicide, as they do not want children to realise someone can choose to end their own life. However, children are much more able to deal with difficult events if they are given open and honest information.

Telling children about a sudden, shocking or unexplained death of someone significant to them is not likely to be a one-off conversation, but a process that may need to happen in stages over the days, weeks, months and even years after the death. By giving the child information in small steps, their understanding gradually grows in a way that everyone involved can more easily handle together.

Accident – Deaths caused by an accident can be difficult to understand because they are so sudden and initially it may not be known how or why it has happened. Knowing how the accident happened is important for children and young people, as it helps them to piece together why their loved one died. They are likely to have lots of thoughts in their head, and so being given factual information is important. Although some parents may feel they do not want to overwhelm their child with too much detail, the child may be making up the missing information in their heads, which could be more distressing than the truth, or feel confused or scared because they do not have all the details.

Murder – With support, children can deal with the truth, no matter how difficult or shocking it may be. What they find harder are untruths. With a natural instinct to protect children, it may be tempting to withhold information from them. However, a death by murder or manslaughter is often picked up by the press, the local community and social media. The chances are that a child will overhear a conversation or be told by someone at school. It is much better that they are told in a safe place, by someone they are close to and who can support them on an ongoing basis.

The principle of telling children remains the same in all situations:

- Use age-appropriate language.
- Give as many details as you can.
- Be prepared for a variety of responses from not seeming to take the information on board to becoming overwrought.

- Do not shy away from the questions they ask and say that you do not know something, if you do not, but will find out if that is the case – but make sure you do go back with an answer as children will remember. What children are not told they make up in their heads and that can be more confusing and frightening than the reality however awful that is.
- A common feature is the need to go over the story time and again especially in the first few weeks and months but there may also be a need to have the situation explained years down the line especially when life is changing or the child is going through a transition such as moving schools or reaching adolescence.
- Helping them to make sense of the loss is necessary from different perspectives and is often helpful for us all as our perception of relationships develops as we grow and experience various changes in our lives.

The following websites have some useful things to say about how children can be supported in these situations: Child Bereavement UK www.childbereavementuk.org and Winston's Wish www.winstonswish.org.

Seeing a Body and Attending Funerals

It is not unusual for a child to ask to see the person who has died. Children are naturally curious and provided they are well-prepared for what they will see, viewing a body can help them to understand what being dead means. Understandably, adults may be unsure about this, and will want to think it through carefully. There may be many reasons why a child may want to see a body; however, even with the best planning and support this may not be possible or not in the way that may be desired. If there is damage to the body which is distressing to see it may be possible to view, or even touch, an undamaged part such as a hand, with the body covered so that only the hand is exposed. It is important to think beforehand about what to do if the child asks to see the rest of the body.

What if There Is No Body?

Sometimes a death or loss can be accompanied by the fact that there is not a body to see or to have funeral for. This may be because a body has not been found in some cases of drowning or disasters or they may have died as part of an explosion or war. This still needs to be explained to the child and, again, any questions answered. Children will often know, or find out the truth, from various sources however much they are 'protected', for example overhearing phone calls, seeing written evidence such as emails or social media, hearing things in the school playground or at friends' houses. Silences or private phone calls may also give clues as to what might be going on. These behaviours can lead to children feeling that death is something shameful or that it is their fault the person has died.

Coping With Loss and Bereavement

The global Covid-19 pandemic, which started in 2019, has produced significant losses of various kinds. Many people had relatives and friends who died from a previously unknown virus that appeared to have no clear trajectory. Alongside that the existential threat that the virus posed, to most, added to the insecurity of lockdowns and food shortages. These events appear to have added another layer of insecurity to children as they worked out what was happening alongside witnessing the concerns of their parents. Many children missed out on transitions and rites of passage during this time which added to the number of losses they may have already been experiencing. These experiences were replicated the whole world over and as lockdown was easing and things were going back to a new normal, the United Kingdom experienced the death of its longest serving monarch potentially created another layer of loss for some. Even though these losses were not experienced directly by some children their insecurities and uncertainties were far reaching and created low levels of loss across the board.

In 2022, the UK Commission on Bereavement, which included a briefing on children's needs and services, was published. This was the first of its kind to include the recognition and consideration of what children may need when bereaved. This report followed a yearlong research project, prompted by the responses to the pandemic, and was made up of a group of people with a particular interest in bereavement, supported by a steering group of individuals actively involved in research, services and writing about these topics. One of the principles that was established from the survey was the need for children to be supported with one of the aims being that loss and bereavement is included in their education.

Points of Reflection

- Do you agree that children should be educated about loss and bereavement?
- What are the challenges of educating children about loss and bereavement? What are the benefits?

Ages and Stages of Expressions of Grief

Although the following suggestions are useful general guidelines, the subsequent ages and stages of expressions of grief should be held loosely and used as a guide rather than an absolute. They are an amalgamation of recommendations from the major children's bereavement charities such as Winston's Wish and Child Bereavement UK as well as incorporated into some of the reading in the reference section. As stated earlier there is no substitute for watching a child's behaviour and talking with a child to understand what it is they are experiencing and feeling.

0–2 Years

Following a death in the family it is common for babies or toddlers to become withdrawn or display outbursts of loud crying and angry tears. There may be changes, regression or difficulties with their development, for example sleeping or feeding. Although infants do not understand death at this age, they know when things have changed, and may well react to a person's absence. This may show in clinginess and distress. Support can be given by maintaining the child's routine and making them feel secure.

2–5 Years

At this stage the child still does not fully understand death although they are often fascinated by the concept, wanting to see dead birds and animals. They do not realise at this stage that death is permanent and that it will happen to everyone. Their reactions may be limited when they are told someone has died. It is important to use words such as dead or died so they know that they deceased is not simply 'asleep', and that they will not return. They may worry that something they said or did have caused the death, and need to be reassured that it was not their fault. Children often ask the same questions over and over again. Support can be given to the child by encouraging them to ask questions, and answering them openly and simply. Again as with all stages of expressions of grief, regression in development and changes in sleeping and eating pattern are common.

5–8 Years

Within this stage children gradually learn that death is final and that all people will die at some time. This may make them worry that other people close to them will also die. It can help children to talk about these fears. We cannot promise children that no-one will ever die, but we can help them to feel safe by telling them that they will always be looked after and by whom. More curious children in this age group often ask direct questions about what has happened to the body. They may blame themselves in some way for the death and can engage in 'magical thinking', for example filling in the gaps when information has not been given to them. Support can be given to the child by encouraging them to talk about and express their feelings, and reassuring them that all feelings are normal and 'okay'.

8–12 Years

This age group usually understands that death is irreversible, universal and has a cause. Grief can express itself through physical aches and pains and challenging behaviour. It is important not to place unnecessary responsibility on children of this age, particularly older children who may feel responsible for younger siblings, or boys who lose their father and take on the role of 'man of the house'.

Adolescence

Adolescence is a time of great change. Teenagers struggle with issues of identity and independence as they try to bridge the gap between childhood and adulthood. Losing someone can make life very difficult. Adolescents need clear and accurate information at the time of a death. Involving teens in the rituals can help them, but be sure to treat them in a manner appropriate to their stage of development. They may wish to take an active part in funeral arrangements, or to mark the death in their own way. At this age young people know that death is final and inevitable. However, confusion arises as they struggle with the many emotions, thoughts and mood changes that the death creates while trying to fit in with their peers.

In summary bereavement takes adults, and children, back to a much earlier stage of life and often evokes previous losses. It is widely accepted that the emotional age of an adult who is recently bereaved is around eight-years old so it is clear from that to see that children may regress even further. These regressions can enable us to rework some of the pain of previous losses too 'In learning how to grieve we are learning skills for life' (Carter, 2016: 59).

The Importance of Language

The language we use to express death and bereavement with children and young people is important and there are ways of expressing concepts that are more helpful than others. That does not mean to say we need to get it right first time round, or all the time, what it does mean is we are able to have those conversations and be ready to answer any questions or be able to go back and right any mistakes that we may have made. As Carter (2016: 49) points out, 'Starting to talk is difficult'; there is no good time to tell a child bad news. There is no blueprint which indicates the relationship between age and understanding, how much the child wants to know or if the child would rather not know anything.'

Generally the recommendations for these discussions are:

- be clear in the language you use;
- check out that what you have said has been understood;
- be open and honest;
- be available and/or let the child know who is available – very often children will work out for themselves who they would like to talk to;
- use appropriate language such as died or dead rather than euphemisms such as they have gone to sleep or gone away;
- be patient both in the explanation and with any questions they may have – remembering that they may have questions later on, or that they may need to have the conversation time and time again to make sense of it.

Case Study: Using Appropriate Language

Very early on in my career, and first working with bereaved children, I was working with one boy of 8-years old whose mother had died. Initially his father, supported by the rest of the family, had been reluctant for him to know about what was happening or indeed that his mother had died. Eventually his behaviour was alternating between being very withdrawn and then angry. I started to work with him a few months after the funeral, which he had not been able to attend, and established that he had lots of questions about his mother's death that needed answers. So with the aid of his father we tackled these questions about how and why she died alongside the practicalities of the funeral arrangements and who had been there and who had not. He seemed satisfied with the answers and settled at school until a few weeks later the behaviours had returned. So again I was asked to come to the house and continue some of the work we had begun. It transpired that when we had talked about his mother's body being in the coffin, when she was buried, we had omitted to talk about his mother's body being intact. His worry was that his mother's head was somewhere else and he wanted to know where it was and why that had happened.

A salutary lesson to all of us is making sure that language is appropriate and understood by the children involved not just by the adults who have come to understand that when we talk about bodies when it comes to death and funerals that it also, usually, means someone's head too.

- Are there other ways you might tackle this situation?
- What other words or phrases do we use on an everyday basis which could also be misinterpreted?

The case study above also highlights the importance of noticing behaviours that may indicate that something is wrong, providing age-appropriate information and checking out regularly what children understand by the words adults use. Common language suggests that the use of the word 'body' means the whole of someone but to a child it may mean something completely different.

What Concepts Might Need Explaining?

So far, this chapter has given an overview of the needs of grieving children; however, there are a variety of other ways to support children alongside other matters and situations that need to be taken into consideration.

Pre and Post Death Experiences

There are many situations that may occur before a death that need some form of explanation such as what someone may look like if a child visits someone who is dying.

As adults we may have got used to seeing someone lose weight, change colour or the fact that they may not recognise us. All these things can be explained to a child and any questions answered honestly and simply. If a child asks to see a dead body, explanations need to be thorough and an understanding of what they may see or smell or touch had before they visit is vital so the child will have some understanding of what they may experience before they get there. The following is a list of topics and observations that may be helpful to think about:

- Be clear about the purpose of the visits. Is it a regular visit? Is it to say goodbye? Is it to create memories or to just be together?
- Explain how the location of the person may be different. If it is their home maybe there is specialist equipment around or the bed is downstairs (as opposed to upstairs).
- Explain what they may see, hear or smell. Are there any rules that visitors have to adhere to, such as washing hands on entry or certain areas that cannot be accessed?
- Reminders that the person they are visiting is still the same person although they may look different are helpful.
- Give the child some control over how long the visit takes place and what they do there is helpful. Give them the option to take breaks or do activities – maybe even with the person.

Explaining What Happens to Someone After Death

These can be difficult conversations to have but starting with a simple biological explanation can often be very helpful. Explaining that someone's heart does not beat anymore and their lungs no longer work so they do not need to breathe can be useful alongside the fact that the brain stops working. This type of explanation lays out the facts about what someone may need before a death and what they do not need afterwards. If the family have a belief system these can either be introduced here or reinforced.

Explaining Funerals, Burial and Cremation

Most children will be aware at some level that something happens after someone dies but they may not know what or why. An explanation of what a funeral is designed for is useful. Explaining that it is to say goodbye to the person who has died, remember the person, tell stories about them and talk about how we will miss them will help to illustrate what may happen. Including children in a funeral even if they are too young to really remember is helpful as they will feel included and part of the experience, especially later on in life when people talk about the event. That said giving children a choice of whether to attend is also important, remember that they cannot make an informed choice if they have not got the details. Let them know they can also change their minds! They could do a drawing or write poem that can go in or on the coffin, or if it is a coffin that can be decorated they could take part in that activity. They could choose flowers or a song or reading for the funeral. They could also visit the place the funeral will take place. It may well be helpful to ask someone to take responsibility for the child/children during the ceremony if they feel restless or need to go out for whatever reason. This can be especially important if it is a parent that has died and the remaining parent is not able to have the same level of involvement in their care on the day. Explaining how people may grieve in different ways is also helpful to the child (for example some people may cry a lot, some just a little and others not at all).

Explaining Burial and Cremation

Although there are various ways of dealing with a body after a funeral the most common ways are burial or cremation. Burial can be explained by the coffin being lowered into a hole in the ground that has been pre-dug in a designated place such as a churchyard or natural burial ground. The hole will be filled with earth and eventually grass, plants or a tree will grow over it. Cremation can be a bit trickier to explain as fire is often associated with being burnt and pain. However, both methods can be described alongside the previous knowledge of how the body does not feel anything anymore. The description can then continue with the fact that the body, still in the coffin, is put into a furnace and burnt and the ashes are then returned to the family in something called an urn. Then a decision can be taken as to whether to scatter the ashes and where, or whether to keep them somewhere safe.

The Role of Early Years Settings and Schools

Nearly all children in the United Kingdom have experienced bereavement by the time they reach 16, whether that be of a grandparent, parent, friend or sibling (Dawson et al., 2023). Yet very little is taught about the realities of death and bereavement as a subject in schools. Practitioners in early years settings and schools can provide invaluable support and may well be a source of information and comfort for children when families are maybe finding it difficult. Depending on the developmental age of the child, the following gives some ideas as to how practitioners can support children in settings:

- Keep routines as normal as possible.
- Offer comforting foods where possible – for example soft food can often be helpful.
- Provide as much comfort as possible if a child is distressed, such as wrapping them in a blanket, providing favourite or familiar toys.
- Children may well want to ask lots of question about what has happened – discuss how to answer these questions with the parents and/or care givers.
- Providing a safe space where children can use play as a way to work through feelings and emotions.

Children With Special Educational Needs

Support for children with special educational needs is, in essence, no different from the support described above that help most children. And as above if you are caring for a child that is facing or has been bereaved assessing what the child knows and framing things within their sphere of understanding/developmental stage is a good way of providing that support. Winston's Wish and Child Bereavement UK charities have resources that may well be helpful when you are working with a child with special educational needs.

Creating Rituals

The rituals we create to remember someone who has died can be invaluable in both helping a child understand what has happened and to process their feelings and thoughts. These rituals often start with the funeral but can be broader and wider than that and work in all sorts of circumstances. The very act of creating a memory box or scrap book of the person that has died can be helpful alongside reading books specially designed for children. Planning a special meal with all the people's favourite foods or planning a ceremony that can be held in a garden, a community hall or school. These rituals can also be especially helpful if a child has not been able to attend a funeral. They can help them say goodbye and remember the person in their own way.

Diversity and Inclusion

Although what has been written about so far is good general guidance for when we are supporting children, we also need to be mindful of the wider family context. Every family will have their own unique way of practising those traditions and expressions of grief according to their family culture, ethnicity as well as any particular religious beliefs. For instance some families may feel that grieving should be over once the funeral has happened whereas for many others it is recognised that grieving is, probably, a lifetimes process. Another area for discussion is whether children should attend funerals; again in some families they may be excluded but in others they may well be included in the family preparations and attendance. To understand the impact on the children it is always good to have a conversation with the family and the child to understand the context within which the child is living and their stage of development (Thanasiu and Pizza, 2019: 8).

Support for Children and Their Families

Throughout the rest of this chapter the focus is on trying to give pointers as to how children may experience the loss of someone close to them, alongside providing some indicators as to how that support may be offered and ways of providing that support. However much the adults around them assume that children do not know what is happening the reality is that they often do even when they have not been told explicitly. Children pick up on tensions, stress or anxiety and overhear, or are told, pieces of information that they gradually make sense of but sometimes have nowhere to share it as they realise that they are not supposed to know. In my opinion children need continuity and the creation of an environment where they know they can ask questions and trust the answers they receive, as well as making sure all topics can be talked about alongside what questions to ask and to whom.

The American psychologist Esther Shapiro suggests that 'children oscillate, putting their grief down then taking it up again' (Carter 2016: 23). Sometimes this flexibility is confused with children not grieving, however, make no mistake they do grieve but their expression is more in the moment and they have not yet learnt to succumb to the social conformities of having to behave in a particular way. This is illustrated beautifully in the book Muddles, Puddles and Sunshine (Crossley 2001) and illustrates the complexity of a child's response to a bereavement. Children, and adults, need to know they can have fun as well as grieve and, in fact, that is vital for everyone's mental health. There are many books and games available now to help children express their feelings and process a loss or bereavement and I have included some of the organisations that produce some of these in the reference list at the end of the chapter. There may also be times when it is important for children to receive more specialist help, a list of organisations that offer this is also listed at the end of the chapter. Occasionally, counselling may be required and this can also be sourced through the organisations listed or through specialist services such as the Young Minds charity or Play Therapy.

Although I have recognised that there may be times when specialist services may be required, this is not to be confused with times in a child's life when the grief may be reawakened, for example special occasions such as birthdays and significant religious holiday. Grief may also be reawakened at points of transitions such as going to school, leaving school and going to university. Later in life they may be reawakened again when getting married, getting a first job, having children, as you can see these are not one-off conversations, they are lifelong conversations and adjustments.

Chapter Summary

This chapter has gone some way to describe the losses that children may experience together with ideas as to how to support them given the development age of that child. One of the ongoing concerns parents and carers often have is around whether the events in a child's life will affect their future mental health. When we look at what is needed to support a child through the death of a loved one, and their experiences of bereavement, it is important to remember to look after ourselves. To do this work well we need to be available to children both physically and emotionally and to do that we need to make sure that we get the support we need. I do not mean the superficial nod at saying we are going for a walk or reading a book or having a glass of wine. I mean the deep work of grief that we need to do for ourselves both for our own losses but also for the losses of the children we support. I am a great advocate of supervision and good quality supervision can enable us to process all the losses we are carrying. While they cannot make us forget the losses they can help us with the feelings and experiences of those losses. Working in a trauma informed way is also a good start to understanding the impact that our own or someone else's trauma may be having on us and alert us to what we need to support the children.

Key points to supporting children who have experienced bereavement and loss include:

- continue to provide the child with loving and consistent care from those they trust and know well;
- maintain normal routines and structure as much as is possible;
- If children display challenging and/or regressive behaviour, try to understand it is their way of communicating what they are not able to verbalise.

Further Reading

In addition to the valuable reading presented in the Reference list, I have also included three texts which provide a good starting point:

Anti-Bullying Alliance (nd) At risk groups. Available at: https://anti-bullyingalliance.org.uk/tools-information/all-about-bullying/at-risk-groups (accessed 23.10.23).

Childhood Bereavement Network (nd) Welcome to the Childhood Bereavement Network. Available at: https://childhoodbereavementnetwork.org.uk/ (accessed 23.10.23).

Child Bereavement UK (nda) Available at: www.childbereavementuk.org (accessed 23.10.23).

Child Bereavement UK (ndb) For adults bereaved as children. Available at: https://www.gov.uk/government/statistics/online-bullying-in-england-and-wales-year-ending-march-2020 (accessed 23.10.23).

Child Bereavement UK (ndc) Supporting bereaved children and young people with special educational needs. Available at: https://www.childbereavementuk.org/information-bereaved-children-with-special-needs (accessed 23.10.23).

Crossley, D. (2001) *Muddles, Puddles and Sunshine*. Hawthorne Press

Di Ciacco, J.A. (2008) *The Colours of Grief: Understanding a Child's Journey through Loss from Birth to Adulthood*. Jessica Kingsley

Furikman, E. (1974) *When a Childs Parent Dies*. Karnac Books.

Grollman, E. (1993) *Straight Talk about Death for Teenagers*. Beacon Press.

Harmer, J. (2021) Grief hierarchy: who has the right to grieve? www.mariecurie.org.uk/talkabout/articles/grief-hierarchy-who-has-the-right-to-grieve

Jackson, M. and Colwell, J. (2001) *A Teachers Handbook of Death*. Jessica Kingsley.

Masur, C. (2022) *When a Child Grieves: Psychoanalytical Understanding and Techniques*. Phoenix Publishing House.

Office for National Statistics [ONS] (2020) Official Statistics: Online Bullying in England and Wales: Year Ending March 2020. Available at: https://www.gov.uk/government/statistics/online-bullying-in-england-and-wales-year-ending-march-2020 (accessed 23.10.23).

Smith, S.S. (1999) *The Forgotten Mourners* (2nd ed). Jessica Kingsley

Special Educational Needs (nd) Grief unspoken. SEN Magazine. https://senmagazine.co.uk/content/care/social/2069/grief-unspoken/

UK Commission on Children's Bereavement (Part of The UK Commission on Bereavement) (2022). Available at: https://bereavementcommission.org.uk (accessed 23.10.23).

UNICEF (1989) United Nations Convention on the Rights of the Child. Available at: https://www.unicef.org/child-rights-convention (accessed 23.10.23).

United Nations (nd) Cyber bulling – What Is It and How to Stop It. Available at: https://www.unicef.org/end-violence/how-to-stop-cyberbullying (accessed 23.10.23).

Winston's Wish (nd) Bereavement Support for Children with SEND. Available at: https://www.winstonswish.org/supporting-children-with-send/ (accessed 23.10.23).

References

Arnold, C. (2017) *Understanding Child and Adolescent Grief: Supporting Loss and Facilitating Growth* Routledge.

Carter, M. (2016) *Helping Children and adolescents think about death, dying, and bereavement.* Jessica Kingsley.

Crossley, D. (2001) *Muddles, Puddles and Sunshine*. Hawthorne Press.

Dawson, L., Hare, R., Selman, L.E., Boseley, T. and Penny, A. (2023) 'The one thing guaranteed in life and yet they won't teach you about it': The case for mandatory grief education in schools Bereavement Journal of grief and responses to death.

Di Ciacco, J.A. (2008) *The Colors of Grief: Understanding a Child's Journey through Loss from Birth to Adulthood*. Jessica Kingsley.

Masur, C. (2022) *When a Child Grieves: Psychoanalytical Understanding and Techniques.* Phoenix Publishing House.

Pennells, M. and Smith, S. (1999) *The Forgotten Mourners: Guidelines for Working With Bereaved Children* (2nd ed.). London: Jessica Kingsley Publishers.

Thanasiu, P.L. and Pizza, N. (2019) Constructing culturally sensitive creative interventions for use with grieving children and adolescents. *Journal of Creativity in Mental Health,* 14(3): 270–279.

Part III
Children's Minds

11

Dreaming the Child Awake

Carol Lloyd

After reading this chapter, readers will be able to:

- Consider the value of empirical evidence from the child's voice, that sharing dream experiences with children in any setting is a developmentally valid activity.
- Reflect upon the skills necessary for the integration of group work with dreams in an early year's context.
- Personally re-evaluate the importance of sharing dreams with a trusted practitioner.

Introduction

So, she told them her dreams and they said she was mad

They told her they'd listen then covered their ears

And gave her a hug whilst they laughed at her fears. (Hemsley, 2022)

Humans are born unconscious and evolve into a state of consciousness, although leaving potential new self and world awareness. The world of sleep dreams, whether we think we dream or not (Foulkes, 1982). This chapter will present the findings of research on the dream worlds of children within an educational context. It outlines the approach of a social dream matrix (Lawrence, 2005) and how dream sharing can be implemented and valued in professional interactions with children in your care. It does not involve analysing the dream as in the traditional Freudian (Freud,1997) sense, sharing our inner worlds is a collective need to gain a sense of self as it affects our emotional regulation.

The Value of Sharing Children's Dreams Within Education

This chapter is based on empirical qualitative research using a social dream matrix approach while researching into children's dreams. Children's dreams were shared within an educational setting, and the research fits the curriculum activity known generically as circle time (Mosley, 1996). The research enquired into sharing children's dreams and analysed and interpreted the phenomena of their lived experience of dreaming and dream sharing within a social, dream matrix and school context. The findings indicate that sharing dreams in a group enhanced their confidence both personally and socially. The literature review is based on other researcher's findings from dream sharing in schools especially conceptual views on children's dreams and nightmares.

Having acknowledged dreaming as a human phenomenon, it is important to stress how diversity and inclusion of the individual can be explored. When sharing the dreams in a group the personality of the child is acknowledged as unique, but also creates a binding of thinking through collective experiences (Lawrence, 2005), for example dreams can be similar in the script but unique and different in their images, feelings and relevance to the dreamer. Just as storytelling, myths and fairy stories have been part of community ritual for centuries (Bainbridge and Formenti, 2021), so has dream sharing, although not given the same status, therefore creating a split in the psyche both personally and collectively. So, the research argues there is a real potential within sharing dream worlds within educational contexts (Adams, 2005; 2010; Mallon, 2002; 2018).

The Origins of Empirical Dream Research With Children

The idea that dreams are a precious unconscious and natural phenomenon and therefore important to the development of a child's personality is not new. Over time, dream work became increasingly aligned to the therapeutic context due to the work of Freud and to Jung's dream analysis (Punnett, 2018; Van de Castle, 1994). However, from the more recent research findings (Adams 2010; Gambini, 2012; Hoffmann and Lewis, 2014), the 21st century counter movement towards integrating the sharing of dreams within a school curriculum is increasingly advocated and considered worthy of practice and further research. Psychosocial research by Lawrence and others into the sharing and expression of sleep dream activity indicated that this was without doubt beneficial to children's development (Adams, 2010; Adams et al., 2016; Gambini, 2003; Lawrence, 2005, 2010; Mallon, 2002; Selvaggi as cited in Lawrence, 2010; Agresta and Planera, 2010). Research into the social dream matrix method suggested 'sharing dreams collectively within a school context' is feasible, as it provides a 'pedagogical extension to understanding how children think' (Lawrence, 2010: 22). It includes the collective unconscious (Jung, 1971), and as Agresta and Planera's (2010) discuss, it is a successful method to consider unconscious elements of school life, indicating that Lawrence's 'four modes of thinking' can be educationally developed. Jung wrote four seminars about children's dreams between 1941–1943 and postulated the beginnings of consciousness in his theory of 'individuation' (Jung, 1971, 2008: 100). He explains dream sharing as a relational process that young children need to thrive. The post-Jungian theorists Fordham (1944, 1969) and Neumann (1954, 1988) went on to develop theory on early childhood ego development within the theory of individuation. Piaget (1962, 1969) and subsequent researchers have focused on children's dreaming and symbolic thinking; Piaget (1962) indicated that children's dream content can be harnessed as a possible assessment tool for various domains and stages of cognitive ability, in which creativity and imagination are included.

The Child's Inner World

The child's inner world is experienced differently to the outer world; it involves emotional experiences, fantasies, feelings, imagination and dreams, and informs our responses to the outer world. In 1938, Wickes was the first to write about the aspect of the inner world of childhood from a Jungian perspective (Wickes, 1963). The works of Jung, Wickes and contemporary Jungians (Gambini, 2003, 2012; Semetsky, 2013) focus on the inner world being expressed into the outer world in a social context and validate how the transcendent processes of consciousness can be nurtured through a sensitive approach to sharing dreams. The creative, ethical and delicate bridging of the child's inner dream worlds to the outer world has been explored as a key thread through the research Dream Time Project (Lloyd, 2020).

Watson (2010) questioned existing models of naturalistic or secular humanist perspectives in state education. Watson's findings suggest that education tends to ignore how spirituality can be used to nurture the spiritual or non-material aspects of development in school children. However, there is extensive contemporary interest in defining the spiritual domains of childhood through the study of dreams (Adams et al., 2008; Adams et al., 2016; Hay & Nye, 2006; Nye, 2009).

Adams (2005, 2010, 2015) considers the dream world as soul or spirit, manifesting from the inner world of the child. It is important when considering the early child psychology theory to note that Jung (Wickes, 1963: xxi) suggested 'the child's psyche, prior to the stage of ego consciousness, is very far from being empty and devoid of content'. He stated his view on early childhood, confirming that it is the pre-ego stage of a child's development in which the collective, the symbolic and the archetypal are found. For example children will dream about something that they may never have seen or experienced. Thus, the pre-ego stage of consciousness is not a part of individuation; this comes later. This view is confronted later in Fordham (1969) and Neumann's (1988) evolving views of the individuation process starting from birth.

Educational Perspectives and Policy on Spirituality

Inclusion of spiritual aspects of development in children was originally defined by the Department for Education (DfE) (Department for Education, 2011, archived 2013), it stated:

> Pupils' spiritual development involves the growth of their sense of self, their unique potential, their understanding of their strengths and weaknesses, and their will to achieve. As their curiosity about themselves and their place in the

> world increases, they try to answer for themselves some of life's fundamental questions. They develop the knowledge, skills, understanding, qualities, and attitudes they need to foster their own inner lives and non-material wellbeing. (Department for Education, 2011)

It is notable that the word *spiritual* as a developmental domain was removed from the Early Years Foundation Stage (EYFS) curriculum in 2008. This omission raises two questions; how is children's spiritual development currently perceived by teachers and how is the idea of a sense of self (personality) being nurtured within schooling?

Policy Versus Child Development: An Ongoing Paradox

The intention was not to analyse the children's dreams with the children in a classical analytic form; the social dream matrix approach specifically kept the child and their dreams safely contained within the group (Lawrence, 2005). The dreams were not interfered with; they were shared without duress and expressed as the children chose. This method of implementing a social dream matrix was adapted from the pioneer and contemporary researchers Lawrence (2005) and Manley (2014). The Dream Time project matrices created an established safe, transitional space (Winnicott, 2012), which involved free association and amplification and obviated any sense of judgement (Lawrence, 2005).

The Dream Project in Relationship to Circle Time

The Dream Project was undertaken with six-year olds over one school year, included and utilised activities such as drawing, drama, story books, sand trays with miniature figures, a dream journal interest table and making dream catchers. The six class social dream matrices and dreams from eight of the 22 children interviewed were analysed, and two teacher interviews were evaluated. This analytical process explores how a child's dream and consciousness can be perceived developmentally and contextually appropriate within educational settings.

Six whole class social dream matrices were implemented in line with the existing pedagogical approach and national curriculum hour within the English Early Years and Primary curriculum weekly timetable: by combining these circle time (Mosley, 1996) meetings. This structured group activity aimed to develop positive relationships, self-discipline, assertive communication and democratic group processes, alongside the skills of speaking, listening, observing, thinking, playing and concentrating (Department for Education, 2014). These educational aims amalgamate with the aims of a social dream matrix (Lawrence, 2005). Children in this early developmental phase of schooling are encouraged to paint, draw to allow for the inner world of imagination, ideas and fantasy to be amply expressed and developed.

Points of Reflection

- Have you encouraged children to share their dreams when you are working with them, or have you dismissed their dream experiences?
- What is your relationship to your dream world?
- How do you perceive spirituality as a developmental domain?

The Key Ideas and Implementation of Social Dream Matrixes

The social dream matrix method suggests that affirmation of dreaming creates a depth or expansion of thinking to develop an 'authority of the mind' for children, which can be carried on into adult hood rather than supressed (Lawrence, 2005: 23–26). Lawrence's hypothesis of thinking, dreaming and consciousness has been part of the research into the 'continuum of thinking' (2005: 31) and the 'continuum of consciousness' (2005: 32) where the mind can be perceived as the conscious and unconscious. Research by Hartmann (2000: 67) suggested that valuing the unconscious could enhance a more holistic approach to dreaming. Hartmann's theory of the wake-to-dreaming continuum as a way of removing the boundaries between waking life, and unconscious dream life, taps into creative aspects of thinking. Continuum research offers potential to demonstrate how the conscious and unconscious influence how humans learn, and dreaming is a natural conduit to more awareness. This opens up discussion of the possibility of balancing the highly debated heavily weighted subject-based curriculum in the United Kingdom (Ecclestone and Hayes, 2009; House, 2011, 2018; House and Loewenthal, 2009). Gambini (2012), a Jungian analyst and author, undertook dream research within Brazilian schools and reported that children's well-being and academic writing skills were enhanced by sharing dreams in schools. However, there is contrasting debate around the barriers to accepting therapeutic attitudes in the relationship between teachers and pupils in British schools (Ecclestone and Hayes, 2009; Mallon, 2002). The main issue is the capacity for schools to firstly accept and then to develop feasible ways of containing a child's unconscious world as a resource to enhance learning (Douglas, 2007).

There are ethical questions surrounding the theory; implementation using a social dream matrix in a school context is illustrated in *The Infinite Possibilities of Social Dreaming* (Lawrence, 2007). However, Selvaggi suggests that a social dream matrix is an informative tool, informing researchers/practitioners about how the media culture influences young children and how to help them cope or integrate the messages they absorb. The use of social dreaming as a 'pedagogic instrument' can build social containers and develop imagination (Selvaggi, 2010: 63). Once ground rules and expectations are explained, the social dream matrix is no different from how any social Circle Time in an infant school is practised (Mosley, 1996).

The Case Study Implementation of the Research Is Described Below Followed by a Checklist of the Implementation Process

The children were enthusiastic and interested in searching for dreams, and the children grasped that the focus of the project was about sleep, not conscious dreams. The point and expectations of the 'Circle Dream Time' were explained. This included established Personal, Social, Health and Economic Education (PSHE) routines and prosocial skills: happening at a regular time and place, using small toys in a sand tray, sharing dreams, acting out dreams and listening to each other, not interrupting. Big Friendly Giant and Sophie dolls were introduced as the speaking objects, some story books about dreams were given to the class and that dream catchers would be made by the children. A final interview to reflect about their thoughts and feelings about sharing dreams in school was presented as an option.

Of the 22 children taking part, some children could wait and take turns, others were not yet socially mature enough to listen to others; the capacity to listen to others involves 'decentring' or empathic waiting (Piaget, 1969). Stickers were used as a behavioural approach to encourage a social skillset of speaking and listening in a group in school (Wheldall, 2012). Dream Time stickers were prepared for this purpose. It was not possible to use a traditional social matrix snowflake seating arrangement as proposed by the literature on social dream matrices (Lawrence, 2005: 100).

The prominent finding of the introduction to a Social Dream Time clarified that the concept of sleep dreams for the children was quite straightforward. When asked if they could recall some dreams, the replies were immediate and contained subjects such as Halloween dreams, bad dreams, nightmares, zombie dreams, Christmas dreams, my nanny's tortoise dream, dinosaur and stegosaurus dreams, skeletons, pirates, monsters, Ninjas, my toys and I think they are alive, imagination dreams, Danger Mouse dreams, a video game dream and a dream about people turning into anything. Overall, the children were excited, and a spontaneous chatty response started especially when The Big Friendly Giant film (Spielberg et al., 2016) was mentioned. Several children had seen the film in the holidays and wanted to share their experience.

Points of Reflection

- Can you imagine doing a dream time circle time?
- What would your initial thoughts be?

The Voices of the Children: Case Studies

Case Study: Dream Catchers

The reaction to making dream catchers as part of the project was varied. One child replied:

> 'I have one and it is amazing.' Adding that 'it works some days, and it is used to catch bad dreams, I have good dreams at my daddy's.'
>
> (Child 3): 'I have a dream catcher. I made it and it actually works.'
>
> (Child 6): 'I have a dream catcher, but it doesn't work.'

Grandmother's Dreamcatcher (McCain and Schuett, 2014), a story of a child's bad dreams and of making a dream catcher to help her in her transition to a new home, was shared with the children. Following this story, some dreams were shared within the group.

> Child 24 (boy with autism age 6): 'I dreamt about a Batman, Superman superhero; Batman is best because he rescues people. Superman comes to play, comes to fight bad guys, bad guys kick Superman, Batman hits like this.' (He uses the small toy figures of superhero to kick at each other.)
>
> Child 17 (boy aged 6), using toys: 'A giant aeroplane came and shooted [*shot*] it, then in came a flying parachute and dropped dinosaur to the ground, then tried to...' (In the background a child called out, 'I liked that dream').

Point of Reflection

Personal reflexivity around dreams is an essential part of being able to host a dream matrix. As you read these dream offerings, reflect upon what is going on in your professional mind what are you perceiving?

The children gave each other affirmations, supporting each other's self-esteem and friendships, but this could influence the children to make up dream stories to gain peer kudos. However, Cicogna (1991) argues this is not of importance as children do quickly know if daydreams or sleep dreams are presented, as illustrated below. Themes in the first matrix were flying, fighting and death, and the group was not inhibited in raising darker aspects of life.

Case Study: Power Rangers and Bad Guys

Child 10 (boy age 6, with Attention-deficit/hyperactivity disorder [ADHD]) using the toy figures in an animated drama as he dialogues: Power ranger and bad guy, power ranger tries to battle him and he (with toy figures bashes them together) fighting it, comes through volcano to get all bad guys, and jump on him and eat him, into ocean then to get hands off, spooky house to make plans, ghost go out digging and hole, power ranger goes higher.

A child in the background said, 'It's a good one, like a film last night'.

One boy became excited and physically animated with much of the play action taking place up in the air around his head with flying involving fighting and rescuing between the characters. However, although it appeared to be a spontaneous, it was difficult to tell if it was a sleep dream. The work of Cicogna (1991, as cited in Colace, 2010) and Selvaggi (2010: 59), indicated that children will tell stories which are made up rather than actual sleep dream content, and the way the recall is 'told with a faltering voice or too many details' can indicate the extent to which it is or is not from the dream unconscious. However, one aspect of a social dream matrix is to observe and draw out patterns of unconscious themes from the participants within the institution in which the group is working (Lawrence, 2005).

Considering Special Educational Needs (SEN) and Dream Time Research Findings

A boy, with ADHD, repeated negative dream content and flying actions compare to a study by Schredl and Sartorius (2010). Schredl indicated that the dreams of children with ADHD were more negatively toned and included more misfortunes/threats, negative endings and physical aggression towards the dreamer, of which flying dreams are typical. As he was retelling his story, he was sensitive to see who was watching him and was adapting as he went on and pleased that his peers were listening. It may have started as a sleep dream, but he took it into impulsive imaginative play and, possibly, a way to make friends.

Points of Reflection

The work of Carl Jung refers to personality development all that is emotional, imaginative and the evolving process of consciousness. Children are more unconscious than adults, so be sensitive to their world views and feelings.

- Do you agree that children are more unconscious than adults?
- How can we respond sensitively to children's world views and feelings?

The Research Analysed Against Jung's Famous Seminars on Children's Dreams

Children chose small world toys to share dreams, creating a more detailed or extensive imaginative story with a different vocal animated tone compared to how other memories were being told. Boys in the group were complimentary to each other if adventure and fighting occurred. Both boys when retelling their dreams, demonstrated by holding the characters high in the air as well as having them do lots of flying and falling to the ground. This aligns with Jung's account in 'Seminar Three' (2008: 132–134), where he discussed the dream of a boy in which the boy ascended to heaven and was instructed by St Peter to go back to the Earth. In Pullman's trilogy entitled *His Dark Materials* (2007), he creatively orientated the story between the idea of parallel worlds, and the North Pole was a crucial place, where transcendent transpersonal change happens to the children Lyra and Will.

In further discussing the boy's dream in 'Seminar Three', Jung (2008) explained that this dream illustrated that 'something is happening innately to the child' and discussed the effect of schooling upon the unconscious. 'We have to be careful that the school does not destroy the natural functioning of the psyche' (Jung, 2008: 133). Here Jung proposed that 'the first school years bring about a couple of adjustment difficulties for the child'; the development of the unconscious includes the danger of 'splitting...between consciousness and [fantasy].... This manifests itself in children's being 'in the air', unable to pay attention. They are really devoured by their intuitions' (Jung, 2008: 134). Jung concluded that in the boy's dream, 'flying upward, and floating in the air, are a danger. That is why the unconscious intervenes and tries to stop the process'. Jung was objectively giving his perspective of normalising the child's transition into society and how the unconscious present's the child's experiences felt sense symbolically in the dream as the infant moves into consciousness. The participant boys' movements when retelling their dreams were a balance between flying high in the air and coming back to the ground. This could represent the playing out of the Ego-Self Axis theory (Neumann, 1988: 47). Regarding Jung's model of the psyche, he stated that 'The ego is ... a clown acting as if it were the leading actor' (Jung, 2008: 134). But in fact, 'the centre of a human being lies in the unconscious.... We want to see ourselves as natural superpowers.... [but we] underestimate the unconscious' (Jung, 2008: 47). The children in the first matrix were possibly clowning and laughing to develop ego strength and friends, but something from the network of the collective unconscious seemed to be playing itself out too.

In contrast to Jung's analysis, contemporary research by Garfield (2009) indicates that children as young as four have recalled dreams of flying and that it is a preferred and happy dream experience. The prevalent motifs of 21st century children's dreams from recent research indicates that monsters and TV characters appear in dreams and are more common in boys (Honig & Nealis, 2012; Johnson & Campbell, 2016; Schredl & Hofmann, 2003; Schredl & Sartorius, 2010).

It was clear that the small world toys and the subject of dreams had engaged the children and inspired some imaginative sharing. This group of six-year olds who usually found it hard to listen in a large group surprised the teacher when they managed to stay involved for 40 minutes. The spontaneous responses encouraged pupil engagement to a greater degree than other Circle Time activities, which are more directed towards knowledge than feelings or inner world dialogue.

A Comparative Analysis of Themes and Symbols From the Dream Time Research Project

In the introduction matrix, the collective themes apart from the theme of flying involved dark content: killing, fighting, death and resurrection, such as being rescued or brought back to life by parents, but also lighter themes of family members, pets, TV characters and superheroes. These collective shadowy themes are in line with other researchers' findings of dream content and themes for this developmental age (Beaudet, 1990, 2008; Bulkeley, 2012; King and Welt, 2011; Schredl and Hofmann, 2003; Schredl & Sartorius, 2010; Szmigielska, 2010; Woolley, 1995). It is possible that the school environment affected the dream content specifically if linked to Jung and Neumann's theory of the splitting of the psyche. These children's dreams presented symbolically that something within was being killed off, and this was coming through in the dream compensation.

In one of the earliest studies of children's dreams, undertaken by Kimmins (1920, 2012) in 1918 in London schools, the same pattern of the theme of fighting appeared in young children's dreams, especially boys, but this was contextualised in the First World War. These themes of children and experiences of war and conflict were raised by Mallon in her research of children living in Northern Ireland in 1989 during conflict and unrest (2002) and their dreams helped them to process their lived experiences. These research findings by Kimmins and Mallon demonstrate that external influences can affect dream content.

Points of Reflection

- Why would you be unsure of listening to a child's nightmare?
- Dreams and nightmares are symbolic not literal; they often indicate feeling states about lived experiences and a window into their inner personality. This helps you attune to their regulatory needs.
- Recall a dream or nightmare you have had and how it felt to share it with another person.

Chapter Summary

The research outlines key highlights from the research process of analysis of six matrices through a specific psychological and developmental lens, Jungian theory, and the development of the personality, presenting specific perspectives regarding a practitioner observing unique personality developmental ideas of consciousness, personality traits, ego states and the evolving capacity of young children to conform to group social expectations in educational settings. The children's dreams indicated the possible effects of school on the children's emotions, and gender different themes were apparent, with boys dreaming of fighting, flying and rescue situations, while girls dreamt more about animals, insects and Disney characters. The research raises questions surrounding dreams of children with ADHD, with themes of flying and fear of bad dreams, also common experiences in other research findings of children with ADHD (Schredl and Sartorius, 2010). The key to hosting the children's social interactions and maintaining the essence of the method's aims was due to preparation of relevant resources: the dream journal entries, toys, stories and name pegs randomly pulled out for turn taking.

The greatest social and emotional developments were the children's improved natural spontaneity in questioning and their sustained interest in dreams, therefore indicating the matrices experience improved listening, empathy and prosocial skills. The integration by the researcher of creative tools such as sand trays, small toys and acting out were unique to this dream matrix group and encouraged the children's development of listening and the amplification of the children's dreams. The individual choices of props or delivery indicated how the child's personality typology of introvert or extrovert can be assessed (Jung, 1971). The interactions indicated how emotionally charged a dream matrix can become for a child. These observations open the potential for further researcher to discuss children's unconscious and conscious prosocial behaviours and attitudes towards validating emotional containment in school environments. As Cullingford (1991: 175) suggested in *The Inner World of the School*, 'many of the attitudes' children derive from their school experiences are a result of wide-ranging discussions with their peer groups. . .. Many of the moral issues that concern children appear to be left to the children to talk about with each other. The prosocial skills practised or observed in a social dream matrix can be developed through subjective issues more than objective thoughts. These perceptions and the value of peer group sharing would contribute to the discourses of other protagonists who promote developing a move towards merging existing educational psychology and holistic education, which supports a child's inner world as an important resource within an educational context (Adams, 2014; Jones et al., 2008; King and Welt, 2011; Neville, 1989; Semetsky, 2012).

The findings from the children's unprompted reactions show that sharing dreams is an exciting and stimulating social exercise even if bad dreams are shared. The themes and dream content across the matrices, which showed numerous archetypal images of animals, monsters and mythical creatures, correlates with Jung's (2008) theories of the symbolism of the collective unconscious and concurs with other researchers who found archetypal dream images and examples of Jung's dream story schema (Kimmins, 1920/2012, Johnson & Campbell, 2016).

School life can also influence a child's dream content and felt sense in positive and stimulating ways as evidenced by the children's sustained eagerness to share dreams, and the expressed feelings of confidence during the dream matrices analysis. In addition, it is evident that Circle Time is an effective activity in which to integrate Dream Time into the existing curriculum, although there are other opportunities, as discussed by Adams (2014).

Key Points

- Social dream matrices and dream time have demonstrated the value and positive activity within an educational setting.
- Children need to share their dream worlds and emotional inner experiences to a trusted adult.
- Jungian psychology, specifically the theory of consciousness could be utilised more in teaching training and educational policy.

Further Reading

Lloyd, C. (2020) Dreaming at School: A Qualitative Depth Psychological Research Project on Sharing Dreams in a British Infant School. PhD thesis, University of Essex. https://repository.essex.ac.uk/28086/

Children's Dreams: An exploration of Jung's concept of big dreams https://www.tandfonline.com/doi/abs/10.1080/13644360304632

Dream Time with Children https://www.brendamallon.com/books/dream-time-with-children/

Bibliography

Adams, K., Hyde, B., & Woolley, R. (2008). *The spiritual dimension of childhood*. London: Jessica Kingsley.

Adams, K., (2010). *Unseen worlds: Looking through the lens of childhood*. London: Jessica Kingsley.

Adams, K., Koet, J., & Koning, B. (Eds.). (2015). *Dreams and spirituality: A handbook for ministry, spiritual direction and counselling*. Norwich: Canterbury Press.

Adams, K. (2005). Voices in my dream: Children's interpretation of auditory messages in divine dreams. *Dreaming*, 15(3), 195–204. Retrieved from doi:10.1037/1053-0797.15.3.195

Adams, K., Bull, R., & Maynes, M. L. (2016). Early childhood spirituality in education: Towards an understanding of the distinctive features of young children's spirituality. *European Early Childhood Education Research Journal*, 24(5), 760–774. Retrieved from doi:10.1080/1350293X.2014.996425

Adams, K., & Hyde, B. (2008). Children's grief dreams and the theory of spiritual intelligence. *Dreaming*, 18(1), 58–67. Retrieved from doi:10.1037/1053-0797.18.1.5

Adams as cited in Hoffmann & Lewis (2014): 17.

Agresta & Planera, as cited in Lawrence, The creativity of social dreaming (2010).

Bainbridge, A., Formenti, L et al. (Eds.). (2021). *Discourses, Dialogue and Diversity in Biographical Research: An Ecology of Life and Learning*. Leiden: Brill Sense.

Beaudet, D. (1990). *Encountering the monster: Pathways in children's dreams*. London: Continuum.

Beaudet, D. (2008). *Dreamguider: Open the door to your child's dreams*. Charlottesville: Hampton Roads Pub.

Colace, C. (2010). *Children's dreams: From Freud's observations to modern dream research*. London: Karnac Books.

Cullingford, C. (1991). *The inner world of the school: Children's ideas about schools*. London: Cassell Education Ltd.

Department for Education. (2011) *Early years foundation stage*. Retrieved from https://www.gov.uk/early-years-foundation-stage

Department for Education. (2014). *The National Curriculum for England: Key stages 1-4*. London. Retrieved from https://www.gov.uk/government/publications/national-curriculum-in-england-framework-for-key-stages-1-to-4

Department for Education. (2011). *Spiritual development*. Retrieved from http://webarchive.nationalarchives.gov.uk/20130903160914/http://www.education.gov.uk/schools/teachingandlearning/curriculum/a00199700/spiritual-and-moral Archived September 2013

Douglas, H. (2007). *Containment and reciprocity: Integrating psychoanalytic theory and child development research for work with children*. London: Taylor & Francis.

Ecclestone, K., & Hayes, D. (2009). *The dangerous rise of therapeutic education*. London: Taylor & Francis.

Fordham, M. (1944). *The life of childhood: A contribution to analytical psychology*. London: Kegan Paul, Trench, Trubner company.

Fordham, M. (1969). *Children as individuals*. London: Hodder & Stoughton.

Foulkes, D. (1982). *Children's dreams: Longitudinal studies*. New Jersey: John Wiley & Sons Inc. First Printing, Highlighting edition.

Freud, S. (1997). *Freud's interpretation of dreams* (A. Brill, Trans.). Hertfordshire: Wordsworth Editions.

Gambini, R. (2003). *Soul and culture*. Texas: Texas A & M University Press.

Gambini, R. (2012). Dreams can see through. *Spring Journal. Winter 2012* (Environmental disasters and collective trauma).

Garfield, P. (1984). *Your child's dreams*. New York: Ballantine Books.

Garfield, P. (2009). *The dream book: A young person's guide to understanding Dreams*. Toronto: Tundra.

Hartmann, E. (2000). The waking-to-dreaming continuum and the effects of emotion. *Behavioral and Brain Sciences*, 23(6), 947–950. Retrieved from doi:10.1017/S0140525X00474029

Hay, D., & Nye, R. (2006). *The spirit of the child*. London: Jessica Kingsley.

Hemsley. (2022). *Breathe* (n.p.). Wildmark Publishing.

Hoffmann, C. & Lewis, J. E. (2014). *Weaving dreams into the classroom*. Florida: Brown Walker Press.

Honig, A. S., & Nealis, A. L. (2012). What do young children dream about? *Early Child Development and Care*, 182(6), 771–795. Retrieved from doi:10.1080/03004430.2011.579797

House, R (2011). *Too much, too soon? Early learning and the erosion of childhood*. Stroud: Hawthorn Press Ltd.

House, R. (2018). *Too much too soon initiative*. Retrieved from http://www.toomuchtoosoon.org/latest-news.html

House, R., & Loewenthal, D. (2009). *Childhood, well-being and a therapeutic ethos*. London: Karnac Books.

Johnson, & Campbell, J. M. (2016). *Sleep monsters and superheroes: Empowering children through creative dreamplay*. California: ABC-CLIO Publishing Company.

Jones, R., Clarkson, A., Congram, S., & Stratton, N. (2008). *Education and imagination: Post-Jungian perspectives*. Hove: Taylor & Francis.

Jung. (1971). *CW 6. Psychological types*. New York: Pantheon Books.

Jung, C. G. (2008). Children's dreams. In J. Lorenz & M. Meyer-Grass (Eds.), (E. Felzeder, Trans.) (English). *Woodstock*. Oxfordshire: Princeton University Press.

Kimmins, C. (1920). *Childrens dreams*. Penguin: Longmans, Green and Company.

Kimmins, C. W. (2012). *Children's dreams*. Los Angeles: HardPress.

King, P. B., K., & Welt, B. (2011). *Dreaming in the classroom: Practices, methods, and resources in dream education*. New York: SUNY PRESS.

Lawrence, W. G. (2005). *Introduction to social dreaming: Transforming thinking*. London: Karnac.

Lawrence, W. G. (2007). *Infinite possibilities of social dreaming*. London: Karnac Books.

Lawrence, W. G. (2010). *The creativity of social dreaming*. London: Karnac Books.

Lloyd, C. (2020). *Dreaming at School: A Qualitative Depth Psychological Research Project on Sharing Dreams in a British Infant School*. PhD thesis, University of Essex. https://repository.essex.ac.uk/28086/

Lloyd, C. (2020). *Dreaming at School: A Qualitative Depth Psychological Research Project on Sharing Dreams in a British Infant School*. PhD thesis, University of Essex. https://repository.essex.ac.uk/28086/

McDonald, K. (2019). *Unschooled: Raising curious well-educated children outside the conventional classroom*. Chicago: Chicago Review Press Incorporated.

Manley, J. (2014). Gordon Lawrence's social dreaming matrix: Backgrounds, origins, history and developments. *Journal of Organisational and Social Dynamics*, 14(2), 322–341.

Mallon, B. (2002). *Dream time with children*. London: Jessica Kingsley.

Mallon, B. (2018). *Building continuing bonds for grieving and bereaved children: A*

McCain, B., & Schuett, S. (1998, 2014). *Grandmother's dreamcatcher*. Park Ridge, Illinois: Albert Whitman.

Mosley, J. (1996) *Circle time in the primary classroom*. London: Learning Development Ideas.

Neumann, E. (1954). *Origins and history of consciousness*. New York: Pantheon.

Neumann, E. (1988). *The child: Structure & dynamics of the nascent personality*. London: Karnac.

Neville, B. (1989). *Educating psyche: Emotion, imagination, and the unconscious in learning.* Melbourne: Collins Dove.

Nye, R. (2009). *Children's spirituality: What it is and why it matters.* London: Church House Publishing.

Piaget, J. (1962). *Play, dreams, and imitation in childhood.* New York: W. W. Norton & Co.

Piaget, J. (1969). *The theory of stages in cognitive development: An address by Jean Piaget to the CTB/McGraw-Hill Invitational Conference on Ordinal Scales of Cognitive Development, Monterey, California, February 9, 1969.* New York: CTB/McGraw-Hill.

Pullman, P. (2007). *His dark materials.* New York: Alfred A. Knopf Publishers.

Punnett, A. (Ed.). (2018). *Jungian child analysis.* Sheridan, Wyoming: Fisher King Press.

Schredl, M., & Hofmann, F. (2003). Continuity between waking activities and dream activities. *Consciousness and Cognition,* 12(2), 298–308. Retrieved from doi:10.1016/S1053-8100(02)00072-7

Schredl, M., & Sartorius, H. (2010). Dream recall and dream content in children with attention deficit/hyperactivity disorder. *Child Psychiatry and Human Development,* 41(2), 230–238. Retrieved from doi:10.1007/s10578-009-0163-8

Semetsky, I. (2012). *Jung and educational theory.* New York: Wiley.

Semetsky, I. (2013). *Jung and educational theory.* New Jersy: Wiley.

Spielberg, S., Marshall, F., & Mercer, S. (Producers), & Spielberg, S. (Director). (2016). *The BFG [Motion Picture].* Walt Disney Studios.

Szmigielska, B. (2010). *Children's dreams.* New York: Nova Science Publisher Inc.

Taylor, B., & Francis, K. (2013). *Qualitative research in the health sciences: Methodologies, methods and processes.* London: Taylor & Francis.

Van de Castle, R. L. (1994). *Our dreaming mind.* University of California: Ballantine Books.

Watson, J. (2010). Whose model of spirituality should be used in the spiritual development of school children? *International Journal of Children's Spirituality,* 5(1), 91–101.

Wheldall, K. (2012). *The behaviourist in the classroom.* Abingdon-On-Thames.

Wickes, F. G. (1963). *The inner world of childhood.* Lanham, Maryland: Sigo Press, U.S.

Winnicott, D. W. (2012). *Playing and reality.* London: Taylor & Francis.

Woolley, J. (1995). The fictional mind: Young children's understanding of imagination, pretense, and dreams. *Developmental Review,* 15(2), 172–211. Retrieved from doi: 10.1006/drev.1995.1008

Young-Eisendrath, P., & Dawson, T. (1997). *The Cambridge companion to Jung.* Cambridge: Cambridge University Press.

Zwiers, M., & Morrissette, P. J. (2013). *Effective interviewing of children: A comprehensive guide for counsellors and human service workers.* London: Taylor & Francis.

12 Emotional Safety

Becky Edwards

After reading this chapter, readers will be able to:

- Outline what is meant by emotional safety.
- Analyse the role of practitioners in helping to support children to feel emotionally safe.
- Explore how to create an environment where children feel emotionally safe.

Introduction

We are living in precarious times. We are experiencing a period of unprecedented social and economic upheaval in a world ravaged by war, hunger, poverty and inequity. We are inhabitants of a planet that is struggling to survive the growing impact of global warming and climate change. We are a society emerging from a pandemic which has left many of our children and young adults feeling anxious and vulnerable and we do not know how long it will last and how far its shadow has been cast. It is easy to feel overwhelmed by a sense of helplessness, by the fear that we are watching a global and societal unravelling. The future for our children is full of uncertainty and unknown challenges. As educators, teachers and practitioners, we may not have the answers to the problems they will face but we do have the capacity to improve their present by ensuring that they feel emotionally safe, that schools and settings are 'islands of safety' in an often-chaotic world (Van der Kolk, 2015). By developing positive relationships and predictable, nurturing environments, by ensuring that they feel constantly valued and cared for, we can help our children to grow and flourish without fear of failure. Children who feel emotionally safe learn better, have a stronger sense of self and agency and will be better prepared to face what lies ahead of them (Shean and Mander, 2020; Van der Kolk, 2015).

If children do not feel emotionally safe, they will struggle to become effective learners, develop trusting relationships or to achieve their potential (Shean and Mander, 2020). Yet the concept of how to develop a sense of emotional safety in the early years is rarely discussed or prioritised. This chapter will explore what is meant by emotional safety and how to create an early years environment where children feel emotionally safe, valued and able to learn.

What Does Emotional Safety Mean?

Emotional safety is a subjective, individual and fluctuating feeling (Vincent, 1995) which depends on a sense of acceptance and belonging (Whalley-Hammell, 2014) and on the consistency and predictability of an environment free from physical and emotional threat. When all these elements come together, when trusted adults can hold and contain the fears and anxieties of the children they support (Bion, 1962), emotional safety begins to develop. But environment alone is not enough. For children to feel emotionally safe, positive and trusting relationships must be built with key adults who set consistent boundaries and are predictable in their responses. Once trust and safety are established, children can relax, and are ready to engage, explore and learn. Quiros et al. (2012) state that emotional safety is created when certain conditions are met:

- a space where there are familiar, trusted adults is a safe space;
- an environment which sets consistent and familiar expectations is a safe environment;
- a predictable world is a safe world.

Predictability removes the anxiety created by fear of the unknown and the unexpected; it is enhanced by a structured and clear curriculum but it is the consistent behaviour of the adults children trust that is most important. For children the knowledge that key adults will behave today as they did yesterday brings order, calmness and certainty. Emotional safety is created when children know what to expect from the spaces and people that matter the most.

The Building Blocks of Emotional Safety

Attachment

Emotional safety is built upon an 'invisible network of relationships', (Perry, 2000). Children in an early years setting, often leaving their parent for the first time, will experience an initial sense of loss and separation. It is only with the gradual development of a trusting relationship and a sense of emotional bonding with key people that children begin to feel safe and secure. Children need to find someone who can safely hold their feelings and who can safeguard their sense of wholeness (Van der Kolk, 2015). Healthy attachments ensure that children have a secure base from which to explore, that they have an emotional anchor point in an unfamiliar environment and that they can be certain that they have someone to return to if they become anxious or overwhelmed. Children learn best when they are healthy, safe and secure, when their individual needs are met, and when they have positive relationships with the adults caring for them (DfE, 2023).

Healthy attachments depend on the skill of practitioners to contain the emotions of the children they work with (Bion, 1962) and to be attuned and emotionally synchronised, with their feelings, needs and actions (Trevarthen and Aitken, 2001).

Secure attachments are integral to the development of emotional safety. They form the foundations from which children develop a sense of self, a meta-awareness of who they are and how they are perceived by others, safe in the knowledge that there is always someone close by who can help them to make sense of the world around them. When they are terrified, nothing calms children down like the reassuring voice of someone they trust. The knowledge that someone bigger and stronger than them is taking care of things allows them to let go of their fear and to relax and re-focus.

What helps:

- home visits before the child starts school or nursery so that the teacher or key person is familiar;
- a photo of their key person which they can keep at home before they join the school or nursery;
- being greeted by their key person as they come into the setting each day;
- ensuring that there is a 'buddy', system so that if the key person is absent, children still know have a familiar adult to turn to for support;
- consistent and predictable responses from key people.

Belonging

While positive attachments are key to emotional safety, a sense of belonging also plays an essential role in ensuring that children feel safe and secure. In 1943, Maslow included the concepts of both safety and belonging in his hierarchy of physiological and emotional needs. According to Maslow (1943), safety, which links to being part of a family and the ability to make social connections, must be in place before a sense of belonging – linked to friendship, family, intimacy and a sense of connection – can be achieved. For children, this division between feeling safe and a sense of belonging is less clear. Emotional safety is created when children feel a sense of connection with their peers and trusted adults, when they feel that they are part of something bigger than themselves and that they are included and valued within a group. Involvement in collaborative play and positive social interactions creates a sense of connection and a feeling of wholeness that has been linked to feelings of well-being and happiness (Tonneijck et al., 2008; Ware et al., 2007). A sense of belonging engenders feelings of self-worth and identity (Van der Kolk, 2015). When children do not feel included, when they remain on the edges of the micro-communities that develop in schools and settings, they are likely to feel excluded, marginalised and lonely. Being able to feel safe with other people is linked to positive mental health (Van der Kolk, 2014) and is fundamental to the development of a sense of emotional safety.

What helps:

- photos and names on coat pegs from the day the children arrive;
- children's names available for self-registration from the first day;
- ensuring that children gain a strong sense of being part of a group through daily group-time activities at the end of sessions;
- ensure children see themselves and their families reflected in displays and photos;

- support engagement with small group activities during nursery sessions;
- help children to bridge the developmental stage between parallel play and working together to enhance collaboration and opportunities for friendships to develop;
- help children to understand that their views are welcomed;
- allow enough time for children to process information before expecting a response (for example count to 10).

The Amygdala Hijack

When emotional safety is lacking, children can feel overwhelmed or threatened. When this happens, they become hyper-vigilant and their brain, sensing danger prioritises survival, responding by letting the emotional brain (the limbic system) flood the logical brain (the neocortex) which is responsible for learning. This triggers a tiny part of the limbic system, the amygdala, to prepare the body to fight, to run away or to freeze to avoid being noticed (Goleman, 2007) The emotional impact of the amygdala hijack causes children to behave in different ways: they can become confrontational (fight), escape mentally by ignoring what is said to them (flight) or hold their breath or appear to be absent (freeze). While children are feeling threatened or fearful (or hungry or tired), while their brains are flooded with emotions and their bodies are preparing to defend themselves, they cannot learn or focus; they will not care about new experiences or exploring, instead they will search for the safe and the familiar (Perry, 2000). They depend on adults to intuitively understand this need for survival (Ditter, 1988). While meeting physiological needs ensures survival (Maslow, 1943), meeting emotional needs ensures a sense of safety. Emotional safety depends on adults being able to meet both these needs. Children need support to stop or prevent an amygdala hijack, to regulate their feelings, to re-anchor themselves, emotionally, in the present and physically, in their environment. This depends on the development of reciprocal relationships with key adults and on the capacity of those trusted key people to contain the emotions that are threatening safety and preventing learning and engaging.

What helps:

- know the potential triggers for fight, flight and freeze reactions in each child;
- calming activities such as breathing exercises;
- ensure that there are relaxing, quiet spaces.

Reciprocity and Containment

Effective reciprocal relationships in childhood are transactional, based on a continual cycle of emotional giving and receiving (Schwarz et al., 2005). Secure attachments ensure healthy reciprocal relationships where children are confident that if they cry or point, they will be comforted or given what they need, in response parents and/or carers feel valued and fulfiled. Effective reciprocal actions form the basis of positive relationships and create a world that is safe and predictable; and if the world becomes too overwhelming, children depend on those reciprocal adults to contain and hold their emotions (Bion, 1962), filtering and absorbing their anxieties and fears. In a new and unfamiliar environment, children search for reciprocal certainty, for someone who will fulfil their needs and contain their concerns and safeguard their sense of wholeness (Van der Kolk, 2015). When reciprocity breaks down, when children do not know who to turn to for their needs to be met and are uncertain who will hold their emotions when they feel overwhelmed, emotional safety is lost. For overworked often emotionally and physically exhausted practitioners, developing effective emotional transactions with every child can be challenging. It demands time and 'headspace', empathy and understanding, but if successful, it gives children the courage to be curious, to follow their innate desire to explore and to learn new things. When children feel contained and that their needs are reciprocally responded to, independence is enhanced and a sense of agency, the belief that they have control over what happens to them, is created.

What helps:

- an effective key person and buddy system;
- time and patience to develop trusting relationships;
- train staff in trauma informed practice and interventions.

Point of Reflection

- What happens when relationships are not reciprocal?

Locus of Control

If children feel in control of what is happening to them, if their world is predictable and the actions of others are consistent, if they are given ownership of their learning and input into their environment, they develop a strong internal locus of control (Rotter, 1966). This creates a sense of agency where children feel that they matter and that their actions make a difference to themselves and others. A strong internal locus is linked to academic achievement and emotional maturity (Kalter et al., 1984). Children with an external locus of control are more likely to grow up believing that they cannot influence what happens to them, that they are unimportant and that their actions are meaningless. This evokes feelings of powerless and causes anxiety. Children cannot feel safe when their world feels out of their control. By giving children ownership of their learning through child-centred activities and ensuring they have a voice, they are more likely to engage in activities, build social connections and grow in self-esteem. The role of the practitioner is key to the creation of emotionally safe environments where children feel safe enough to express their feelings and to explore and learn. By containing feelings, creating a sense of belonging empowering the children they teach, they support the emotional growth and safety that is necessary for children to grow and achieve.

What helps:

- create an environment where children feel confident to express their views and feelings;
- ensure that every child is praised for succeeding at something;
- remind children of the ways in which their views are reflected in displays and activities.

Points of Reflection

- Are loci of control fixed?
- Does a sense of agency alter depending on the situation and environment?

Transitions

Transitions are an integral part of life. But while adults have control over when transitions occur, children are often transitioned by others as they move between environments and activities: such as from home to school or setting; from inside to outside; from structured activities to unstructured play time; from informal social time to formal learning time; from mealtime to activity time; from school or setting, back home. A child's day is a ceaseless series of transitions, a constant movement between periods of stability (Levinson, 1986). Transitions are unpredictable and can create feelings of anxiety and stress (Green and Edwards, 2023), and necessitate adaptation (Schlossberg, 2005), and implicit in even micro-transitions is the knowledge that they begin with an ending (Chickering and Schlossberg, 2002). While emotional safety depends on predictability and consistency, transitions represent uncertainty and disruption. With each movement between environments and activities, children need to re-calibrate and re-assess, to re-focus and re-attach, to anticipate altered expectations and adapt their actions to meet changing demands. For children in search of emotional safety, the perpetual temporariness of a daily routine punctuated by transitions can cause a heightened sense of uncertainty which can begin as they walk through the door. In order to counteract the anxiety engendered by the transitioning process, it is essential that children understand that they matter to someone in the places that they are transitioning from and to (Anderson et al., 2012), that wherever they end up they are important to people who are interested in and concerned about them (Marshall, 2001). If children, can be consistently certain that a trusted adult will be waiting for them in an unfamiliar environment, the anxiety caused by transition will be lessened and emotional safety can be re-asserted. For some children, a transitional object (Winnicott, 1951), a toy or object which they bring from home to the setting can provide a safe bridge between their familiar home and their new and unfamiliar setting. The transitional object offers security, in an insecure world. It is important that a setting understands the importance of these to emotional safety and rather than trying to prevent the child from holding on to them, gives them time to engage with their surroundings and emotionally transition and are ready to store it in a designated safe space (box or bag) which they can see but which is not accessible to ensure that transitional objects are not 'borrowed' by other children. As they begin to feel safer in the setting, they can leave their transitional object in the box or bag as they enter the room, secure in the knowledge that it will always be there if they need it. If the setting represents a child's safe space, it is important to let them choose a transitional object from the setting to take home, a link to the sense of emotional safety that might be missing for some children who may experience a chaotic or complicated home environment.

What helps:

- consistency and predictability,
- trusting relationships,
- visual timetables and
- awareness of the emotional impact of continual micro and macro-transitions.

Point of Reflection

- How do children know that they 'matter' to someone?

The Role of Practitioners in Creating Emotional Safety

To create emotional safety, practitioners must build secure attachments with (Bowlby, 1988) and contain the emotions of (Bion, 1962) the children they work with. Our brains are wired to find new environments threatening, without the support of a trusted person, the child is likely to experience fear in these circumstances. As Perry (2000: 35), a leading brain development scientist, points out: 'Fear kills curiosity and inhibits exploration'. A safe base to explore and learn is created when children can be certain that when they need assurance, a trusted adult will be there. Attunement between the practitioner and the child, the presence of an emotional synchronicity (Mukherji and Dryden, 2014) connoting empathy, understanding and containment ensures that children can explore a new environment free from the anxiety caused by emotional uncertainty.

Key Person Approach

An effective key person in an early years setting must possess many qualities and play many roles. As teachers and educators, they must have a holistic understanding of the intrinsic motivations of the children they work with. This is based on empathetic observation and understanding of lived experience of the child both in the setting and outside the setting. Effective key persons must be able to hold the whole child in mind

(Winnicott), while being consistently 'present', during interactions. A sense of congruent presence from the key person, the belief that they are truly listening and valuing what the child is doing and saying, supports the development of self-esteem, ensures that children feel emotionally and physically connected to their surroundings and that they gain a sense of belonging (Quiros et al., 2012). In a time-pressured, busy environment, being consistently present can be the greatest challenge for a key person but is also one of the most reciprocally rewarding experiences. Ensuring that all children are contained, receiving the attention they need, understand that they matter and are engaged in homeostatic activities, involves a complicated and complex tacit intertwining of individual and group needs, of planning developmentally appropriate activities and of creating a predictable yet stimulating environment where all children feel included and valued. An experienced key person can hold many children in mind (Winnicott, 1960) while interacting with individual children and reflecting in action (Schon, 1984) while maintaining a professional overview. Children, constantly transitioning to and from settings, tread a thin line between certainty and uncertainty, anxiety and confidence, threat and security, safety and lack of safety. A skilled practitioner, who has developed positive attachments and created non-threatening emotionally supportive environments, is able to help children to feel anchored, both physically and emotionally, in their learning. By creating environments that are predictable with clear expectations and consistent boundaries, children feel safe and grounded. By creating nurturing, caring and safe environments, children feel welcomed and unjudged, by allowing children to co-produce their learning, they will feel valued and understand that they belong. Caring practitioners who know the children well enough must constantly use their skills and knowledge to develop a sense of emotional safety in the children they work with.

Working With the Whole Family – Knowing the Whole Child

Effective practitioners understand the importance of working holistically with children. The creation of an emotionally safe environment depends not only on the development of positive relationships between the child and their key person but also on the relationships that are built with the whole family. Positive relationships between the setting and the home, where parents and/or carers and key people model trust and honesty, sends a message to children that they too can trust the adults in their setting to contain and support them (Mukherji and Dryden, 2014). A practitioner who only knows their key children from the time they spend in the setting, only knows part of those children. To provide the emotional support and consistency that children need, an effective practitioner must try to understand the whole child. At home children are often part of a complex microsystem with key people leaving or returning, in a blended family they might spend time with one parent and then another, or with siblings who are only present for the weekend. Their mesosystems, the connections between the people in the child's microsystem, can become a complicated moving web of interlinked relationships. A positive, honest, trusting relationship between parents, carers and practitioners ensures a holistic understanding of the child and is integral to the creation of quality interactions in the setting (Elfer et al., 2012) and a sense of well-being for the child. This commences with supporting the child as they transition from home to the nursery and from nursery to school. In order to ensure that these transitions are a time of positive emerging growth (Anderson et al., 2012) rather than of anxiety and stress (Green and Edwards, 2023), it is essential that the key person helps children to understand that they have someone in the setting who is interested in them, concerned about them and believes in them (Marshall, 2001). Settings that include initial home visits before children attend begin to build home-school bridges from the moment they meet the child. This can comfort both children and parents. Where messages from home and school are consistent, where children are continually aware of a positive relationship between their key person and their parents or carers, children will thrive.

Consistency and Predictability – Familiarity and Trust

When children feel that the world around them is safe and predictable, they are ready to learn and explore. Perry (2000: 2) describes children as 'drowning in novelt'y' when they start at a new setting. They must learn to navigate a new and unfamiliar world, bereft of the emotional attachments that keep them feeling 'safe' and anchored. Unpredictability causes uncertainty and uncertainty causes heightened levels of anxiety which trigger the fear response in the brain. Children experiencing an amygdala hijack, will not see a well-resourced early years setting as stimulating and inviting, but will instead be constantly scanning for threat and danger. A sense of emotional safety depends on consistent, nurturing and sensitive attention in an environment that is predictable with educators who are knowledgeable and caring (Perry, 2000). Expectations must be clear, timetables predictable and interactions consistent. Children feel comforted when those they trust respond in ways that they can predict and understand. Predictable, stable relationships with trusted adults assuage fears and create safety. For some children, experiencing trauma or chaotic home lives, their setting or school, their relationship with their key person, may become a beacon of emotional certainty in an uncertain world. Through careful planning, expert knowledge and a compassionate child-centred approach, practitioners can create environments that reduce anxiety and enhance emotional safety.

Environment

While it is the relationship with familiar adults that is key to emotional safety for children, the importance of creating an environment that evokes a sense of belonging and ownership cannot be underestimated. An environment that can lower anxiety levels, support smooth transitions and ensure children feel in control of their learning and relationships is an environment that feels emotionally safe. The subliminal messages received by children from what they see and hear as they enter a school or setting will tacitly impact their perception of the setting as a place of safety or of threat.

Emotionally Safe Environments – Owning and Belonging

Slaughter (2015) suggests that in order for children to engage positively with early years environments, they must be both inviting and potentiating, involving a mixture of child-initiated and adult-led activities which challenge and support problem-solving through sustained-shared thinking and co-created learning opportunities. If a child believes that their voice is always heard, that their views are consistently valued and that they regularly have ownership of their learning, they will gain a sense of self-worth and belonging that promotes emotional safety. An effective early years environment needs to reflect emotional warmth (Whitebread and Cardenas, 2012) ensuring children and families feel welcomed and included. For settings that have both indoor and outdoor environments, this must be true wherever children choose to play. Activities must be open-ended, designed to tacitly invite, encourage, challenge and develop learning without fear of failure. While an unchanging layout and design of learning spaces, ensures consistency and predictability, the available resources should be constantly changed to reflect interest and curiosity and to encourage exploration and learning. This demands careful planning and organisation of the physical space.

Physical Environment – Subliminal Messages

The design and organisation of physical spaces in settings provides subliminal messages to children, for example 'Come and play', 'You are welcome here', 'This is a big and busy place – be careful', 'Everything here is unfamiliar – I need to stay with the person I trust'. Practitioners need to think carefully about spaces, places and displays.

Spaces – to encourage co-construction and ownership of learning there must be unfilled space where children can create their own activities. Ephgrave (2018: 37) discusses the importance of ensuring that a rich variety of open-ended resources are available and accessible in all areas at all times, but nothing is set out. In such a potentialising environment, a child's locus of control is internal because they are in charge of their learning, using space to create activities which are interesting and personally meaningful. Spaces must be kept tidy, resources changed regularly (based on emerging interests) and kept in labelled spaces on shelves so that children always know where to find what they are looking for and where to put them away. Clear, well-organised resources set up around uncluttered spaces, prevent children from feeling overwhelmed. Open space means emotional space while organised, enticing, open-ended, non-prescriptive resources offer an invitation to play. It is clear where children should play – there is an empty space waiting to be filled; it is clear what they are expected to use – they are surrounded by inviting resources; and it is clear that they can decide what to play with. In this way the environment allows them to take control of their learning, if they make the rules and choose the tools, then they cannot get it wrong. Expectations are clear, anxiety is lowered, the threat of failure is removed and children are free to safely lose themselves in their play.

Places – while space connotes opportunity, an area that is waiting to be filled, a physical place is understood to be a space invested with social meaning, conventions and cultural understanding. We are located in 'space', but we act in 'place'. Just as a house protects us from the elements, a home is where we live. The places that children create in the space of an early years setting build a sense of belonging. Place for children links to emotional safety because it is familiar, predictable and part of a routine: children arrive and hang their coats in the place where their pegs are found, they know the place where their key worker will greet them, at the end of their session they go to their group room (which might be used as a different space for the rest of the session), for group time and this is often the place where their parents pick them up. Place is a familiar space that represents safety but also has an emotional meaning that enhances emotional safety. If children believe they have a place in a setting, that they are accepted for who they are, that what they do matters and makes a difference, then they will feel that they belong. While this is an abstract feeling, it can be made concrete through displays and resources. Human beings have an innate desire to feel at home wherever they find themselves (Angelou, 1984). Emotionally safe places in a setting play an essential role in an overall sense of well-being. For many children, easily overwhelmed by a busy environment and constant stimulation, it is important that a setting also contains quiet corners where they can hide themselves away, places of space and solitude where they can observe, process and reflect (Perry, 2000).

Displays – In the busyness of teaching days, displays can often be overlooked or left unchanged for many weeks. While this is understandable the subliminal messages given by what children see around them, cannot be underestimated. The sense that a child has ownership and control of their surroundings is visually transmitted if they see themselves or children like them in pictures and photos on the walls of their setting. Recognising their own names, seeing their own work displayed for everyone to see evokes a sense of pride and gives a clear message that their input is valued and celebrated. For children with English as an additional language (EAL), seeing signs written in their home language(s) ensures that the children and their families understand that they belong and that their culture is celebrated and valued, while the use of signs and symbols means that children with SEND feel included. Effective displays need no explanation but relay clear messages, creating a sense of visual emotional safety where children understand that effort is prioritised over results (Dweck, 2000).

Reception area – First impressions are more important than any other. The way in which a child and their family are greeted when they first arrive in a setting, the images on the walls, comfortable furniture, all these things matter. Ensuring that a setting feels welcoming to all whatever their needs or cultural background, takes time, thought and effort but can make the difference between a sense of emotional safety or a sense of confusion and uncertainty. Parents, sometimes separating from their children for the first time, are likely to be anxious and upset, parents with English as a second language will have the added worry that they or their children might not be understood. Initial impressions matter. From the moment they walk through the door, families need to be assured that they are welcome and that they are leaving their children in safe hands. A sense of nurture and warmth should emanate from the entrance. If families walk through the doors of a setting and see themselves and their children represented all around them, they will feel valued, welcomed and accepted. Children, attuned to the emotions of their parents and care givers, will sense this too. Emotional safety is not experienced in isolation, emotions are contagious, if children are secure in the knowledge that their primary carer is feeling calm and safe, the transition from home to school will feel less daunting.

Case Study: Elias

Elias is 3-years old. His family is asylum seekers from who have been living in a hotel room for the past year. He has two older brothers and a younger baby sister who was born in the United Kingdom. The family has been living together in one hotel room for the past year. He has very little English. His dad who brings him to nursery can speak a little English and explains that Elias used to be 'a good boy', but since the arrival of his sister he has begun to bite his mum and often has tantrums. The hotel has no outdoor area and Elias spends most of his day watching TV or running around the hotel room and sometimes the foyer. The country the family has fled from is war-torn and although the father cannot explain exactly what Elias might have seen, a case worker from the council has explained that it is likely that Elias has seen people killed in front of him. The family is currently awaiting the outcome of an application to become refugees and gain permanent leave to remain, but this could take up to 2 years.

On arrival at nursery school Elias clings to his father, screaming. After his father has left, Elias remains anxious and upset throughout his time at nursery. The only place where he calms down is when he is outside playing in the sandpit. He finds it difficult to share and bites and hits other children when they try to come and play next to him.

Points of Reflection

- You are Elias' key person.
- What can you do to help Elias to feel emotionally safe in the setting?
- How can you build a secure and trusting relationship with Elias and his family?

Chapter Summary

To the human brain, novelty, the unfamiliar and the unpredictable, all signal danger and threat. Fear and anxiety are innate human responses to new situations. Where boundaries and expectations are unclear, where trusting relationships are not built because staff are continually changing, where the layout and organisation of the physical environment is inconsistent and transitions are not carefully planned, children will not thrive. Emotional safety is key to learning. Early years environments must create safe places for children to talk about their emotions and feelings and calm containing spaces where they can sit and watch. Opportunities for play must be open-ended, resource rich and child-led. It is only when children feel completely safe that they can lose themselves in the flow of creativity and exploration, temporarily abandoning their worries and inhibitions to the all-consuming pleasure of play. Emotional safety depends on the skill of practitioners to build positive relationships, their holistic knowledge of a child and the creation of warm and welcoming environments that engender a sense of belonging and ownership. It depends on reciprocity, on children hearing and being heard, seeing, and being seen and on practitioners who care enough about every child, despite the constant demands and time pressures imposed upon them. Emotional safety is an innate human need. If its seeds are planted during a child's first experience of independent learning, if emotional safety is implicit in every part of their day, in each area of their setting and in all their relationships with trusted adults, their future will be rooted in a sense of self-worth and self-belief and anchored in their learning and experience. Emotional safety in the early years creates children who are socially competent and educationally confident. As educators, teachers and early years practitioners, we cannot predict the future but we can make the present predictable; we cannot provide solutions but we can help children to search for answers; we cannot map their path but we can help them to build an emotional compass to guide them through the challenges that lie ahead.

Key Points

- Emotional safety is key to children's development and learning.
- Emotional safety depends on the skill of practitioners to build positive trusting relationships with children and the creation of a warm and welcoming environment which engenders a sense of belonging and ownership.
- Emotional safety depends on consistency and predictability.

Further Reading

Ephgrave, A. (2018) *Planning in the Moment with Young Children. A Practical Guide for Early Years Practitioners and Parents* London, Routledge.

Quiros, L., Kay, L. and Montijo, A., (2012) Creating emotional safety in the classroom and in the field. *Reflections: Narratives of professional helping, 18*(2), pp.42–47.

Van der Kolk, B. (2015) *The Body Keeps the Score. Mind Brain and Body in the transformation of Trauma*. London, Penguin Books

References

Anderson, M., Goodman, J., and Schlossberg, N. (2012) *Counseling Adults in Transition: Linking Schlossberg's Theory with Practice in a Diverse World*, 4th ed. New York: Springer Publishing Company.

Angelou, M. (1984) *I Know Why the Caged Bird Sings*. London: Virago Press.

Bion, W. (1962). *Learning from Experience*. London: Heinemann.

Bowlby, J. (1988) *A secure base: Parent-child Attachment and Healthy Human Development*. New York: Basic Books.

Chickering, A., and Schlossberg, N. (2002) *Getting the Most Out of College*. New Jersey: Prentice Hall.

Department for Education [DfE] (2023) *EYFS Statutory Framework for Group and School Based Providers*. Available at: https://www.gov.uk/government/publications/early-years-foundation-stage-framework--2 (accessed 4.1.23).

Ditter, B. (1988, Winter) Emotional safety and growing up. *Journal School Safety*, 12–15.

Dweck, C. (2000) *Self-theories. Their Role in Motivation, Personality and Development*. New York and London: Taylor and Francis Psychology Press.

Elfer, P., Goldschmied, E., and Selleck, D. (2012) *Key Persons in the Nursery*, 2nd ed. London: David Fulton Publishers.

Ephgrave, A. (2018) *Planning in the Moment with Young Children. A Practical Guide for Early Years Practitioners and Parents*. London: Routledge.

Goleman, D. (2007) *Emotional Intelligence*, 10th ed. New York: Bantam Books.

Green, H., and Edwards, B. (2023) *True Partnerships in SEND*. London: Routledge.

Kalter, N., Alpern, D., Spence, R., and Plunkett, J. (1984) Locus of control in children of divorce. *Journal of Personality Assessment*, 48(4): 410–414.

Levinson, D. J. (1986) A conception of adult development. *American Psychologist*, 41(1): 3–13. doi:10.1037/0003-066X.41.1.3

Marshall, S. (2001) Do I matter? Construct validation of adolescents' perceived mattering to parents and friends. *Journal of Adolescence*, 24(4): 473–490.

Maslow, A. (1943) A theory of human motivation. *Psychological Review*, 50: 370–396.

Mukherji, P., and Dryden, L. (2014) *Foundations of Early Childhood. Principles and Practice*. London: SAGE.

Perry, B. (2000) Creating an emotionally safe classroom. *Early Childhood Today*, 15(1): 35.

Quiros, L., Kay, L., and Montijo, A. (2012) Creating emotional safety in the classroom and in the field. *Reflections: Narratives of professional helping*, 18(2): 42–47.

Rotter, J. (1966) Generalized expectancies for internal versus external control of reinforcement. *Psychological Monographs*, 80(1): 1–28.

Schon, D. (1984) The architectural studio as an exemplar of education for reflection-in-action. *Journal of Architectural Education*, 38(1): 2–9.

Schwarz, B., Trommsdorff, G., Albert, I., and Mayer, B. (2005) Adult parent–child relationships: Relationship quality, support, and reciprocity. *Applied Psychology*, 54(3): 396–417.

Shean, M., and Mander, D. (2020) Building emotional safety for students in school environments: Challenges and opportunities. In *Health and Education Interdependence: Thriving from Birth to Adulthood* (pp. 225–248). New York: Springer.

Slaughter, E. (2015) *Quality in the Early Years.* London: Open University Press.

Tonneijck, H., Kinébanian, A., and Josephsson, S. (2008) An exploration of choir singing: Achieving wholeness through challenge. *Journal of Occupational Science*, 15: 173–180. doi:10.1080/14427591.2008.9686627

Trevarthen, C. and Aitken, K. (2001) Infant Inter-subjectivity. Research Theory and clinical applications. *Journal of Child Psychology and Psychiatry*, 42(1): 3–48.

Van der Kolk, B. (2015) *The Body Keeps the Score. Mind Brain and Body in the Transformation of Trauma.* London: Penguin Books.

Vincent, S. (1995). Emotional safety in adventure therapy programs: can it be defined? *Journal of Experiential Education*, 18(2): 76–81. doi:10.1177/105382599501800204

Ware, N., Hopper, K., Tugenberg, T., Dickey, B., and Fisher, D. (2007) Connectedness and citizenship: Redefining social integration. *Psychiatric Services*, 58: 469–474. doi:10.1176/appi.ps.58.4.469

Whalley-Hammell, K. (2014) Belonging, occupation, and human well-being: An exploration. *Canadian Journal of Occupational Therapy*. 81(1): 39–50. doi:10.1177/0008417413520489

Whitebread, D. and Cárdenas, V. (2012) Self-regulated learning and conceptual development in young children: The development of biological understanding. In Zohar, A., and Dori, Y. (eds.), *Metacognition in Science Education. Contemporary Trends and Issues in Science Education*, vol 40. Dordrecht: Springer. doi:10.1007/978-94-007-2132-6_6

Winnicott, D. (1951) *Transitional Objects and Transitional Phenomena.* London: Tavistock.

Winnicott, D. (1960) The theory of the parent-infant relationship. *International Journal of Psycho-Analysis*, 41: 585–595.

13
Childhood and Resilience

Christopher Smethurst

After reading this chapter, readers will be able to:

- Consider a range of definitions of the concept of resilience.
- Explain the significance of how the term resilience has permeated into contemporary British culture.
- Apply the models of resilience to the experience of children.

Introduction

Resilience can be a difficult concept to define. Although it has been in the popular consciousness for many years, in one form or another, in more recent times it has been used as a means of signalling intervention with children and families. Drawing on recent developments in the fields of psychology, sociology and social policy, this chapter outlines different features of resilience and examines situations where resilience is necessary. It demonstrates links between self-concept and problem-solving abilities, and in the light of contemporary political discourse and emphasis on the individual, shows the importance of understanding the concept of resilience for children living in conditions of social deprivation.

Defining Resilience

Resilience is a word that can incorporate a range of interpretations; Southwick et al. (2014) suggests that resilience is often viewed as being one or all the following: a trait, a process or an outcome. WeinrebIn doing so, it is possible to suggest that resilience may have a broad range of individualised, definitions and, if that is the case, that the usage of the word may not be underpinned by a shared understanding. For example Is resilience something you have? Is it something you do? Is it constant? Does it depend on context? Is it an individual or a collective phenomenon? Has the word been so overused that it has lost its meaning (Smethurst, 2023)?

Fletcher and Sarkar (2013) provide a useful summary of the way the term resilience is applied contexts as diverse as sporting performance, educational attainment and workforce development. They note that there are a range of different definitions of resilience; however, most share a common theme: positive adaptation to adversity. In short, resilience develops through exposure to challenges which one learns to accommodate, overcome and then be better able to manage similar, or new, challenges in the future. 'Grit', 'determination', 'perseverance'; 'bouncing back' are words that are typically associated with human resilience (Smethurst, 2023). Watson et al. (2006) note similar terms: 'hardiness' and 'coping'.

However, the use of the term resilience did not originate with its application to human characteristics. Resilience has its origins in the Latin word 'resilire', which means 'to rebound'. It first entered the English language approximately 500 years ago. For much of the intervening period, resilience has been applied, not to human beings, Faberbut to materials, for example how well wood, stone and metal used in construction could withstand the impact of the elements, or the extent to which the materials used in Bellisle, F. (2004). Effects of Diet on Behaviour and Cognition in Children. British Journal of Nutrition, 92, S227-S232. shipbuilding could resist the onslaught of the sea (McAslan, 2010; Tasan-Kok et al., 2013). When used in these contexts, resilience does not merely refer to standing rigid in the face of a storm, but to be able to flex and then, as the Latin verb suggests, rebound. In material science, resilience also encompasses the ability to withstand continuous stresses: our understanding of 'metal fatigue' largely arose in the aftermath of aircraft accidents, where it was discovered that repeated exposure to stressors could lead to aircraft components breaking, with often catastrophic consequences.

The application of resilience to understand human behaviour originated in the 20th century, and from the 1950s onwards resilience emerged as a term increasingly applied to themes as varied as: Holocaust survival (Frankl, 1959); burnout (Maslach and Jackson,1981, 1997); child poverty, (Garmezy, 1971); loss and bereavement (Coifman et al., 2007); abuse and trauma, (Van der Kolk, 2014). However, the theoretical understanding of resilience in adults, is relatively new, drawing heavily on research conducted with children (Stacey et al., 1970; Elder,1974; 1979; Garmezy, 1974,1985).

Although the theoretical underpinnings of resilience in adults are relatively new, one could tentatively suggest that many of the phenomena understood by engineers, architects and material scientists were, and are, unknowingly reflected in the everyday phrases people use to describe human behaviour under stress. Consider the following:

Cracking under the strain

The straw that breaks the camel's back

Standing firm

These colloquial descriptions of human experience appear to resonate with our scientific understanding of how ships, planes and buildings respond to physical stressors. However, in the human context, resilience refers to a response to both physical and/or *mental* stressors. Consequently, it is necessary to emphasise the limitations of comparing humans with inanimate objects. Similarly, it is important to note that language does not merely reflect our understanding of the world; it shapes it (Bonvillain,

2019; Thibodeau et al., 2019). This can be problematic; people commonly demonstrate resilience when coping with demanding situations (Bonanno, 2004), yet there is a tendency to view resilience as rare and heroic (Collins, 2008). This is perhaps reinforced by the language that is used to describe resilience, for example 'grit', 'hardiness' and' bouncing back'. This tends to, 'reinforce the misperception that only rare individuals with 'exceptional emotional strength' are capable of resilience' (Bonanno, 2004: 24). Masten (2015: 4) argues that resilience 'arises from ordinary resources and processes', resilience is not the only demonstrated by exceptional people, but most people are resilient most of the time.

Points of Reflection

Masten (2015: 4) refers to resilience as 'ordinary magic' and arguably reinforces both the ambiguity and mystique of resilience.

- What does resilience mean to you?
- Think back to your own childhood: in what ways do you think you were resilient?
- Do you think your own resilience was the result of your personality characteristics, the support of others, including adults or social factors?

The Emergence of the Resilience in Public Discourse

Smethurst (2023) suggests that, within the past 20 years resilience has emerged from a place of relative obscurity to one of ubiquity, in policy documents, in self-help literature and in the life-affirming slogans on mugs and T shirts. McAslan (2010) notes that the UK government has rewritten a range of policies, plans and initiatives to place resilience at their centre. In addition, the phrase 'Keep Calm and Carry On' has made the transition from a long-forgotten Second World War public information poster to a place a of near universal recognition in the British public consciousness (Smethurst, 2023). Although advances in neuroscience and other aspects of behavioural psychology might explain, at least in part, our greater understanding of human responses to stressors, they do not necessarily account for the greater public and political awareness in contemporary society. There is a risk of conducting a simplistic and reductionist analysis of the political, economic and sociological factors that may have impacted on the emergence of resilience within British culture; however, the following may be relevant.

First, heightened anxiety about the state of the world and human vulnerability within it. Although technological and social advances have arguably increased objective measures of safety, security and well-being, people feel vulnerable, insecure and exposed to risk (Douglas 1994; Joffe, 2003; Mcinnes and Roemer-Mahler, 2017). With increased scepticism about both the intentions and ability of governments, business and science to promote security and well-being, people have an increasing awareness that modern society produces, not only 'goods', but also 'bads' (Beck et al., 2013). Recent events and developments, including the global economic crash of 2008, the Covid-19 pandemic and the climate emergency have exacerbated this anxiety to create a sense that we are living in times of perpetual crisis and that individuals are increasingly vulnerable to events and phenomena beyond their control (Roitman, 2022; Reitter and Wellmon, 2023).

Second, having evolved over the past 40 years, the dominance of neoliberal discourses in economic and social policy has entailed a move away from collective to individualised approaches to understanding and responding to life's challenges. Responsibility has shifted to the individual and away from the state or society, so that individuals are ultimately deemed responsible for their own emotional well-being and material welfare; crises are personal ones, divorced from their wider political and economic context (Bottrell, 2013). One of the central problems with this individualised view of resilience is that it can be underpinned by distinctly moral overtones 'Resilience is not a static trait that some have and others lack,' (Lown et al., 2015: 708); yet, it remains associated with character, specifically, self-reliance and resourcefulness. As such, it aligns with neoliberal conceptualisations of the ideal citizen who, when facing adversity, looks first to their own resources and those of their families and places few expectations and demands on the state (Bull and Allen, 2018; Burman, 2018; Walker and Cooper, 2011).

Finally, there has been enhanced societal awareness and interest in the way the demands of modern life can wear people down; emotionally, physically and cognitively (Hochschild, 1983; 2013; Jackson, 2014; Lown et al., 2015). Simultaneously, and not coincidentally, there has been a burgeoning interest in psychological and other interventions to combat stress, and to promote well-being. The work of Seligman and Csikszentmihalyi (2000) in the field of Positive Psychology has been influential in focusing on the positives as opposed to the negative aspects of human functioning. This aligns to a growing awareness in Western science, of what had been understood for centuries in the East, of the interrelationship between subjective well-being and physical health (Antonovsky, 1987). In addition, these approaches resonated with theories that identify the human need to find meaning and purpose in life (Maslow, 1954; Frankl, 1985). However, a non-critical acceptance of individualised approaches to promoting resilience and well-being may tacitly affirm that stress, anxiety and material and psychological insecurity are the natural human condition, and it is for the individual, neither the state, nor indeed wider society, to ameliorate their effects (Evans and Reid, 2015). From here, it is not too great a step for resilience to be weaponised, for individuals and families to be blamed for being not resilient, or not resilient enough (Walsh, 2003; Bottrell, 2013; Hickman, 2018; Vasquez, 2022).

Some authors have noted that the rise of resilience in policy discourse has existed in parallel with cuts to public services and real-term erosion of household income levels (Bottrell, 2013; McRobbie, 2020). Failure to navigate these, often catastrophic, consequences for individual and family well-being are, at least for the working class, reframed as psychological deficits; the product of fecklessness, psychological dependency and lifestyle choice (Smethurst, 2017).

Where does this leave our understanding of resilience and, specifically, its application in understanding the lives of children? Some authors hold that resilience is too nebulous a concept to have much relevance in understanding the complex and varied means by which individuals navigate adversity. For example Kaplan (2005: 39) states that:

> The deceptively simple construct of resilience is in fact rife with hidden complexities, contradictions and ambiguities... arguably, any consensus that exists regarding the nature of resilience rests upon the idea of achievement of positively (or the avoidance of negatively) valued outcomes in circumstances where adverse outcomes would normally be expected. A close examination of this idea, however, reveals a number of unresolved questions that at best render the concept less than useful, and at worse impede progress in understanding human adaptation.

Kaplan (2005) provides a useful warning for those who may take an uncritical view of the various conceptualisations of resilience. Nevertheless, McAslan (2010) surveys the contemporary definitions of resilience and identifies some common themes. These are helpful in navigating the complexities and ambiguities of the concept:

Threats and Events

Definitions of resilience have a common focus on abnormal or unusual stressors, be they of short duration or sustained over time. In this context resilience is the ability to accommodate these without incurring significant, lasting harm.

Positive Outcomes

All definitions emphasise a positive outcome, whether this is a recovery, or return to the state or conditions that existed before the disruption, or an improvement in functioning or well-being.

Being Prepared

Definitions focus on creating the conditions that support resilience, be this through policies or plans or providing individuals with the necessary support or skills to be resilient. Resilience can thus be seen as being not merely a reaction to stressors but a product of pre-emptive action and preparedness.

Desire/Commitment to Survive

Resilience in individuals is strongest where there is a will to survive and recover from the impact of stressors or traumatic events.

Adaptability

Resilience correlates with adaptability, which is both a product of ability to adapt and willingness to do so.

Gaining Experience

For those who are resilient, exposure to stressors leads to learning, for example the development of new coping skills or an ability to recognise similar stressors in future and respond appropriately.

Interdependency

Literature highlights the value of mutual support, cooperation in the face of adversity, in terms of both psychological and practical benefits. This provides a marked contrast to the neoliberal construct of individuals and families as sole actors stoically facing life's challenges alone (Smethurst, 2017, 2023).

Case Study: George

George has spent his early childhood largely separated from his parents, with whom he has regular but brief contact. His care has largely been shared out between his grandmother (with whom George has a strong bond) and assorted carers. On one occasion, George failed to recognise his mother when she returned to collect him. Teachers report that George has a poor attention span, finds it difficult to concentrate and daydreams in class, although he is not disruptive and is eager to please. He spends much of his time alone, lacks self-confidence and is described as being sensitive and easily upset. He is not popular with other children and is frequently bullied. George appears to have a difficult relationship with his father, who is irritated by George's sensitivity and lack of physical strength. George's father is very critical of him and often humiliates him in public.

Taking as a starting point your own understanding of resilience:

- What are your first impressions of the life George leads?
- Do you think George's experiences will make him more, or less resilient as a child and then as an adult?

It may surprise you to know that the case study of George is based on the documented early life of King Charles. Does this change your initial impression, or lead you to speculate about how King Charles' childhood experiences may have shaped his adult responses to life's challenges? On the latter, caution is recommended: adult human beings are not merely a product of their childhood experiences, nor do adults or children respond in entirely predictable ways to those experiences. Child and adult social and emotional development are not a simple equation of cause and effect. Similarly,

Kelly (2012: 944) cautions against a contemporary tendency to view young people as 'brains in a jar': in short, the application of neuroscience to understanding personality and behaviour without sufficient consideration of either individual variances or the impact of other, environmental factors.

Resilience in Children

The review of the construct of resilience conducted by McAslan (2010) drew upon literature from a diverse range of disciplines: human behavioural science, ecology, engineering, politics and organisational theory. It is interesting that common themes identified have resonance with the work undertaken by Grotberg (1995, 1997). In developing an understanding of resilience in children, Grotberg's conceptualisation of resilience was holistic, in blending personality traits, skills and environmental factors. Crucially, it focused on a human rights approach to resilience and in particular the preconditions necessary for human flourishing. In order to thrive, children have a right to expect: trusting relationships; to be supported to be autonomous and independent; access to adequate health, welfare and educational services; to be encouraged to communicate, which involves being heard. Grotberg (1997) identifies three domains which are the foundations of resilience:

'I am', incorporates the child's self-concept;

'I can', focuses on the child's perception of their own skills and capabilities;

'I have', encompasses the child's awareness of their environment, as either supportive or hostile.

Notably, Grotberg understood resilience from the child's perspective, looking out from the child's experience rather than looking in. An example was Grotberg's (1995: 24) elaboration of the domains 'I am', 'I can' and 'I have' through a number of statements.

I Have

- people around me I trust and who love me, no matter what;
- people who set limits for me, so I know when to stop before there is danger or trouble;
- people who show me how to do things right by the way they do things;
- people who want me to learn to do things on my own;
- people who help me when I am sick, in danger or need to learn.

I Am

- a person people can like and love;
- glad to do nice things for others and show my concern;
- respectful of myself and others;
- willing to be responsible for what I do;
- sure things will be all right.

I Can

- talk to others about things that frighten me or bother me;
- find ways to solve problems that I face;
- control myself when I feel like doing something not right or dangerous;
- figure out when it is a good time to talk to someone or to take action;
- find someone to help me when I need it.

Grotberg (1995) A Guide to Promoting Resilience in Children: Strengthening the Human Spirit. The Hague: Bernard van Leer Foundation.

In essence, Grotberg's work encourages us not to think of resilience as merely something that is focused on an individual's or family's skills or attributes, but on the wider social, economic and political dimensions. Consider the following case study and apply Grotberg's framework.

Case Study: Joe

Joe is seven-years old. He is the youngest of four children. Last year his father left. Prior to this Joe witnessed frequent domestic abuse perpetrated by his father. Joe and his other siblings were also frequently beaten by their father.

Soon after his father left the family, they were made homeless. They are currently living in temporary accommodation, which is damp and frequently cold. Joe's mother has long struggled with depression, this has been exacerbated by recent events; she tries to be a good parent but feels overwhelmed. The family struggles financially and hunger is a constant presence.

Joe's teachers find him to be easily distracted in class; he is often disruptive and finds it hard to sit still. Recently, his school attendance has become more sporadic. Joe and his siblings often spend their days wandering the streets and have become involved in low-level criminal activity such as stealing from shops.

Consider Grotberg's statements under the domains I am, I can and I have:

- How many of these reflect Joe's life?
- How might Joe learn to cope with adversity as he progresses through life?
- As Grotberg (1997) was writing from a human rights perspective, what do you think should be done, if anything, and by whom?

'Joe' is a fictional character, but the features of his life are not, they reflect the reality of the lives of many children in contemporary Britain (Smethurst, 2017; Thapar et al., 2021; Flew, 2023). Grotberg (1995, 1997) also examined personality traits, behaviours and attitudes; but, crucially, without the right support, these are not likely to be enough to sustain resilience, certainly over an extended period (Seccombe, 2002; Hickman, 2018). Joe's case study has been included to illustrate the potential limits to conceptualisations of resilience based upon personality traits, and personal skills and behaviours.

From the 1980s and into the 1990s resilience developed as an alternative to risk-focused social or health work with children (Rutter, 1987). It resonated with strengths-based approaches to achieving change and aligned, in the early years of the 21st century, with emerging interest in positive psychology. The aim was to emphasise the positive rather than the maladaptive (Rutter, 2012), to mobilise and strengthen existing resources and, in doing so, to work with children and families rather than perceive them as passive recipients of expert intervention (Smethurst, 2023). Consequently:

> Resilience can be defined as reduced vulnerability to environmental risk experiences, the overcoming of a stress or adversity, or a relatively good outcome despite risk experiences. Thus, it is an interactive concept in which the presence of resilience has to be inferred from individual variations in outcome among individuals who have experienced significant major stress or adversity. (Rutter, 2012: 36)

Rutter (2012) identifies three important strands in the evolution of resilience theory and practice:

Identifying: the nature of challenging or protective factors, be these individual, systemic or ecological, for example the work of Garmezy et al. (1984).

Prevention: having identified stressors or challenge factors, what interventions are effective in strengthening protective factors (Rutter, 1987)? Similarly, can individuals learn new coping skills? This strand aligns with the 'Being prepared' and 'Gaining experience' themes identified by McAslan (2010) in the generic resilience literature.

Cumulative Effects: a focus on the interaction of multiple factors, for example how several stressors acting at once, or in quick succession, can overwhelm. Hobfoll describes now cumulative stressors can result in 'loss spirals' where stressors can act as accelerators, prompting additional losses while diminishing the ability to cope (Hobfoll, 1991; Hobfoll et al., 2007, 2016).

At this point it may be worth returning to the case study of Joe to consider whether any lossspirals can be identified.

Underpinning the early approaches to understanding children's resilience was an attempt to identify why, in similar circumstances and with similar stressors, some children demonstrated characteristics that might be termed resilient, yet others did not (Rutter, 2012). Research in the 1970s began to illustrate some of the ways in which children developed resilience. Stacey et al. (1970) explored the experiences of children who, following hospital admission, were separated from their parents. The research identified an 'inoculation effect' where children who had prior experience of mini separations from parents seemed better able to cope with long stay hospital admissions.

The research into children's experience of hospital stays aligned with attachment theories (Bowlby, 1958, 1960; Ainsworth, 1969), in particular, the phenomenon of 'separation anxiety'. More recently, there have been numerous studies which highlight a close correlation between childhood attachment and resilience: in understanding transitions in early years (O'Connor, 2017; Rolfe 2020); in the prevention of mental ill health in adolescence and adulthood (Svanberg, 1998; Winston and Chicot, 2016); and surviving the care system (Atwool, 2006; Sebba and Luke, 2019).

The role of adults in supporting children to navigate adversity aligns with Grotberg's analysis from the 1990's (Grotberg, 1995, 1997) but also with contemporary interest in the impact of 'toxic stress' upon children and the longer term consequences of 'Adverse Childhood Experiences' (Van der Kolk, 2014). The study of toxic stress focuses on the consequences of the prolonged or extreme activation of the human stress response, resulting in negative physiological and psychological impacts. These can range from hypersensitivity to potential stressors to maladaptive changes to body and brain development (Garner et al., 2021). An understanding of toxic stress provides the conceptual framework for demonstrating how the experience of adverse childhood experiences can have profound and lasting impacts on both physical and mental health (Garner et al., 2021). The impact of stress is exacerbated by the absence of mitigating factors including the support of adult caregivers (Van der Kolk, 2014; Madigan et al., 2023). In addition, many children experience a toxic mix of multiple adversities, or Adverse Childhood Experiences (ACEs), which both challenge and can overwhelm their ability to cope (Webster, 2022; Elmore and Crouch, 2023) ACEs can include: abuse and neglect, trauma, loss and bereavement, the experience of domestic abuse and the experience of abandonment (Van der Kolk, 2014; Thomas, 2016; Spratt et al., 2019).

Being overwhelmed, being unable to control, to avoid or to escape the stressor(s) correlates strongly with long term, negative impacts of trauma (Van der Kolk, 2014). This aligns with contemporary understanding of how stress impacts upon both children and adults (Folkman,1984; Hobfoll, 1991, 2004; Theorell, 2020). Within the literature on children's resilience, having both experience and a self-perception of personal agency, control and capability correlates strongly with the child's ability to cope (Elder, 1974; Grotberg, 1995; Rutter, 2012; Van der Kolk, 2014; Davidson et al., 2021). Consequently, models aimed at promoting resilience in young people focus on the development of capabilities that enhance self-concept and problem-solving abilities, for example the '7 Cs' model focuses on strengthening the following:

- **Confidence:** adults should notice and acknowledge children's effort, not just achievement, as a route to nurturing confidence;
- **Competence:** interventions should support the development of communication skills, self-advocacy skill and peer negotiation skills;
- **Connection:** support to enhance connection with others and reduce isolation;
- **Character:** Support children to 'Do the right thing'. This involves observing others to doing right thing; it is not merely an exercise in being told what to do;
- **Contribution:** Resilience is enhanced through the child's experience of giving, receiving gratitude and of making a difference;

- **Coping:** enhancing the skills and strategies that children need to both recognise and navigate adversity;
- **Control:** The development of problem-solving skills and the opportunity to exercise these mitigate against feelings of helplessness. (Ginsburg, 2011; Ginsburg & Jablow, 2015)

Resilience Is Not Enough

There is a risk that resilience can be viewed through a lens of individual responsibility, capability and psychological predisposition. Consequently, for every individual who demonstrates resilience in the face of adversity, what are the implications for those who do not, or more specifically are deemed by others to be not resilient (Smethurst, 2023). It is notable that the disparaging term 'snowflake' has entered the British lexicon to refer to young people, who are deemed lacking in comparison with mythical earlier generations, forged in the 'school of hard knocks' (Turner, 2017; Finn et al., 2021). Nostalgia is a British cultural phenomenon, along with a tendency to look backwards into history not outwards to other the countries when evaluating social progress (Woods, 2022). Once these parochial filters are removed, we get a clearer sense of the challenges taxing the resilience of young people in Britain. The 'Good Childhood Report' of 2020 concluded that: 'Modern life has been chipping away at children's happiness over time' (Children's Society 2020: 6). In addition, in 2021, the United Kingdom ranked lowest of 24 European countries in its proportion of children with high life satisfaction, it was lowest in its proportion of children with a positive sense of purpose in life and second highest in its proportion with high sadness levels (Thapar et al., 2021).

The Good Childhood Report (2020, 2022) focused on children's subjective sense of their own well-being. Fear of failure and fear of being judged were perhaps surprising themes to emerge from the research. However, on closer inspection, these themes resonate with the 'I am' and 'I can' domains in Grotberg's (1995, 1997) analysis. If we return to consider the 'I have' domain, recent UK research highlighting children's experience of poverty is both illuminating and disturbing.

Research by the Joseph Rowntree Foundation concluded that 3.8 million people in the United Kingdom experienced destitution in 2022, of this number approximately one million were children. 'Destitution' is defined as the absence of two or more of six items needed for the most basic need to stay warm, dry, clean and fed (Fitzpatrick et al., 2023: 4). The number of children experiencing destitution since 2017 has increased 186% (Fitzpatrick et al. 2023). Devereux et al. (2022) write of the normalisation of poverty and the societal tendency not to consider the specific impacts on those affected. Consequently, if one focuses on hunger, the implications for young people's well-being become clearer. Childhood hunger correlates with suicide ideation (McIntyre et al., 2013; Koyanagi et al., 2019); heightened levels of aggression (Bellisle, 2004; Pumariega et al., 2022); hyperactivity (Lu et al., 2019); impaired social functioning (Faber and Häusser, 2022); child anxiety, depression and behavioural problems (Weinreb et al., 2002; Cain et al., 2016).

Chapter Summary

In summary, this chapter has reviewed the evolution of resilience as a construct in psychology, child development and social policy. It has explored a range of theories and models which are useful for practitioners working with children. However, if there is a consistent theme that emerges from these pages it is this: we should not rely on the resilience of children to compensate for the failures of adults.

Key Points

- The concept of resilience is a relatively recent innovation in the field of childhood.
- Resilience is a useful tool for making decisions about children's well-being.
- The entrance of resilience into national discourse is linked to ideas about the primacy of the individual in contemporary Britain.

Further Reading

Smethurst, C. (2023). Resilience: Magic Bullet; Buzz Word, or Something Else? In H. Green and B. Edwards (eds) *True Partnerships in SEND* (pp. 87–99). London: Routledge.

References

Ainsworth, M. D. S. (1969). Object relations, dependency, and attachment: A theoretical review of the infant-mother relationship. *Child Development*, 40, 969–1025.

Antonovsky, A. (1987). *Unravelling the Mystery of Health: How People Manage Stress and Stay Well*. San Francisco, CA: Jossey-Bass Publishers.

Atwool, N. (2006). Attachment and resilience: Implications for children in care. *Child Care in Practice*, 12(4), 315–330.

Beck, U., Blok, A., Tyfield, D., and Zhang, J. Y. (2013) Cosmopolitan communities of climate risk: Conceptual and empirical suggestions for a new research agenda. *Global Networks*. 13(1), 1–21.

Bellisle, F. (2004). Effects of diet on behaviour and cognition in children. *British Journal of Nutrition*, 92, S227–S232.

Bowlby, J. (1958). The nature of the child's tie to his mother. *The International Journal of Psychoanalysis*, 39, 350–373.

Bowlby, J. (1960). Separation anxiety. *The International Journal of Psychoanalysis*, 41, 89–113.

Bonanno, G. (2004). Loss, Trauma & Human Resilience: Have we underestimated the human capacity to thrive after extremely aversive events. *American Psychologist*, 59(1), 20–28.

Bonvillain, N. (2019). *Language, culture, and communication: The meaning of messages*. Lanham, MD: Rowman & Littlefield.

Bottrell, D. (2013). Responsibilised resilience? Reworking neoliberal social policy texts. *M/C Journal*, 16(5).

Bull, A., and Allen, K. (2018). Introduction: Sociological interrogations of the turn to character. *Sociological Research*, 23(2), 392–398.

Burman, J. T. (2018). Through the looking-glass: PsycINFO as an historical archive of trends in psychology. *History of Psychology*, 21(4), 302–333.

Cain, M., Leonard, J., Gabrieli, J., and Finn, A. (2016). Media multitasking in adolescence. *Psychonomic Bulletin & Review*, 1–10.

Coifman, K. G., Bonanno, G. A., and Rafaeli, E. (2007). Affect dynamics, bereavement and resilience to loss. *Journal of Happiness Studies*, 8(3), 371–392.

Collins, S. (2008). Statutory social workers: Stress, job satisfaction, coping, social support and individual differences. *British Journal of Social Work*, 38(1), 173–1193.

Davidson, B., Schmidt, E., Mallar, C., Mahmoud, F., Rothenberg, W., Hernandez, J., and Natale, R. (2021). *Risk and resilience of well-being in caregivers of young children in response to the COVID-19 pandemic. Translational behavioral medicine*. Oxford: Oxford University Press.

Devereux, S., Haysom, G., Maluf, R., and Scott-Villiers, P. (2022). *Challenging the normalisation of hunger in highly unequal societies*. Institute of Development Studies, Working Paper, Volume 2022 Number 582.

Douglas, M. (1994). *Risk and blame: Essays in cultural theory*. London: Routledge.

Elder, G. H. (1974). *Children of the great depression*. Chicago: University of Chicago Press.

Elmore, A. L., and Crouch, E. (2023). Anxiety, depression, and adverse childhood experiences: An update on risks and protective factors among children and youth. *Academic Paediatrics*, 23(4), 720–721.

Evans, B., and Reid, J. (2015). Exhausted by resilience: Response to the commentaries. *Resilience*, 3(2), 154–159.

Faber, N. S., and Häusser, J. A. (2022). Why stress and hunger both increase and decrease prosocial behaviour. *Current Opinion in Psychology*, 44, 49–57.

Finn, K., Ingram, N., and Allen, K. (2021). Student millennials/millennial students: How the lens of generation constructs understandings of the contemporary HE student. In *Reimagining the higher education student* (pp. 187–204). London: Routledge.

Fitzpatrick, S., Bramley, G., Treanor, M., Blenkinsopp, J., McIntyre, J., Johnsen, S., and McMordie, L. (2023). *Destitution in the UK 2023*. London: Joseph Rowntree Foundation.

Flew, L. (2023) *The Cost of Child Poverty in 2023*. London: Child Poverty Action Group.

Fletcher, D., and Sarkar, M. (2013). Psychological resilience: A review and critique of definitions, concepts, and theory. *European Psychologist*, 18(1), 12–23.

Folkman, S. (1984). Personal control and stress and coping processes: A theoretical analysis. *Journal of Personality and Social Psychology*, 46(4), 839.

Frankl, V. E. (1959). The spiritual dimension in existential analysis and logotherapy. *Journal of Individual Psychology*, 15, 157–165.

Frankl, V. E. (1985). *Man's search for meaning*. New York: Simon and Schuster.

Garmezy, N. (1971). Vulnerability research and the issue of primary prevention. *American Journal of Orthopsychiatry*, 41, 101–116.

Garmezy, N. (1974). The study of competence in children at risk for severe psychopathology. In E. J. Anthony, and C. Koupernik (Eds.), *The child in his family: Children at psychiatric risk* (Vol. 3, pp. 77–97). New York: Wiley.

Garmezy, N. (1985). Stress-resistant children: The search for protective factors. In A. Davids (Ed.), *Recent research in developmental psychopathology* (pp. 213–233). Elmsford: Pergamon Press.

Garmezy, N., Masten, A.S, and Tellegen, A. (1984) The study of stress and competence in children: A building block for developmental psychopathology. *Child Development*, 55, 97–111.

Garner, A., Yogman, M., and Committee on Psychosocial Aspects of Child and Family Health. (2021). Preventing childhood toxic stress: Partnering with families and communities to promote relational health. *Pediatrics*, 148(2).

Ginsburg, K. R. (2011). (2nd ed.). *Building resilience in children and teens*. Elk Grove: Academy of Pediatrics.

Ginsburg, K. R., and Jablow, M. M. (2015). *Building resilience in children and teens: Giving kids roots and wings*. Elk Grove: American Academy of Pediatrics.

Grotberg, E. H. (1995). *A guide to promoting resilience in children: Strengthening the human spirit*. The Hague: Bernard van Leer Foundation.

Grotberg, E. (1997). *The international resilience project. A charge against society: The child's right to protection* (pp. 19–32). London: Jessica Kingsley.

Hickman, P. (2018). A flawed construct? Understanding and unpicking the concept of resilience in the context of economic hardship. *Social Policy and Society*, 17(3), 409–424.

Hobfoll, S. E. (1991). Traumatic stress: A theory based on rapid loss of resources. *Anxiety Research*, 4(3), 187–197.

Hobfoll, S. E. (2004). *Stress, culture, and community: The psychology and philosophy of stress*. New York: Springer Science & Business Media.

Hobfoll, S. E., Watson, P., Bell, C. C., Bryant, R. A., Brymer, M. J., Friedman, M. J., and Ursano, R. J. (2007). Five essential elements of immediate and mid–term mass trauma intervention: Empirical evidence. *Psychiatry: Interpersonal and Biological Processes*, 70(4), 283–315.

Hobfoll, S. E., Tirone, V., Holmgreen, L., and Gerhart, J. (2016). Conservation of resources theory applied to major stress. In *Stress: Concepts, cognition, emotion, and behavior* (pp. 65–71). New York: Academic Press.

Hochschild, A. (1983). *The managed heart: Commercialization of human feeling*. Berkeley: University of California Press.

Jackson, M. (2014). The stress of life: A modern complaint? *The Lancet*, 383(9914), 300–301.

Joffe, H. (2003). Risk: From perception to social representation. *British Journal of Social Psychology*. 42(1), 55–73.

Kaplan, H. B. (2005). Understanding the concept of resilience. In S. Goldstein and R. B. Brooks (Eds.), *Handbook of resilience in children* (pp. 39–47). New York: Springer.

Kelly, P. (2012). The brain in the jar: A critique of discourses of adolescent brain development. *Journal of Youth Studies*, 15(7), 944–959.

Koyanagi, A., Oh, H., Carvalho, A. F., Smith, L., Haro, J. M., Vancampfort, D., Stubbs, B., and DeVylder, J. E. (2019, September). Bullying Victimization and Suicide Attempt Among Adolescents Aged 12-15 Years From 48 Countries. *Journal of the American Academy of Child & Adolescent Psychiatry*, 58(9), 907–918.

Lown, M., Lewith, G., Simon, C., & Peters, D. (2015). Resilience: What is it, why do we need it, and can it help us? *British Journal of General Practice*, 65(639), e708–e710.

Lu, L., Lianqinga, Z., Shia, T., Xuana, B., Yinga, C., Xinyua, H., Xiaoxiaoa, H., Hailonga, L., Lantingb, G., Sweeney, J., Qiyong, G., and Xiaoqi, H. (2019). Characterization of cortical and subcortical abnormalities in drug-naive boys with attention-deficit/hyperactivity disorder. *Journal of Affective Disorders*, 250, 397–403.

McIntyre, L., Williams, J., Lavorato, D., and Patten, S. (2013, August 15). Depression and suicide ideation in late adolescence and early adulthood are an outcome of child hunger. *Journal of Affective Disorders*, 150(1), 123–9.

Madigan, S., Deneault, A. A., Racine, N., Park, J., Thiemann, R., Zhu, J., & Neville, R. D. (2023). Adverse childhood experiences: A meta-analysis of prevalence and moderators among half a million adults in 206 studies. *World psychiatry*, 22(3), 463–471.

Maslach, C., & Jackson, S. (1981). The measurement of experienced burnout. *Journal of* Occupational Behavior, 2, 99–113.

Maslow, A. H. (1954). The instinctoid nature of basic needs. *Journal of Personality*, 22, 326–347.

Masten, A. S. (2015). *Ordinary magic: Resilience in development*. London: Guilford Publications.

McAslan, A. (2010). *The concept of resilience: Understanding its origins, meaning and utility* (p. 1). Adelaide: Torrens Resilience Institute.

Mcinnes, C. and Roemer-Mahler, A. (2017). From security to risk: Reframing global health threats. *International Affairs*. 93(6), 1313–1337.

McRobbie, A. (2020). *Feminism and the politics of resilience: Essays on gender, media and the end of welfare*. Chichester: John Wiley & Sons.

O'Connor, A. (2017). *Understanding transitions in the early years: Supporting change through attachment and resilience*. London: Routledge.

Pumariega, A., Jo, Y., Beck, B., and Rahmani, M. (2022, April). Trauma and US Minority Children and Youth. *Current Psychiatry Reports*, 24(4), 285–295.

Reitter, P., and Wellmon, C. (2023). *Permanent crisis: The humanities in a disenchanted age*. Chicago: University of Chicago Press.

Rolfe, S. A. (2020). *Rethinking attachment for early childhood practice: Promoting security, autonomy and resilience in young children*. London: Routledge.

Roitman, J. (2022). The ends of perpetual crisis. *Global Discourse*, 12(3-4), 692–696.

Rufat, S. (2015). Critique of pure resilience. *Resilience Imperative*, 201–228.

Rutter, M. (1987). Psychosocial resilience and protective mechanisms. *American Journal of Orthopsychiatry*, 57(3), 316–331.

Rutter, M. (2012, May). Resilience as a dynamic concept. *Development and Psychopathology*, 24(2), 335–44.

Sebba, J., and Luke, N. (2019). The educational progress and outcomes of children in care. *Oxford Review of Education*, 45(4), 435–442.

Seccombe, K. (2002). "Beating the odds" versus "changing the odds": Poverty, resilience, and family policy. *Journal of Marriage and Family*, 64(2), 384–394.

Seligman, M. E. P., and Csikszentmihalyi, M. (2000). Positive psychology: An introduction. *American Psychologist*, 55, 5–14.

Smethurst, C. (2017). Class inequality and social work: We're all in this together? In Bhatti-Sinclair, K., and Smethurst, C. (eds) *Diversity difference and professional dilemmas: Developing skills in challenging times*. London: Open University McGraw Hill.

Smethurst, C. (2023). Resilience: Magic Bullet; Buzz Word, or something else? InGreen, H., and Edwards, B. (eds) *True partnerships in SEND* (pp. 87–99). London: Routledge.

Southwick, S., Bonanno, G., Masten, A., Panter-Brick, C., and Yehuda, R. (2014, October). Resilience definitions, theory, and challenges: Interdisciplinary perspectives. *European Journal of Psychotraumatology*, 1, 5.

Spratt, T., Devaney, J., and Frederick, J. (2019). Adverse childhood experiences: Beyond signs of safety; reimagining the organisation and practice of social work with children and families. *British Journal of Social Work*, 49(8), 2042–2058.

Stacey, M., Dearden, R., Pill, R., and Robinson, D. (1970). *Hospitals, children and their families: The report of a pilot study*. London: Routledge and Kegan Paul Ltd.

Svanberg, P. O. (1998). Attachment, resilience, and prevention. *Journal of Mental Health*, 7(6), 543–578.

Tasan-Kok, T., Stead, D., and Lu, P. (2013). *Conceptual overview of resilience: History and context. Resilience thinking in urban planning* (pp. 39–51). Dordrecht: Springer.

Thapar., Stewart-Brown, S., and Gordon, T. H (2021). What has happened to children's wellbeing in the UK? *The Lancet Psychiatry*, 8(1), 5–6.

Theorell, T. (2020). The demand control support work stress model. In *Handbook of socioeconomic determinants of occupational health: From macro-level to micro-level evidence* (pp. 339–353). Berlin: Springer.

Thibodeau, P. H., Matlock, T., and Flusberg, S. J. (2019). The role of metaphor in communication and thought. *Language and Linguistics Compass*, 13(5), e12327.

Thomas, J. T. (2016). Adverse childhood experiences among MSW students. *Journal of Teaching in Social Work*, 36(3), 235–255.

Turner, R. J., Wheaton, B., and Lloyd, D. A. (1995). The epidemiology of social stress. *American Sociological Review*, 60(1), 104–125.

Turner, C. (2017, January 8). Universities warned over "snowflake" student demands. *The Daily Telegraph*. https://www.telegraph.co.uk/news/2017/01/08/universities-warned-snowflake-student-demands/

Van der Kolk, B. (2014). *The body keeps the score: Mind, brain and body in the transformation of trauma*. Harmondsworth: Penguin.

Vasquez, R. (2022). You just need more resilience: Racial gaslighting as "Othering". *Journal of Critical Thought and Praxis*, 11(3).

Walker, J., and Cooper, M. (2011). Genealogies of resilience: From systems ecology to the political economy of crisis adaptation. *Security Dialogue*, 42(2), 143–160.

Walsh, F. (2003, Spring). Family resilience: A framework for clinical practice. *Family Process*. 42(1), 1–18.

Watson, P., Ritchie, E., Demer, J., Bartone, P., and Pfefferbaum, B. (2006). 'Improving resilience trajectories following mass violence and disasters'. In Richie, E., Watson, P., and Friedman, M. (eds), *Interventions following mass violence and disasters*. New York, Guildford.

Webster, E. M. (2022). The impact of adverse childhood experiences on health and development in young children. *Global Pediatric Health*, 9, https://doi.org/10.1177/2333794X221078708

Weinreb, L., Wehler, C., Perloff, J., Scott, R., Hosmer, D., Sagor, L., and Gundersen, C. (2002, October). Hunger: Its impact on children's health and mental health. *Pediatrics*, 110(4), e41.

Winston, R., & Chicot, R. (2016). The importance of early bonding on the long-term mental health and resilience of children. *London Journal of Primary Care*, 8(1), 12–14.

Woods, H. R. (2022). *Rule, Nostalgia: A backwards history of Britain*. London: Random House.

14

Working Therapeutically with Children

Sam McNally

After reading this chapter, readers will be able to:

- understand the need for, and benefits of working therapeutically with children and young people.
- explore what working therapeutically might look like and how it differs from providing therapy.
- give an overview of how all practitioners can use therapeutic approaches including the therapeutic use of play to build secure and trusting professional relationships with the children they support.

Introduction

The cornerstone of therapeutic work is the relationship; respectful of prior experience and permissive of creative expression. The child is afforded the emotional and temporal space necessary to work through challenges, in a dynamic process where they can make sense of their experience in relation to the world around them. This chapter will consider the distinction between providing therapy and working therapeutically and offer an overview of some therapeutic approaches. One approach that is particularly effective with children is the use of play.

Play gives children the autonomy and control needed to process their problems through a safe and familiar medium at their own pace and without adult interference or overbearing direction. Play offers catharsis, the opportunity to develop problem-solving skills and an outlet for self-expression. It validates feelings and promotes positive self-concept. Working therapeutically with children is reparative, helping children to develop strategies and approaches to regulate their emotions and build resilience.

The discussion of something that is 'therapeutic' often refers to an intervention that is associated with healing, recovery or treatment. It is a term that may be considered synonymous with the prevention or alleviation of something that is problematic. It may also be that it suggests engagement with another that is reparative or restorative in nature. There are numerous ways of working that may be considered therapeutic and a plethora of reasons why this type of interaction may be positively indicated.

The Problem

Research suggests that around half of all mental health problems are apparent by the time young people reach their mid-teens (Kessler et al., 2007). In the wake of the Covid-19 pandemic, there has been an exacerbation of young people grappling with issues relating to poor mental health. In 2022, the Mental Health of Children and Young People (MHCYP) Survey provided statistics for England on trends in children's mental health. The survey revealed that 18% of children aged 7–17 years of age had a probable mental disorder. The authors also revealed experimental data suggesting that 5.5% of preschool aged children may also have a mental disorder (Newlove-Delgado et al., 2022). This is the first time that the prevalence of mental disorders has been measured in children aged 2–4 years of age (Newlove-Delgado et al., 2022). This data is significant because of a correlation between poor mental well-being in young people and the likelihood of less favourable outcomes including involvement in criminal activity, poor academic outcomes and the misuse of drugs and alcohol, later in life (Chanfreau et al., 2008). One area of mental health presentation which has been seen to rise in children and young people is that of emotional disorders including anxiety (RCPCH, 2021). Some children's biological make-up results in them being more anxious than others, and less able to manage stress in the face of adversity, but we are also acutely aware of the impact of trauma and adverse events on some children (Felitti et al., 1998). The dominant discourse for many years was that children did not experience anxiety, but as our understanding of anxiety disorders has increased, it is now accepted that 8%–11% of children and young people will be affected by anxiety (Mental Health Foundation, 2022). Some anxiety is normal, welcome even, because it promotes action and keeps us safe. Anxiety becomes problematic when it affects our ability to engage with normal day-to-day activities. Problematic anxiety can be categorised into specific diagnosable disorders, but a key characteristic of all anxiety is worry. Flannery-Schroeder (in Morris and March, 2004) asserts that childhood worry does not receive the same attention or clinical concern as worry in adults and that much of the aetiology remains under researched. What is known, however, is that there are notable risk factors for childhood anxiety disorders and these include parenting characteristics and attachment style (Flannery-Schroeder, 2004).

The Importance of Authentic Relationships

Humans are inherently relationship seeking (Bowlby, 1969). If anxiety is not responded to or contained in early childhood, this may lead to pushing overwhelming experience out of the conscious mind as part of the body's defence mechanism to protect from emotional distress and psychological harm, or elevating attachment-seeking behaviours to meet the need. Early relationships play a significant role in shaping our resilience or vulnerability when faced with challenge later in life. Denying or not validating this unmanageable emotion may lead to the child or young person lacking agency over their emotions and emotional responses in adulthood. Understanding attachment-needs helps us to understand the need for authentic and secure connection to another.

Holmes and Slade (2018) poignantly assert 'secure people *survive* as infants, *thrive* as children, and *flourish* as adults' (p. 17).

When we work with children and young people, we offer the opportunity to build new, authentic relationships. Some children will have been fortunate enough to have experienced responsive, reciprocal relationships in their lives, but for others, those who have barely *survived* and are yet to *thrive*, we may be offering a relational connection that is new and unfamiliar. Even for those with secure attachment relationships, the impact of the Covid-19 pandemic may have ruptured relationships and heightened anxiety levels. For many, this period of uncertainty was bound up in fear and unpredictability which also led to some people becoming socially isolated and relationships being irreparably damaged. The Government's 'Staying at home and away from others (social distancing)' guidance (2020) gave a clear message that the fight against coronavirus required us to stay away from other people. Key measures within the document were underpinned by law making sure we stayed apart from one another or risk fines or even arrest. At the time, there was valid justification for such extreme public health intervention to prevent the spread of disease. These stay-at-home orders were enforced globally in an attempt to minimise the impact of the pandemic, but for children, who were less likely to become seriously unwell with the virus, they threatened to leave a devastating alternative legacy (Triggle, 2021). The negative effects of these stay-at-home orders has been recognised to be associated with greater health anxiety, damaged social connections and loneliness (Tull et al., 2020). In fact, some commentators have suggested that the negative social and economic consequences of the stay-at-home orders, along with distressing media coverage of the pandemic may have themselves been the cause of adverse psychological outcomes for some (Asmundson and Taylor, 2020; Reger et al., 2020).

The Impact of Social Media

Another issue thought to be impacting mental health and well-being in young people is the rising use of social media platforms. A longitudinal study of adolescent neural development and use of technology which was undertaken in North Carolina, US, has indicated that young people's habitual checking of their social media accounts is causing changes to their brains affecting how they respond to the world including evidence of hypersensitivity to the feedback that they receive from peers (Maza et al., 2023). It would be valid to assume that this experience is likely to be mirrored in other Western countries including the United Kingdom. This may indicate a pattern of adolescent social media usage impacting the levels of sensitivity experienced relating to social rewards and punishment which has the potential to lead to adaptive relational behaviours including conditioning to checking social media more frequently for social feedback and validation which may in turn negatively impact their self-esteem and social interactions both on and offline. This issue is interrelated to the wider psychological issue of online bullying which has become an increasingly prevalent issue among children and young people in the digital age.

Working Therapeutically Towards a Solution

> The act of therapeutic connection is not owned by any one profession. The responsibility to offer authentic and compassionate care to another human being is something we all share. (Koloroutis and Trout, 2012)

It is a view held by some that to work therapeutically, one must hold the position as a trained, qualified therapist (Burlingame and Barlow, 1996). Undoubtedly, there are people who need the specialised interventions of those adequately trained to navigate the challenges that their clients face, and provide psychological containment. It would be irresponsible to suggest that somebody without the appropriate credentials or systems of support should be adopting the role of an untrained therapist, but there is a distinction between providing therapy and working in a way that is therapeutic. It may be helpful to consider the distinction between working therapeutically and providing therapy, as similar to the concepts of first aid and physical medical treatment. A person that has fallen and injured their elbow may benefit from a caring person asking if they are okay or if they need help, cleaning a graze, and possibly applying a plaster. This action shows compassion and kindness and demonstrates an interest in their condition and an effort to improve the situation. This may be enough to resolve the issue. If they have also fractured a bone in their arm, they will need attention from a qualified medical professional. The immediate care they have received will not have been wasted or in vain, but they require something more to remedy the physical damage. The same tenets can be applied to those who have experienced emotional harm. A competent, caring person may be enough, or they may be the first step in a healing process.

The fundamental and qualitative difference of working ***therapeutically*** with children is the reparative nature of the interaction. It involves time, space and permissiveness, but most importantly it involves forging a relationship rooted in trust and congruence (Rogers, 1957). It can be an approach that is good for all, and pivotal for many. Treating everyone in such a way that we assume they may be impacted in the here and now by negative experiences or events from their past involves applying 'universal precautions' (Brummer, 2020). Not so long ago we were in the grips of the Covid-19 pandemic. During this time, we were faced with avoiding a virus that is invisible to the naked eye. We did this by applying universal precautions – that is we assumed everyone was carrying Covid-19, unless we knew otherwise. This did not cause any harm to the people around us, in fact by being mindful that the virus COULD be there, unseen, we went some way to keeping everyone safe. If we apply the same tenets when we do not know a child's history, by applying these universal precautions we follow the golden rule of 'Do no harm'.

Building Positive Attachments

When we are born into this world we are entirely dependent upon another person to meet our needs. We rely on a parent or other primary care-giver to feed us, clothe us, protect and love us. This (usually) safe and nurturing connection leads to the formation of an attachment, a connection which, for that baby, means life or death. Securely attached children learn independence and they also come to recognise when they need support to navigate new or unfamiliar situations (Ainsworth and Bell, 1970). It is this fine balance between autonomy and seeking help that helps to build resilience. It is relevant to note that when Bowlby (cited in Holmes and Slade, 2018) defined what qualified as an attachment relationship, he focused upon the position of the child rather than the parental side of the attachment system because he elevated the significance of the relationship being *safety seeking*, rather than *safety providing* (Holmes and Slade, 2018). This suggests that when working with children or young people who inherently look to professional practitioners to keep them safe, the nature of the interaction has the conditions needed to qualify as an attachment relationship. Children who lack these early attachment relationships, where their physical and emotional needs are not attended to, learn to shy away from challenge and see little merit in asking for support as they have been conditioned to believe that help is not forthcoming (Van der Kolk, 2014). Thus, the building of positive relationships is key to promoting healing within a therapeutic alliance: 'When a person has been hurt in a relationship, they can only be healed in a relationship' (De Thierry, 2017: 27). By offering an approach that is therapeutic, practitioners can help children to develop strategies and approaches to regulate their emotions and build resilience. Working this way to promote positive change, empowers children and young people and elevates their sense of personal autonomy, in addition to modelling respectful, congruent relationships.

A 'Person-Centred' Approach

Carl Rogers (1902–1987) was the architect of an approach of relating to another which became known as a 'person-centred' way of being. A humanistic psychotherapist, Rogers challenged the belief that some therapeutic modalities were superior to others arguing instead that approaches were likely to be equally effective so long as the relationship between the therapist and the client contained specific key qualities (Rogers, 1957). These became known as 'core conditions' and are often referred to in relation to psychological work in various therapeutic orientations (Egan, 1998). These conditions are empathy, unconditional positive regard (UPR) and congruence. It was Rogers' assertion that what really mattered was the relationship between the client and the therapist and that with these conditions present, positive change can occur.

Empathy

Empathy can be described as the ability to understand the feelings of another by imagining what it would be like to themselves be in that situation (Hodgkins, 2021). Empathy has been considered as an emotion related to work with children across numerous disciplines. In fact, it may be argued that emotion is integral to work with children and young people. Empathy comprises of cognitive, affective and behavioural elements (Telle and Pfister, 2016). Social work research identifies empathy as a key component of the professional role. Ruch et al. (2018) writing about relationship-based practice suggest that empathy is skill which social workers have a natural tendency to possess, but also a skill which can be taught. Morse et al. (2006) investigated the use of empathy in nurse–patient interactions and assert that empathy is itself therapeutic. Moudatsou et al. (2020) concur, asserting that empathy is one of the fundamental tools of the therapeutic relationship. When children feel supported and understood, they are better equipped to navigate challenges and build a positive self-image. Empathy therefore plays a vital part in promoting children's positive mental health and well-being.

Unconditional Positive Regard (UPR)

Unconditional Positive Regard (UPR) is synonymous with respect. It is not about approval or friendship, but involves taking the position that each child is doing their best with the resources that they have available to them. This is possibly the most challenging of Roger's (1957) core conditions as we are called upon to acknowledge our underlying attitudes and biases and frame our thinking to assume children are inherently good and doing what they can to get their needs met. This sometimes requires that we look beyond behaviours that we are challenged by without feeling that we should be attempting to change them. This should not be confused with approval of the behaviour, but a respectful acknowledgement that a child is valued for their self-determined efforts to get things right. Children acting out are often accused of 'attention-seeking' but with a shift in attitude and employing affective empathy we can reframe this as 'attachment-seeking' behaviour. As practitioners we separate the behaviour from the child; humans make mistakes, they have flaws and get things wrong, but reminding them that they are valued and accepted despite this can be an effective therapeutic tool.

Congruence

Congruence involves authentic and genuine interactions with the children and young people that we work with. Every child is unique and approaches need to be adapted and tailored to meet individual needs. A congruent relationship has the power to be transformative for a child who lacks prior experience of this authentic interaction. An example of this may include respecting a child's autonomy by offering genuine opportunities for expressing choices and making decisions, within appropriate boundaries related to age and developmental stage.

It can be argued that the application of Roger's (1957) core conditions is appropriate at any relational level without qualified therapeutic endeavour (even if only as a first aid level intervention). We can demonstrate these relationship qualities and potentially promote healing through forging a respectful relationship without requiring therapeutic expertise. Rogers' (1986) suggested that the *presence* of another incorporating these qualities was likely sufficient for psychological change to occur. Much of Rogers' work, in common with Play Therapy approaches, was non-directive. This process respects the autonomy of the child and builds upon a fundamental belief that all people have the capacity to heal, grow and self-actualise (Goldstein, 1939). In applying Roger's core conditions in working with children we can build an environment which promotes healing and growth. Permissive Play Therapy approaches apply Rogers' non-directive person-centred model to promote a non-authoritarian attitude, taking the view that each person is unique and will work through their challenges in a different way, without the need to be controlled or directed (Merry, 1999). Undoubtedly, some will need more. Some of the children and young people we support will require professional therapeutic expertise. They will require intervention that is beyond the capabilities of the lay helper, but if we start from a position of offering a reparative relationship, we all have the power to be part of the catalyst of a healing process.

Case Study: Millie

Millie is eight-years old and has grown up with her care shared by her mother and her maternal aunt. Millie is of mixed ethnic background with her mother being white British and her biological father being black Caribbean. Millie's father left before she was born and she has never had any contact with him.

Millie's mother has struggled with alcohol addiction for many years and despite periods of successful withdrawal she tends to relapse when things become overwhelming in her life. When her mother has entered rehabilitation for her addiction, Millie has been cared for by her mother's sister. When Millie is living with her aunt she sleeps on a bed-settee in the lounge and is aware that this causes her aunt inconvenience and disruption. Millie's aunt is kind, but she has a stressful job, three young children of her own to care for and money is tight.

Millie says that she does not really feel as though she belongs anywhere as she spends time at the two addresses and nowhere feels like home. There have been times when Millie has found her mother unconscious due to the alcohol abuse and she has often witnessed her mother being taken from the home in an ambulance.

- What might be the emotional impact of Millie's home circumstances?
- How might a therapeutic approach benefit Millie?
- Why is a relationship that prioritises attachment important for Millie?

Attachment-Informed and Trauma-Informed Approaches

Children like Millie may benefit from professionals working in ways that consider her prior life experiences and recognise the impact that these previous experiences may have on her future relationships. Two approaches that are effective when working therapeutically with children and young people are attachment-informed and trauma-informed approaches. While these approaches have different foci, they share the aims of supporting the emotional resilience and well-being in children and young people who are facing or have been faced with adversity. The integration of frameworks such as these can go some way towards creating a safe and inclusive environment where the approach is responsive to addressing the effects of trauma and promoting the importance of healthy attachment relationships for healing.

Attachment-informed ways of working focus upon the importance of secure, congruent relationships in promoting emotional well-being. They prioritise the child's need for consistent, responsive and nurturing caregiving and recognise the significance of early experience in shaping attachment later in life. By employing Roger's (1957) core conditions and elevating the status of a therapeutic relationship, the practitioner acknowledges the importance of the attachment relationship in building children and young people's emotional resilience.

Research confirms that the effects of trauma can place a heavy burden on people (SAMHSA, 2014). Although many people who experience trauma will bounce back without significant impact, others will grapple with the pervasive effects for many years to come. The Substance Abuse and Mental Health Services Administration (SAMHSA) in the United States of America (2014) have developed an evidence-based framework for interventions which promotes services being more responsive to the experience of those who have experienced trauma recognising that the exposure may have impacted an individual's biological, neurological, psychological and social development.

Trauma-informed approaches see beyond the presenting behaviours and instead of asking 'what is wrong with them?' encourage the reframing of this position to 'what happened to them?'. Trauma-informed practice does not promote encouraging lay persons to make attempts to treat the presenting trauma-related difficulties, as this would likely require the intervention of a trained professional, instead it offers a way of working which addresses barriers to people burdened with a trauma-history accessing services. Trauma-informed approaches are guided by six principles (SAMSHA, 2014). The principles provide a framework for working in a way that recognises the significance of trauma. **Safety**: This is fundamental to success. Before any meaningful work can begin, we must ensure that the children we work with feel safe, not just physically but psychologically. The provision of a safe and supportive environment relies upon us establishing clear and consistent expectations and boundaries that we communicate to the child. **Trustworthiness**: Involves building a relationship with the child or young person that is reliable and transparent. Children develop trust by experiencing consistent, reliable and predictable interactions with an adult who does not make promises that they fail to fulfil. **Choice and Control**: This ensures that interventions with children are undertaken *with* them and not *to* them. It is important that children are offered a sense of control over the processes that they are involved with and this includes choices about their involvement and approaches that are adopted enabling them to retain control over their own healing journey. **Collaboration and peer support**: This principle involves working more widely than with just the child. The practitioner commits to working in partnership with the child or young person and their family or carers to ensure a coordinated and integrated approach. This ensures that interventions are holistic and child-centred. **Empowerment**: The practitioner encourages the child they are working with to take an active role in decision-making and supports them to have an active voice in the strategies used and the skills developed to promote self-help. The practitioner also provides opportunities for building resilience, while maintaining the principles of choice and collaboration. The final principle that forms the basis of the trauma-informed approach is **Cultural Consideration**: This requires that children's cultural experience and background is recognised and respected. To achieve this, practitioners must move beyond personal bias and cultural stereotypes towards authentic cultural connections which acknowledge the potential impact of historical and generational trauma.

Clinical Supervision

Working in a way that is authentic to either of these approaches requires practitioners to be aware of their relational style and their world view and accept that they will have biases as a consequence of their own lived-experiences. Some practitioners will carry their own trauma-history, and this is why being trauma-informed is just as important for practitioners as it is for the children and young people with whom they work (Thomas et al., 2019). When practitioners support people affected by trauma and adversity, they risk being affected themselves by secondary or vicarious trauma. Clinical supervision is a process of engagement between a practitioner and a professionally trained supervisor to work through the material that arises in their work and mitigate the risk of emotional harm to the practitioner. Supervision is routinely utilised in social work, mental health nursing and psychotherapy, but much less likely to be made available to professionals holding roles within the education sector (Sturt and Rowe, 2018). To be able to effectively contain a child or young person, the practitioner too must be emotionally contained. This is one of the reasons that practitioners dealing with significant trauma need not only adequate training, but also a supportive framework to maintain their own well-being.

Points of Reflection

- Can you think of situations in your professional work with children or young people where utilising attachment-informed or trauma-informed approaches may have been effective?
- What might be the barriers to employing these approaches in your workplace?
- Do you think that a move towards these therapeutic ways of working would require significant changes? If so, are there small adjustments that you could make that would provide a meaningful starting point?

Using Therapeutic Play

Engagement with play is natural for children and may be as important to their well-being as being loved (Schaefer, 1993). Play is a symbolic communication (West,

1996) and children tend to express themselves most freely through their play (Bray, 1986). For young children it is the most effective medium to illicit self-expression and establishes a therapeutic relationship, with play providing an effective therapeutic tool (Gavshon, 1989). Non-directive play is often an effective starting point for establishing communication with children. Working in this way offers children a permissive space and utilises Rogers' (1957) condition of unconditional positive regard, adopting the position that children have the internal resources to heal if afforded supportive conditions in which to do so. Some more directive approaches can also be effective, particularly those that promote symbolic communication, and these will often be used if the intervention is time limited. Small world toys, dolls and puppets are valuable because they allow children to tell their story while maintaining emotional distance and without the need for complex language. Oaklander (1978) asserted that children experience things in their lives that they cannot express in language and they utilise play as a means to assimilate and formulate their real-life experiences. With our knowledge and understanding of the value of building relationships with the children with whom we work, practitioners are well-placed to explore the most effective means of communication to facilitate this connection. Therapeutic play can be an effective way to promote emotional well-being by offering children a means to both express and process their emotions without fear of judgement. Engagement with play in the presence of another helps to facilitate the development of social skills such as cooperation, conflict resolution and build skills such as learning to read social cues and building empathy (McMahon, 2009). Play is a child's natural medium to communicate and encourages self-expression and emotional regulation. Children are able to rehearse life experiences safe in the knowledge that the adult holding the space does so with an attitude that is non-judgemental and while viewing the child with unconditional positive regard. As practitioners our role is to provide a safe physical, emotional and temporal space for children to express feelings that may be difficult to language or even unsayable (Gendlin, 1997; Schneier, 1989). Through play, children enhance their problem-solving skills in a way that is enjoyable, and they can build their confidence and resilience in the face of challenge.

Play Therapists

Play Therapists are trained professionals who carefully select their resources and draw upon a strong theoretical basis for their work with child clients known to be facing specific challenges. These practitioners have expertise in recognising nuances in children's presentations and indicative themes in their play, but they are also supported in their professional practice by engaging with clinical supervision. Some Play Therapists will work with specific client groups such as children with a history of abuse, children who have experienced the care system and children who have faced adversity in their formative years, and this may require very tailored approaches and specialist understanding of the risks of re-traumatisation. These children will likely have a level of need which demands the intervention of trained experts, but there are some children with whom lay practitioners can make a positive difference using therapeutic play techniques. Creativity and creative expression are often harnessed to prevent or alleviate emotional difficulties in children (Moula, 2020) and these are approaches that can be applied in many playful contexts. As discussed earlier in this chapter, there can be merit in applying universal precautions and affording all children warm, congruent and respectful relationships where their voices are heard. Creative endeavours can be particularly useful for relationship building in many multi-professional contexts when faced with language barriers such as when the children are from refugee populations for example. With young children, creative and sensory play offer valuable therapeutic media. Those engaging with creative arts as part of their mental health recovery report that the artistic engagement can provide a welcome distraction, promote healing and offer a way to communicate what they are experiencing (Gwinner, 2016), and this may be particularly significant for children.

Chapter Summary

Post the Covid-19 pandemic, children and young people are increasingly presenting with mental health issues including various forms of anxiety. These challenges are not simply the reserve of specialist services but require first line approaches by all practitioners tasked with regular professional interactions with children and young people. While acknowledging that some will require referral onto specialist services for targeted support, there are also approaches that can be adopted which begin to go some way towards providing a supportive environment that does no harm and has the potential to promote healing. Attachment-informed approaches use attachment theory as the guiding framework for building secure, congruent relationships and using these strong relational connections to build trust and resilience. It is an approach that recognises that some children's early attachment relationships may not have offered nurturing caregiving or have provided them with a safe base to which they feel able to return. By offering new opportunities to forge these attachment relationships, practitioners are able to offer relational safety and model patterns of positive interactions that children and young people can use as a blueprint for their future relationships. Trauma-informed approaches use six key principles to recognise the pervasive impact that trauma can have upon a child's biological, neurological, psychological and social development. Working in a way that is trauma-informed helps practitioners to reframe thinking about behavioural presentations from 'what is wrong with them?' to 'what happened to them?' appreciating that those with a history of significant trauma may experience the world differently and may need to be worked with in a way that pays particular attention to ensuring re-traumatisation is avoided. Both approaches elevate the importance of the relationship and focus on the use of effective communication.

One of the most effective ways to communicate with children and young people is through the medium of play. Play offers autonomy and a way to communicate that which a child may not have the vocabulary to share, or which may feel unsayable. In addition to facilitating communication, play offers catharsis and a permissive space to work through challenges and build resilience without overbearing direction that often comes with adult interference. Play levels the playing field when it comes to power and control for this is a child's world where they can adopt the role of the expert. Childhood is socially constructed and experienced differently dependent on a range of factors. As a lay practitioner you may not be able to change the world, but you have the potential to change the world for one small person at a time; moving hopefully towards improvement and a belief that small shifts in practice and professional thinking can be the catalysts for driving change.

Key Points

- There is value in professionals working *therapeutically* with children outside of the therapist–client relationship.
- Play offers children a safe and familiar medium for expression and exploration when making sense of their lived experience and the world around them.
- Attachment-informed and trauma-informed approaches can be used to create a safe and inclusive environment where healthy relationships are cultivated.

Further Reading

Holmes, J. and Slade, H. (2018) *Attachment in Therapeutic Practice.* SAGE.

Newlove-Delgado, T., Marcheselli, F., Williams, T., Mandalia, D., Davis, J., McManus, S., Savic, M., Treloar, W. and Ford, T. (2022) Mental Health of Children and Young People in England, NHS Digital, Leeds

Office for Health Improvements and Disparities (2022) Working definition of Trauma-Informed Practice. Available at https://www.gov.uk/government/publications/working-definition-of-trauma-informed-practice/working-definition-of-trauma-informed-practice#:~:text=Trauma%2Dinformed%20practice%20is%20an,biological%2C%20psychological%20and%20social%20development.

SAMSHA (2014) *6 Guiding Principles to Trauma-Informed Approach.* Available at https://www.samhsa.gov/resource/dbhis/infographic-6-guiding-principles-trauma-informed-approach

References

Ainsworth, M. and Bell, S. (1970) Attachment, exploration, and separation: Illustrated by the behaviour of one-year-olds in a strange situation. *Child Development*, 41, 49–67.

Asmundson, G.J. and Taylor, S. (2020) How health anxiety influences responses to viral outbreaks like COVID-19: What all decision-makers, health authorities, and health care professionals need to know. *Journal of Anxiety Disorders*, 71, 102211.

Bowlby, J. (1969) *Attachment. Attachment and loss: Vol. 1. Loss.* Basic Books.

Bray, M. (1986) Communicating with young children, *Childright*, 31, 18–20.

Brummer, J. (2020) *Building a Trauma-Informed Restorative School: Skills and Approaches for Improving Culture and Behaviour.* London: Jessica Kingsley Publisher.

Burlingame, G. and Barlow, S. (1996) Outcome and process differences between professional and nonprofessional therapists in time-limited group psychotherapy. *International Journal of Group Psychotherapy*, 46(4), 455–478.

Chanfreau, J., Lloyd, C., Byron, C., Roberts, C., Craig, R., De Feo, D. and McManus, S. (2008) *Predicting wellbeing*. NatCen Social Research, DoH.

De Thierry, B. (2017) *The Simple Guide to Child Trauma*. Jessica Kingsley Publishers.

Egan, G. (1998) *The Skilled Helper*. Brooks Cole.

Felitti, V. J., Anda, R. F., Nordenberg, D., Williamson, D. F., Spitz, A. M., Edwards, V., Koss, M. P. and Marks, J. S. (1998). Relationship of childhood abuse and household dysfunction to many of the leading causes of death in adults: The Adverse Childhood Experiences (ACE) Study. *American Journal of Preventive Medicine*, 14(4), 245–258.

Flannery-Schroeder, E.C. (2004) 'Generalized anxiety disorder'. In Morris, T.L. and March, J.S. (Eds.) *Anxiety Disorders in Children and Adolescents*. Guildford Publications, pp. 127–142.

Gavshon, A. (1989) Playing: Its role in child analysis, *Journal of Child Psychotherapy*, 15(1), 47–62.

Gendlin, E.T. (1997) How philosophy cannot appeal tp reason and how it can. In Levin, D.M. (Ed.) *Language beyond Postmodernism: Saying and Thinking in Gendlin's Philosophy*. Northwestern University Press, pp. 3–41.

Goldstein, K. (1939) *The Organism: A Holistic Approach to Biology Derived from Pathological Data in Man*. Zone Books.

Gwinner, K. (2016) Arts, therapy, and health: Three stakeholder viewpoints related to young people's mental health and wellbeing in Australia, *The Arts in Psychotherapy*, 50, 9–16.

Hodgkins, A. (2021) Exploring early childhood practitioners' perceptions of empathy with children and families: Initial findings. *Educational Review*, https://doi.org/10.1080/00131911.2021.2023471

Holmes, J. and Slade, H. (2018) *Attachment in Therapeutic Practice*. SAGE.

Kessler, R.C., Amminger, G.P., Aguilar-Gaxiola, S., Alonso, J., Lee, S. and Ustun, T.B. (2007) Age of onset of mental disorders: A review of recent literature. *Current Opinion in Psychiatry*, 20(4), 359–364.

Koloroutis, M. and Trout, M. (2012) *See Me as a Person: Creating Therapeutic Relationships with Patients and Their Families*. Creative Healthcare Management Inc.

Maza, M.T., Fox, K.A., Kwon, S.J., Flannery, J.E., Lindquist, K.A., Prinstein, M.J. and Telzer, E.H. (2023) Association of Habitual checking behaviors on social media with longitudinal functional brain development. *JAMA Pediatrics*, 177(2), 160–167.

McMahon, L. (2009) *The Handbook of Play Therapy and Therapeutic Play*. Routledge.

Mental Health Foundation (2022) *The Anxious Child*. https://www.mentalhealth.org.uk/explore-mental-health/publications/anxious-child

Merry, T. (1999) *Learning and Being in Person-Centred Counselling*. PCCS Books.

Morse, J., Bottorff, J., Anderson, G., O'Brien, B. and Solberg, S. (2006). Beyond empathy: Expanding expressions of caring. *Journal of Advanced Nursing*, 53(1), 75–87.

Morris, T.L. and March, J.S. (Eds.). (2004). *Anxiety Disorders in Children and Adolescents* (2nd ed.). New York: Guilford.

Moudatsou, M., Stavropoulou, A., Philalithis, A. and Koukouli, S. (2020) The role of empathy in health and social care professionals, *Healthcare (Basel)*, 8(1), 26.

Moula, Z. (2020) A systematic review of the effectiveness of art therapy delivered in school-based settings to children aged 5–12 years, *International Journal of Art Therapy*, 25(2), 88–99.

Newlove-Delgado, T., Marcheselli, F., Williams, T., Mandalia, D., Davis, J., McManus, S., Savic, M., Treloar, W. and Ford, T. (2022) *Mental Health of Children and Young People in England*, Leeds: NHS Digital.

Oaklander, V. (1978) *Windows to our Children: A Gestalt Therapy Approach to Children and Adolescents*. Gestalt Journal Press.

RCPCH (2021) Conference Online 2021. https://qicentral.rcpch.ac.uk/news/rcpch-conference-2021-qi-highlights/

Reger, M.A., Stanley, I.H. and Joiner, T.E. (2020) Suicide mortality and coronavirus disease 2019 – A perfect storm? *JAMA Psychiatry*, 77(11), 1093–1094.

Rogers, C. R. (1957) The necessary and sufficient conditions of therapeutic personality change, *Journal of Counselling Psychology*, 21, 95–103.

Rogers, C. R. (1986) Carl Rogers on the development of the person-centered approach. *Person-Centered Review*, 1(3), 257–259.

Ruch, G., Turney, D. and Ward, A. (2018). *Relationship-based social work: Getting to the heart of practice* (2nd ed.). Jessica Kingsley Publishers.

SAMSHA (2014) *6 Guiding Principles to Trauma-Informed Approach*. https://www.samhsa.gov/resource/dbhis/infographic-6-guiding-principles-trauma-informed-approach

Schaefer, C. E. (1993) *The therapeutic powers of play*. Jason Aronson.

Schneier, S. (1989) The Imagery in Movement Method: A process tool bridging psychotherapeutic and transpersonal inquiry. In Vale, R.S. and Halling, S. (Eds.) *Existential Phenomenological Perspectives in Psychology: Exploring the Breadth of Human Experience*, Plenum Press, pp. 311–328.

Sturt, P. and Rowe, J. (2018) *Using Supervision in Schools: A Guide to Building Safe Cultures and Providing Emotional Support in a Range of School Settings*. Pavilion.

Telle, N.-T. and Pfister, H.-R. (2016). Positive empathy and prosocial behavior: A neglected link. *Emotion Review*, 8(2), 154–163.

Thomas, M.S., Crosby, S. and Vanderhaar, J. (2019) Trauma-informed practices in schools across two decades: An interdisciplinary review of research. *Review of Research in Education*, 43, 422–452.

Triggle, N. (2021) Covid: The devastating toll of the pandemic on children, *BBC News*. https://www.bbc.co.uk/news/health-55863841.amp

Tull, M.T., Edmonds, K.A., Scamaldo, K.M., Richmond, J.R., Rose, J.P. and Gratz, K.L. (2020) Psychological outcomes associated with stay-at-home orders and the perceived impact of COVID-19 on daily life. *Psychiatry Research*, 289, 113098.

Van Der Kolk, B. (2014) *The body keeps the score*. Penguin.

West, J. (1996) *Child centred play therapy*. Hodder Arnold.

15

Futures of Childhood

Andre Kurowski

After reading this chapter, readers will be able to:

- Outline influences on children in the 21st century.
- Analyse conflicting messages to children in the United Kingdom.
- Evaluate the effect of the future on childhood.

Introduction

Childhood has always been changing (Aries, 1962; Postman, 1994), and the 21st century is no different. The concept of childhood in the western world grew out of economic and social changes along with accompanying legal and policy development to protect the category of human beings we call children. At certain times, the concept of childhood has been fairly simple; children were seen as in need of protection and caring, and social institutions accommodated this, and children have become a privileged group in receipt of unprecedented sympathy from adults. However, in recent times, various factors have conspired to challenge the status quo. It is difficult to make general statements about all children because children's experience varies due to social class, gender, ethnicity and other factors. However, in terms of the concept of 'childhood', this chapter will outline fissures between influences to construct young people into vulnerable beings in need of care and protection, with pressures on children in the modern world which assume that children are as competent and able as adults.

The Rise of Childhood

Childhood can be seen as a social construction that varies from culture to culture, and across time. The 'child' is not natural and universal as Piaget might have claimed (Prout and James, 1997). 'The immaturity of children is a biological fact but the ways in which this maturity is understood and made meaningful is a fact of culture'. (Prout and James, 1997: 7). In the western world, the meaning of childhood has developed over many years to what we now see as 'normal'. Aries (1962) informed us that concepts of childhood, adult–child relations, and childhood experiences differ across cultures and time periods. According to Aries, childhood was not understood as a separate stage of life until the 15th century, and children were seen as little adults who shared the same traditions, games and clothing as adults. Events that have affected how children are treated in family and criminal law, education, the world of work, healthcare, as psychological and emotional beings are varied and gradually combined to what we now know as 'childhood'.

One of the most significant drivers of childhood is economic and resulting social change, and the development of the family is central in this. According to Engels (2010), at one point in time, the family as we would recognise it today did not exist. Sexual relations among human beings were unrestricted and random. Engels called this state of relationships the 'promiscuous hoards'. Only when humans began to accumulate wealth and the problem of passing wealth to the next generation, did families develop to ensure paternity rights for the children of the wealthy. Likewise, Shorter (1976) claimed that childhood developed in tangent with capitalism as part of maternal love and domesticity. With capitalism came employment in a different contractual form, and where males were more likely to secure this new work, females were more likely to take on childcaring roles. As a result, ideologies developed regarding the caring and nurturing of children who had no economic role in society. As Zelizer (Bandelj and Spiegel, 2020) put it, between the 19th and 20th centuries children's status changed from being economically useful to emotionally priceless. As a result of these developments, laws and regulations shaped to recognise space as 'not- adult' (Willan, 2017). These laws included the Factory Act (1833) (The National Archives, 2024) which limited the age at which children could start working and restricted the hours of children old enough to work. The 1870 Education Act which facilitated free, compulsory education for all children in England and Wales. Children's fate was sealed. The rights afforded to children continued up to the United Nations Convention on the Rights of a Child 1989 (Unicef, 2024) which contains 54 articles that give civil, political, economic, social and cultural rights that all children everywhere, as well as resulting UK legislation such as various Children Acts.

Infantalisation of Children

Children are protected from modern life in many ways; various pieces of legislation set out children's rights and expectations for those working with children. For example the Children Act 1989 (Gov.UK, 2024) states that in legal proceedings, the child's welfare shall be the court's paramount consideration, and consideration must be given to the ascertainable wishes and feelings of the child concerned. One of the primary functions of the Children Act 2004 is to promote awareness of the views and interests of children. The Child and Social Work Act 2017 (Gov.UK, 2024) states that local authorities must act in the best interests, and promote the physical and mental health and well-being, of those children and young people, and encourage those children and young people to express their views, wishes and feelings. These developments in legislation place the child and their welfare firmly at the centre of policy.

In other areas of social life, the media is protective. Children are shielded from harmful material on television and radio by the 'watershed'. This is a time, 9.00 pm, before which restrictions are placed on content such as sexual content, violence, graphic or distressing imagery and offencive language (Ofcom, 2024). Also, children are protected from misleading, harmful, or offencive material in advertising (Conway, 2023). Children are considered to be adversely affected by 'inappropriate, scary or offensive images' (Conway, 2023: 5) and advertisements must not undermine parental authority or place unfair pressure on children to buy products.

In terms of online activity, children are considered as a group at risk. According to Unicef (2017), children are accessing the internet at increasingly younger ages. Nearly half of children aged 5–10 own mobile phones, and more than half of those admitting to always sleeping with their mobile next to their bed (Childwise, 2022). According to Ofcom (2020), pre-schoolers aged 3–4-years old spend eight hours and 18 minutes a week online. The dangers and harms that can result of children's online activity include grooming, accessing inappropriate material and internet addiction. As a result, the Online Safety Act 2023 (Gov.UK, 2024) has been developed to make the use of internet services safer for individuals in the United Kingdom in general, but also more specifically, provide a higher standard of protection for content and activity that is harmful to children.

It can be seen that across social life, children are considered to be in need of protection from potential harms. However, there has been a backlash against how the status of childhood has developed to protect children. This perspective questions what legislation, policy and society have done to overprotect children. The term 'cotton wool kids' has become part of the lexicon, and refers to risk averse, intensive parenting and stifling children's ability to take risks (Bristow, 2014). Gill (2007) also views the overprotection of children as having adverse effects on children's development. Bristow (2014) goes further with the term 'diseasing of childhood', which refers to adults projecting wider anxieties about adulthood and modern life onto children. Even so, this merely emphasises the lengths contemporary society will go to defend what we have become to view as childhood. Children are seen as innocent, vulnerable to the vagaries of adult life and in need of protection. However, in other ways, children are facing significant challenges, and are behaving and being treated more like adults.

Adultalisation of Children

Childhood as we know it has developed and flourished since industrialisation. However, there is evidence that this version of childhood is under threat. Postman (1994) argued that in mediaeval times, before massed literacy, there was little to distinguish between adults and children as speech was the main way to communicate. Children's experiences in life were similar to those of adults and there was little concern for protecting children from the vagaries of adult life. However, with the development of the printing press and developing widespread literacy, a divide was created between adults and children. As children took time to learn to read and write, this period in their lives set them apart from adults and new ideologies about children began to emerge, and this was the start of the process of social and economic change by which we now understand the concept of childhood. With the advent of mass media, Postman argued that children, after having been separated and protected from the adult world for many years, could have a window into the adult world. As a result, children experience aspects of adult life in a similar way to how they did so before massed literacy.

In general, children feel more pressure placed on themselves. The Good child Report (The Children's Society, 2023) found that about a quarter of children felt unhappy with at least one aspect of their life, while other worries include having enough money and finding a job. Less than half of children feel safe in their local area at night, and girls were more likely to be unhappy with their appearance and friendships. The Good Child Report found that there is a need to support children's well-being and recommends the expansion of mental health support teams to all schools with long-term funding.

With the spread of education in the United Kingdom through since the 1870 Education Act (UK Parliament, 2024), children have been given more responsibility in society, and also face more pressure in the education system; getting good grades at school (The Children's Society, 2023). Despite protective and privileged rights being enshrined in UK law such as the concept of the 'welfare of the child is paramount' (Gov.UK, 2024), policy also gives children more opportunity (and responsibility) to put their views forward through the 'voice of the child' (Gov.UK, 2015). A child remains accountable in criminal law at the age of ten (NSPCC, 2024) and there is little prospect of this changing in the near future (UK Parliament, 2016). Against this policy background, knife crime persists with children. In the year ending March 2018, 6.5% of 10–15-year olds knew someone who carried a knife, and in the year ending March 2023, juveniles (aged 10–17) accounted for around 18% of 19,000 cautions and convictions for possession of a knife or offencive weapon (Grahame Allen et al., 2023).

Children continue to be widespread users of digital technology with nearly half of children aged 5–10 owning mobile phones, and the average child now spending roughly three hours on the internet a day (Childwise, 2022). There are issues about children's privacy online (Information Commissioner's Office, 2021) and the Online Safety Act 2023 (Legislation.Gov, 2023) has been developed because there is a need to protect children from the vagaries of online activities. Children are increasingly viewed as and expected to take the role of consumers (John and Chaplin, 2022), and children can be persuaded by online influencers promoting products, behaviours and ideas to their followers (NSPCC, 2023), and used as influencers themselves (UK Parliament, 2022).

Gender dysphoria issues have become significant in children's lives; the National Health Service accepts that in children is rare but offer advice to parents on signs of gender dysphoria, and that parents can seek advice when their children are as young as 9 or 10 (NHS, 2024). The NSPCC (2024) give definitions and offer helplines for gender dysphoria, and in 2022–2023, Childline delivered almost 3,400 sessions about sexuality and gender identity. In Scotland, 16-year olds can request gender reassignment surgery, whereas this remains at 17 in England and 18 in Wales. In other European countries, the child's maturity is assessed for gender reassignment surgery (European Agency for Fundamental rights, 2024).

Chapter Summary

From the evidence presented above, there are two contradictory influences on children and childhood. On one hand, children have never been protected as much before. This has led rise to the concept of the 'cotton wool kid' (O'Mally, 2015) where children are over-supervised and controlled, due to parental paranoia. This raises questions about resilience in children. Resilience can be described as successful adaption or recovery in the context of risk or a threat (Mesman et al., 2021). If children are infantilised as suggested, then this suggests that perhaps they are not being prepared appropriately for the future.

On the other hand, children have never been exposed to so much pressure and responsibility. This leads to questioning about the nature of childhood and whether 'childhood' is in demise. Children are expected to have more agency in contemporary society. Agency can be defined as a capacity to do things, to act on the world and to make a difference (Oswell, 2013), and children have been given a licence and, in some case, expectation to exercise agency. As Postman (1994) argued, distinctions between childhood and adulthood are becoming increasingly blurred. This may be moral panic (Cohen, 2002) about the demise of childhood as predicted by Palmer (2006) and Louv (2010) and others, but the current 'contradiction of childhood' may simply be another shift in childhood; childhood is not disappearing, it is morphing (again).

Rousseau (1975) claimed that children should be treated as children in order to thrive, if not allowed to thrive 'we shall get premature fruits which are neither ripe nor well flavoured, and which will soon decay...' (1974: 54). If we are to have healthy children who turn into responsible and useful citizens, the contradictory influences on children need to be adjusted with less adultification but not more infantilisation. Children need to be protected but not enough to be emasculated; they need to be nurtured rather than overprotected; the potential in children needs to be recognised, but not over-emphasised. Above all, children need to be allowed to be themselves for them to be valuable for society.

Key Points

- Childhood is a dynamic concept that changes over time.
- Childhood in the 21st century is subjected to competing influences.
- Children need to be allowed to be children to eventually be useful adults.

Further Reading

James, A. and Prout, A. (1997) *Constructing and reconstructing childhood.* London: Falmer.

Heywood, C. (2017) *A History of Childhood, 2nd Edition.* Oxford: Polity.

Save the Children (2021) The future of childhood. Save the Children. London. https://www.savethechildren.org.uk/content/dam/gb/reports/child-protection/the_future_of_chilhood.pdf (Accessed 31.01.24)

References

Allen, G., Carthew, H., and Zayed, Y. (2023) *Knife crime statistics: England and Wales*. House of Commons Library. https://researchbriefings.files.parliament.uk/documents/SN04304/SN04304.pdf (Accessed 31st January 2024).

Aries, P. (1962) *Centuries of childhood – A social history of family life*. New York: Alfred A. Knopf

Bandelj, N. and Spiegel, M. (2020, December 8) Pricing the priceless child 2.0: children as human capital investment. *Theory and Society*. 1–26. doi: 10.1007/s11186-022-09508-x. https://pubmed.ncbi.nlm.nih.gov/36530595/#:~:text=Zelizer%20documented%20the%20transformation%20between,invested%20with%20significant%20emotional%20value. (Accessed 22nd January 2024).

Bristow, J. (2014). The double bind of parenting culture: Helicopter parents and cotton wool kids. In *Parenting Culture Studies*. London: Palgrave Macmillan. https://doi.org/10.1057/9781137304612_10

Childwise (2022) *The Monitor Report 2022 – Children's media use, purchasing and activities*. https://www.childwise.co.uk/monitor.html (Accessed 22nd January 2024).

Cohen, S. (2002) *Folk Devils and Moral Panics*. Abingdon: Routledge.

Conway, L. (2023) *Advertising to children*. House of Commons Library. https://researchbriefings.files.parliament.uk/documents/CBP-8198/CBP-8198.pdf (Accessed 22nd January 2024).

Engels, F. (2010) *Origin of the family, private property, and the state*. https://www.marxists.org/archive/marx/works/download/pdf/origin_family.pdf (Accessed 22nd January 2024).

European Agency for Fundamental Rights (2024) *Access to sex reassignment surgery*. https://fra.europa.eu/en/publication/2017/mapping-minimum-age-requirements-concerning-rights-child-eu/access-sex-reassignment-surgery#:~:text=In%20the%20United%20Kingdom%20the,the%20child's%20maturity%20is%20assessed (Accessed 31st January 2024).

Gill, T. (2007) *No fear. Growing up in a risk averse society*. London: Calouste Gulbenkian Foundation.

Gov, UK (2015) *Voice of the child: Children to be more clearly heard in decisions about their future*. https://www.gov.uk/government/news/voice-of-the-child-children-to-be-more-clearly-heard-in-decisions-about-their-future (Accessed 31st January 2024).

Gov.UK (2024) *Children Act 1989*. https://www.legislation.gov.uk/ukpga/1989/41/section/1 (Accessed 22nd January 2024).

Gov.UK (2024) *The Children Act 2004*. https://www.legislation.gov.uk/ukpga/2004/31/section/2 (Accessed 22nd January 2024).

Gov.UK (2024) *The Child and Social Work Act 2017*. https://www.legislation.gov.uk/ukpga/2017/16/section/1/enacted (Accessed 22nd January 2024).

Gov.UK (2024) *Online Safety Act 2023*. https://www.legislation.gov.uk/ukpga/2023/50/enacted (Accessed 22nd January 2024).

Information Commissioner's Office (2021) *Applying the children's code harms framework: A gaming sector case study*. https://ico.org.uk/for-organisations/childrens-code-hub/age-appropriate-design-code-blogs/applying-the-children-s-code-harms-framework-a-gaming-sector-case-study/ (Accessed 31st January 2024).

John, D. and Chaplin, L. (2022). Children as consumers: A review of 50 years of research in marketing. In L. R. Kahle, T. M. Lowrey and J. Huber (Eds.), *APA Handbook of Consumer Psychology* (pp. 185–202). American Psychological Association.

Legislation.Gov.UK (2023) *Online Safety Act 2023*. https://www.legislation.gov.uk/ukpga/2023/50/enacted (Accessed on 31 January 2024).

Louv, R. (2010) *Last child in the woods: Saving our children from nature-deficit disorder*. London: Atlantic books.

Mesman, E, Vreeker, A, Hillegers, M. (2021, November 1) Resilience and mental health in children and adolescents: an update of the recent literature and future directions. *Current Opinion in Psychiatry*, 34(6), 586–592.

NHS (2024) *Gender dysphoria*. https://www.nhs.uk/conditions/gender-dysphoria/symptoms/ (Accessed 31st January 2024).

NSPCC (2023) *The influence of influencers. What you need to know about online influencers*. https://www.nspcc.org.uk/keeping-children-safe/online-safety/online-safety-blog/2023-05-16-the-influence-of-influencers/ (Accessed 31st January 2024).

NSPCC (2024) *Children and the law*. https://learning.nspcc.org.uk/child-protectionsystem/children-the law#:~:text=The%20age%20of%20criminal%20responsibility%20in%20England%2C%20Wales%20and%20Northern,(Scotland)%20Act%202019 (Accessed 31st January 2024).

NSPCC (2024) *What is gender identity?* https://www.nspcc.org.uk/keeping-children-safe/sex-relationships/gender-identity/ (Accessed 31st January 2024).

Ofcom (2020) *One Nation 2020 Report – Raising awareness of online harms*. https://www.ofcom.org.uk/__data/assets/pdf_file/0027/196407/online-nation-2020-report.pdf (Accessed 22nd January 2024).

Ofcom (2024) *What is the watershed?* https://www.ofcom.org.uk/tv-radio-and-on-demand/advice-for-consumers/television/what-is-the-watershed (Accessed 22nd January 2024).

O'Mally, S. (2015) *Cotton wool kids*. Cork: The Mercier Press Ltd.

Oswell, D. (2013) *The agency of children: From family to global human rights*. Cambridge: Cambridge University Press.

Palmer, S (2006) *Toxic childhood: How the modern world is damaging our children and what we can do about it*. London: Orion.

Postman, N. (1994) *The disappearance of childhood*. New York: Vintage Books.

Prout, A. and James, A. 'A new paradigm for the sociology of childhood? Provenance, promise and problems' in Prout, A. and James, A. (Eds.) (1997) *Constructing and reconstructing childhood*. London: Routledge Falmer.

Rousseau, J. J., (1975) *Emile* (Trans, Barbara Foxley). London: Everyman's Library.

Shorter, E. (1976) *The making of the modern family*. London: Basic Books.

The Children's Society (2023) *The Good Child Report*. https://www.childrenssociety.org.uk/sites/default/files/2023-09/Good-childhood-report-summary-2023_0.pdf (Accessed 31st January 2024).

The National Archives (2024) *1833 Factory Act*. https://www.nationalarchives.gov.uk/education/resources/1833-factory-act/#:~:text=The%20basic%20act%20was%20as,than%20nine%20hours%20a%20day (Accessed 22nd January 2024).

UK Parliament (2024) *The 1870 Education Act.* https://www.parliament.uk/about/living-heritage/transformingsociety/livinglearning/school/overview/1870educationact/ (Accessed 31st January2024).

UK Parliament (2016) *The age of criminal responsibility.* House of Commons Library. https://commonslibrary.parliament.uk/research-briefings/cbp-7687/ (Accessed 31st January 2024).

UK Parliament (2022) *Influencer culture: MPs call for action on advertising and employment rules to protect children and online performers.* https://committees.parliament.uk/work/1126/influencer-culture/news/170678/influencer-culture-mps-call-for-action-on-advertising-and-employment-rules-to-protect-children-and-online-performers/#:~:text=Children%20as%20influencers&text=The%20Committee%20heard%20concerns%20during,privacy%20and%20bring%20security%20risks (Accessed 31st January 2024).

Unicef (2017) *Children in a digital world.* New York: UNICEF Division of Communication. https://www.unicef.org/media/48601/file

UNICEF (2024) *How we protect children's rights with the UN Convention on the Rights of a Child.* https://www.unicef.org.uk/what-we-do/un-convention-child-rights/ (Accessed 22nd January 2024).

Willan, J. (2017) *Early childhood studies – A multi-disciplinary approach.* London: Palgrave.

Index

D

Zeitfracht Medien GmbH
Ferdinand-Jühlke-Straße 7
99095 Erfurt, Deutschland
produktsicherheit@kolibri360.de